# Dispatches From Kansas

*Thanks for sharing the journey!*

To order additional copies, please contact us.
BookSurge, LLC
www.booksurge.com
1-866-308-6235
orders@booksurge.com

# TOM
# PARKER

# Dispatches From
# Kansas

2005

# Dispatches From Kansas

*To Dan Thalmann, Friend First, Editor Second, Who Always Gave Me Room; And Especially To My Wife, Lori, Who Showed Me That Dreams Can Come True.*

# TABLE OF CONTENTS

# INTRODUCTION

*Serendipity: The faculty of making happy and unexpected discoveries by accident.*—Oxford English Dictionary

One could say the origin of the word "serendipity" was a serendipitous occurrence, if one was into wordplay. Which is exactly what author Horace Walpole was about when he combined an old Arabic name for Sri Lanka with an equally-old Persian fairy tale, the result being, as he wrote in a letter dated January 28, 1754, a "very expressive word."

Walpole coined the word from the title of *The Three Princes of Serendip*, using as his inspiration the adventures of three nobles who, as they traveled around, were "always making discoveries, by accidents and sagacity, of things which they were not in quest of." If not for the fortunate meeting of ancient tale and English wit, the world would never have known such a splendid word.

So, too, is this book an act of serendipity.

Several years ago, my wife, Lori, and I drove to the Blue Rapids Episcopal Church to pick up a SHARE order. This being a small town in northeast Kansas, we first had to visit for a few minutes with our neighbors and friends. At the time I was unemployed, having cut my ties with a former employer. By the time we drove off with our boxes of food, I was a journalist.

This isn't to say that somewhere on the church grounds I miraculously acquired a college degree in journalism. Rather, I'd met Heather Dreith, the writer for the local weekly newspaper, and after exchanging the usual pleasantries she asked, seemingly out of the blue, "Would you want my job?" I was too stunned to say anything other than a weak "Sure."

My wife, who has always been supportive of my dubious adventures, asked, "What do you know about writing for a newspaper?" To which I could only reply, with much more confidence than I possessed, "I've read quite a few of them."

In the back of my mind I was thinking, *How hard could it be?*

Answer: damn hard.

Especially when your first article is about a meeting organized, sponsored, and chaired by your spouse. Not only did I have to dazzle my future readers with my talents, however meager and untested, I also had to please my wife. Who was, and remains, my harshest and truest critic.

In the few days leading up to my debut I read everything I could get my hands on about the basics of journalism. I practically memorized the Associated Press *Stylebook*; boned up on weak grammar skills; queried my two journalism friends— Sally Gray of the *Marysville Advocate* and Dan Thalmann of the *Washington County News*—the latter who turned cagey upon hearing of my new career, with a cryptic, "Not everyone can write news"; learned the five Ws and one H (who, what, when, where, why, and how); and discovered the undisputed formula for all news stories—the inverted pyramid.

This theorem is similar to the USDA's food pyramid only turned upside down and minus the slab of cheese, bottle of milk, and pork chop. Under the pyramid, everything of importance in a story must be compressed within the first few sentences, with each succeeding fact having less relevance than its precedent, until the entire story fades away from lack of anything interesting to say. Most readers have the attention span of, say, a gnat, so it's critically important to provide as much substance as possible before they doze off or turn on the TV.

On the night of the meeting I took copious notes, many of which I could barely interpret, snapped a few photographs, and asked for a copy of an old black-and-white photograph of the inauguration of a circular swimming pool Blue Rapids had back in the thirties. When I got home I started a pot of coffee and settled in to the computer. My deadline was the next morning.

It was a long, frustrating, exhilarating night. By the time I handed my copy to the editor I was frazzled, certain that my efforts would be tried and weighed deficient. For what I had done was break every rule in the book. I had dumped the inverted pyramid, disregarded the *Stylebook*, discounted the advice of professionals, and used a disproportionate amount of description, big words, and lengthy paragraphs. Rather than follow a tired maxim, I went for the *story*. Readers—those without journalism degrees, at any rate—loved it.

The real story wasn't that a meeting was held on such-and-such a date in such-and-such a place but that a stranger had come to town searching for traces of his great-grandfather, that the photograph's blurred smears of moving people evoked ghosts more than reality, that in the eyes of a young boy forever staring silently at the viewer was some unreadable, unknowable thing. That it was the duty of the writer to follow that expression back to its source. It was the journey readers wanted, not mere facts.

I've tried carrying that trend into my personal columns,

though honestly it was never my intention to include myself so intimately. The natural world was what fascinated me, and I as a city boy, an outsider, a newcomer, wanted to share my discoveries with people who had known this place all their lives. I wanted to teach them new things, a new way of looking at the world around them. What I quickly came to understand was that only through personal experience can we touch the world. In order for me to show, I had to become their surrogate. I hope in some minor way I have done that.

Most of the essays in this book were originally published in slightly different form in the *Telegraph*, Waterville, Kansas, and the *Washington County News*, Washington, Kansas.

One final note. A common thread running through many of these essays is the idea of *home*. That I should discover an apparently undetected yearning for home through my columns on the natural world is one of those serendipitous occurrences that writers often encounter. We set out to write one thing and uncover something else entirely. We learn to listen for that still small voice, to follow its whisperings. Even if, or when, the writing takes us into dangerous, painful territory.

I am learning to listen more with each story. And when I'm lost, when darkness is all I know, I close my eyes and sink deep into the underworld of my subconscious, and I allow the voice to carry me as if Charon across the River Styx.

Through my blindness, I hope you can see.

# LEARNING THE LAY OF THE LAND

# FOR ALL HIS SPITE, WHITE HAD IT RIGHT

We were no starry-eyed dreamers, no sufferers of mid-life crises, though we were certainly accused of it. If anything, we preferred to call it our great escape. It was March 2000, a leap year, and we were leaping right out of our home, our careers, our rat-race lives. We took one last look around our empty house in Broomfield, Colorado, snapped shut the padlock on the tailgate of the twenty-eight-foot Ryder truck, and drove off. Behind us, the mountains fell away with the sun in pursuit, and dusk came on, and stars popped out in the deepening night, and we did not pause nor stop, our headlights pointing the way. Kansas bound.

My mind roiled. It held no fear but an unquestioning sense of rightness pervaded, and yet, nagging at the borders of my consciousness was a question whose answer eluded me. After all the harassment we received over the place of our relocation, I kept wondering, "What's the matter with Kansas?" Years later I learned I wasn't the first to ask.

\*\*\*

When William Allen White addressed the question in 1896, he was in lather. Fresh off the street after an altercation with reviled Populists, he wrote a scathing denunciation of both the state and its people. Before the issue hit the streets, White was a little-known editor of an obscure newspaper in eastern Kansas. Afterwards, White was famous, especially among Republican leaders who came into power with the national election that fall.

His polemic, *What's the matter with Kansas?*, in many ways could have been written at the beginning of the twenty-first century. He railed at the loss of population and industry, the lack of large cities, the dismal economic picture, sordid politicians. Though Kansas didn't turn out quite as bad as he predicted, growth certainly hit a snag, and continues to do so in many parts of the state. Marshall County, where we were headed on that March night, had lost population every year for the last century. The latest census figures show we're not alone; fifty of Kansas's one hundred and five counties showed a population decline between 1990 and 2000.

For those raised in the city and flogged with merciless growth, witnesses to an unending procession of subdivisions consuming the shortgrass prairie of the Front Range, the census figures were reassuring. Where we were going there would be no concern over new development crowding us out. Time had barely touched Blue Rapids over the past few decades. Of course, we had no insurance, no jobs, nor any hope of finding work in our past professions. We had nothing but a dream.

And, of course, that irksome question harrying me as the miles dropped away.

\*\*\*

Our friends in Colorado were only too happy to tell us what Kansas's problem was. "It's flat, boring and ugly" went the common refrain, spoken so often and with such disdain that it became a mantra they chanted whenever we appeared. On one level it pleased me knowing that our little secret was safe, but on another level it stung to have what we considered so special reduced to the butt of jokes. They cheapened our dream, made light of our future. They sneered at our prospects for finding work, certain in their smug self-righteousness that we would come crawling back.

For twenty-six years I had climbed the ranks of a security company, starting as a technician and ending in a special position just below the chief of operations. My wife, Lori, had risen from a counterperson at an auto parts store to its lead salesperson. What's the matter with Kansas? For starters we'd have to find something else to do. We weren't just stepping off the corporate ladder; we were toppling it and chopping it up for kindling.

That first night, we slept in a small hotel in Bird City. As we were unloading a few things to drag into the room, I looked at the stars and said, "We're homeless." It probably should have frightened me, but it didn't.

***

In this life I will never again be able to replicate the sense of freedom we felt those first few months after our arrival. It was dizzying, heady, electrifying. The road to our rental house on the outskirts of town saw little traffic. Nights were stardrenched. We planted a big garden. We explored the backroads. We watched the sun set and then watched it rise the next morning. We were hard pressed to find anything wrong with Kansas. As far as we were concerned, it was paradise.

But eventually we needed money, and in short order I burned through more jobs in two years than I had done in the previous thirty. A chance meeting landed me a job as a journalist for a small newspaper. Without training or past experience, I slipped into something as comfortable and natural as my own skin.

A letter from the Social Services Administration arrived

asking if someone had stolen my identity. It charted the rise of my earnings since my first job at a candy warehouse at the age of seventeen. For three decades the numbers climbed, only to collapse like a house of cards. They plunged below an invisible line called the poverty level. This was the non-romantic side of population and industry loss that White raged against.

We'd never been happier.

*\*\**

When I first heard of White's editorial, I thought I had found the answer to the question that had hounded me since our departure from Colorado. Snatches of it in print, notably the last paragraph, piqued my interest. Surely, I thought, here was a rejoinder I could hurl at the witless, ignorant criticisms of those living outside our borders.

But on first reading I didn't understand it. His tone seemed all wrong; if anything, he seemed to be knocking the state rather than praising it. Only later did it make sense, when I understood his words from the context of his era. But I think he had it wrong. He was a little hard on the "clodhoppers," and I think he was blind in seeing the vast open spaces as useless vacuums. He wanted cities spreading across the plains; we came here to avoid them.

It was a well-written article, don't get me wrong. That it got him noticed is more important than what it says to us a century later. Ask anyone familiar with it and they can recite the part where he asks, one final time, "What's the matter with Kansas?" followed by his answer, full of sarcasm and bile, a long time coming: "Nothing under the shining sun." That's the part that sticks in our memory. That's the part we relish, rolling it on our tongues as if enjoying its texture and flavor. I don't think he meant it, though. Blind with rage at the confrontation on the street, his words were meant to cut to the bone, to humiliate, to ridicule.

And yet, indirectly, I found an answer to my question.

***

I watch the sun rise five days a week now. As it lifts from the eastern horizon it pours through windows of the Georgia Pacific plant where I clean. It's one of three part-time jobs I hold, two of them janitorial. Had I known I was trading a lucrative professional career for this I might have hesitated, but now I know better. The exchange was more than worth it.

Thomas Hardy's poem, *A Private Man on Public Men*, uncannily describes our experiences. While his contemporaries are busy trying to make riches, he tells of slipping away to a rural life, where he lived "in quiet, screened, unknown/ pondering upon some stick or stone/or news of some rare book or bird/latterly bought, or seen, or heard." Yes, I say, that's it. That too is the answer to the question. "Shut from the noise of the world without," he concludes, "Hearing but dimly its rush and rout/ unenvying those amid its roar/ little endowed, not wanting more." Yes.

***

What's the matter with Kansas?

I leave work as the sun becomes airborne. Mist chokes the valleys, shadowed yet by dense woods. The road dips into a slight depression and then rises and the Blue River Valley spreads before me as far as the eye can see, a verdant channel winding southward between grassy bluffs. The road descends and leaps the river and curves into town.

I stand on my front porch, the song of dickcissels calling the sun up. A cuckoo cries behind me. Warily eyeing me, a cottontail sucks down a long dandelion stem.

I have an answer now. It's not sarcastic, not vindictive like White's, but heartfelt. "There's nothing the matter with Kansas," I say. The rabbit's ears perk up. "Kansas is all right."

Like I said, White had it wrong, but he also had it right. I open the door and step inside. The day is young and I have many words to write.

# THE LOST ART OF WAVING

Such is the nature of the beast: for all our desire to flaunt our uniqueness to the world, at heart we long to fit in, to seamlessly blend into the fabric of whatever society or customs surround us. Which is what my wife and I did when we moved to Blue Rapids from Broomfield, Colorado, trading two-and-a-half million people for a virtual handful. We knew what we were getting into and knew our capabilities, so we figured it wouldn't be that hard to find our niche. For the most part we were right. But some things seem beyond this city boy's capacity to understand. To wit: I can't figure out when to wave.

It wasn't always this way. Once upon a time everybody waved. I'm not talking about urban people, now, but country people—you people, my esteemed friends and neighbors. You'd wave at people in cars, in trucks, in semis, people walking down the street, people flying overhead—everybody. It was as natural as breathing.

And for a short while after we moved here it seemed that little had changed. Even when people didn't have a clue who we were, most of them still waved at us. It wasn't like old times, say twenty years ago, but it was a pleasant change from the rude, irascible drivers of the metro area, who if they bothered to signal your presence at all preferred a pistol or a middle finger.

Oh, sure, I noticed idiosyncrasies. Men waved to other

men as long as they were both driving trucks. Women neither waved nor responded to waves unless, perhaps, another woman was the initiator; if that was the case, I had no way of knowing it short of donning a wig. Men in trucks rarely waved to men in cars, and vice-versa. If anything could be ascertained from this, it was that waving was predominantly a male trait. Men in trucks, outwardly more macho than men driving cars, therefore set the standard.

Okay, I thought, if that's the way it is, that's the way I'll do it. While driving my truck I waved at men in other trucks and they returned the favor. I refrained from waving at women, not wanting to act like a cad, but every now and then one would wave at me and I'd see it at the last minute and they'd be past me before I could react. And then, of course, I felt like a cad. I couldn't win for losing. Men in cars sometimes waved at me and I tried to be prepared, but remaining in a state of preparedness is tough work and requires more concentration than I like to give when driving. I prefer to look for birds and at the passing countryside.

If a driver approached and neither of us waved, I felt relieved. If the driver waved and I didn't, well, a stab of guilt coursed through me. What kind of unfriendly rural man was I?

When I drove our Ford Taurus I simply refused to wave, though the impulse was strong. I'm a friendly guy and I love the fact that country people are friendly. I found that some men waved sometimes and sometimes they didn't. There was never a rhyme or reason. It was all so very confusing.

I'll finally figure it out, I knew. It just takes time.

But then I began noticing a shift in the pattern, subtle at first, but increasingly noticeable. The act of waving was slipping out of fashion. Drivers seemed to be more preoccupied even as their speed steadily increased. Rural Kansas was turning into a miniature version of the Big City. What's next, I wondered, graffiti on the town square?

Being of a quasi-scientific bent (*bent* at any rate), I decided to experiment to get to the bottom of the waving issue. I would take notes about who waved first, who returned my wave, and who refused to acknowledge that another person was anywhere within a hundred miles of their location. Within time, I reasoned, I would have statistics backing up any claim I might make about whether women were less friendly than men or if men driving trucks were friendlier than those driving cars. A statistical analysis would let me understand my parameters.

For several weeks I waved at every vehicle that I passed. Okay, I admit to not waving at a few because I was daydreaming at the time. There are some in Blue Rapids who will tell you that I'm an unfriendly sort because I didn't return their gesture, but it's not altogether true. My mind was simply elsewhere

The results were varied to say the least. So varied, in fact, that nothing could be discerned from them. It's all a puzzle to me. The only facts I can state with unwavering certainty is that drivers in Nebraska vehicles never, ever wave and they usually drive too fast. By the end of my test I was ready to give up waving for good, keeping both hands on the wheel and my eyes grimly pointed straight ahead.

About this time I was driving home from work when a woman in a maroon Taurus approached. She was waving furiously. The sight was so incongruous that it took me aback, and we passed just as I remembered to raise a finger. It was my wife, I realized, and I felt like a cad for not recognizing the car.

When I got home the phone was ringing.

"You have a wimpy wave," she said.

I am *so* confused.

# AN OUTSIDER'S GUIDE TO RURAL LIVING AND RURAL BUSINESS PRACTICES

L arge or small?"

The question hung in the air, each word a translucent mirage hovering between the cashier and myself, shimmering and drifting, causing her pretty face to dance and waver.

It wasn't so much the *ignis fatuus* that stopped me dead in my tracks but the unexpectedness of the query. My wife and I had just walked out of Hometown Foods and transferred our groceries from cart to car when I realized I'd forgotten to buy ice. I was back in a flash, money in hand, when Kelly, the cashier, popped the question.

She was greeted with a bovine gawk, totally lacking in comprehension.

"Beg pardon?" I croaked.

"You want ice, don't you?"

"How'd you know that?"

"It happens all the time. I recognize the look." Her smile lessened the sting of being branded a forgetful oaf.

"Large," I said, and handed her the money.

I walked out the store a second time, shaking my head in disbelief. I thought I'd done my homework before moving here, poring over such books as *Moving to the Country Once and For All* by Lisa Rogak, *Moving to a Small Town* by Wanda Urbanska and Frank Levering, and *How to Find Your Ideal Country Home* by Gene GeRue, but the authors never mentioned I'd be confronted by a clairvoyant cashier. Clearly, rural living would be bountiful with the unexpected.

This may come as a surprise to my fellow residents of northern Kansas who grew up in small communities but there's a lively trade in educating urbanites about what they'll encounter when relocating to the country. An entire bookshelf could be stuffed with such titles, and none of them—not one—is comprehensive. More than a few are downright absurd.

Rogak promises that inquisitive neighbors will routinely peer through your windows and advises the newcomer to leave the curtains off for a period of six months. "This simple practice will save the natives the embarrassment of having to ask what you are doing and will give them something to do after dark," she says.

Garbage is another problem in rural areas, she adds. To be on the safe side, it's best to crush all alcoholic beverage containers and hide them in the smelliest, rankest food wastes—to deter the determined town sleuth. Be sure to dress properly, emulating the natives by dressing in "ragged discount-store polyester, tweed special, L.L. Bean chic, or just plain casual." And whatever you do, don't volunteer to do anything or serve with any organization for at least one year. "If asked to become involved," she says, "look away, avert eye contact, and feign a blush by holding your breath for several seconds."

I blush just thinking of what would have happened if we'd taken her advice.

I picked up the aforementioned books back when our move to Kansas was in the early planning stages. Actually, there wasn't much to plan. The company I had worked at for twenty-six years was scheduled to move from downtown Denver to its southern fringes. It would require a thirty-five-mile commute, something I was not going to subject myself to. We put the house on the market and started packing. The books were merely a primer, meant to brace me for a culture shock we would soon experience.

It was all much ado about nothing. The only way to understand rural life is to jump into it all elbows and knees, helter-skelter, and even then it will take years to get the hang of it. Which is not a bad thing. Having an open mind and a friendly attitude are requisite. Being yourself and not putting on airs is essential. And understanding that the services that you left behind in the city are just that—left behind.

Yesterday I walked into our basement and found a large puddle on the floor. Water was spraying from a cracked elbow on the feeder line. It wasn't bad yet but it soon would be, so I picked up the phone to find a plumber.

In the city one would use the yellow pages. Here, I called a friend, tapping into the local database. She offered several choices, but when I phoned them there was no answer. I left messages and started tiptoeing through the yellow page listings.

By the time I had gone through my options I was desperate. Several had told me they were too busy, and others had promised to call back. Hours ticked by, the phone mute.

I knew what I had to do: fix it myself.

Being woefully incompetent in plumbing skills, I needed advice. A call to the local hardware store brought the owner, Mark Rowe, running. He said it was a simple repair if I cut the line and installed one T-fitting, two straight fittings, and added a few inches of copper tubing. He would have the parts waiting for me by the time I drove the half-mile to the store.

Try that in the big city!

A few hours later it was done. A slight drip exuded from one fitting, but a dollop of silicone took care of that.

When two plumbers called back, one late in the evening and the other the next day, I proudly told them I'd fixed it myself. When I hung up the phone I was strutting like a Bantam rooster. I hitched up my ragged discount-store polyester overalls with the herringbone tweed knees and puffed out my chest. Yep, I told my wife, that's the way us natives do it.

You know, other than an occasional shock to my system, I think I'm finally getting the hang of rural living.

# SHOOTING HOLES IN MY MORALS

One of the lesser-known qualities of hypocrisy is its degree of difficulty to maintain. While it's morally acceptable to disparage hypocrites, perhaps we should admire them for the strength of their dissimilar convictions. It takes wit and craftiness to simultaneously support opposing beliefs, not to mention the physical effort required for all the stretching and straining of one's moral fibers. After a while they fairly sing from the strain. Being a hypocrite is a deft performance worthy of any Shakespearean play. Which was why I was cradling a rifle while standing atop a chair, our dining room window open wide.

The object of my attention and ethical relapse was a small rodent that had moved in, apparently with its mate, below our concrete porch. *Neotoma floridana,* or eastern wood rat, is a shy creature best know as a pack rat. It differs from the detestable Norway rat by having a furry tail, better manners, and a more rural character, all positive traits to be sure but not necessarily worthy of being considered a valued neighbor. This was my second attempt at snuffing out their candles, so to speak, and though I cut an ignoble and ridiculous figure standing on that chair, and though my emotions fairly roiled with diametrically opposing rhythms, I was determined to end this once and for all.

When it had first shown up, a furtive rustling of grass below the bird feeder, an occasional snatch of sleek gray fur and nearly-hairless tail, I had been cautiously thrilled. One more species to chalk up on my yard list, and welcome indeed it was after its home across the street had been reduced to splinters by a bulldozer in an ongoing act of Manifest Destiny.

My joy, cautious though it was and tempered by the wiry tail which bespoke of fetid stinkholes in the lower bowels of Denver where rats were my constant companions, was dampened when people confided darkly that the wood rat would gnaw the wiring in our car and heist bits and pieces of the engine to decorate its walls. No welcome neighbor this but a scourge. *Get rid of it*, they said.

And yet this clashed with the ideal we envisioned when we left the city. At the core of my environmentalist beliefs was the theme of living in harmony with wildlife, of finding a path where respect is given to the other living beings we share space with. When the only wildlife an urbanite expects to find in his yard is the neighbor's cat, a wood rat is a novelty. Unfortunately, many environmentalists live in a la-la land more attuned to Disneyland than reality. No sooner were our two ducks reduced to piles of feathers blowing in the breeze by a hungry pair of coyotes did I realize that while we may play by the rules, nobody informed the wildlife that there *were* rules.

I looked for a way to humanely dispose of the creatures. Poison was out of the question on account of the other mammals that roam the yard at night. Live-trapping was frowned upon by the Department of Agriculture, because it merely relocates the problem to another place, and anyway the wood rat would then be in another's territory, causing more conflicts. I had two choices, either to kill it or live with it, but my threat level was at yellow and inching toward red. These sorts of things are never dealt with in the pages of the Sierra Club guidebook.

A morning arrived with dark clouds deepening so that

the pale and inconsequential sunlight dimmed to twilight. The yard light came on with an electric buzz. Through the open windows I could hear the scold of a wren, the staccato of a chipping sparrow, and the faint but unmistakable *peent* of a nighthawk. Looking out the window, I saw the wood rat nosing through the flower bed.

I eased the window open, trying to make as little noise as possible, but the rat scurried under the patio. I'd probably blown any chance I might have of surprising him in the open but I left the window ajar and set the pellet rifle on the table. Whenever I crossed the room to refill my coffee cup I'd glance out the window. On my third refill the rat was drinking water from the dish.

Only its head was visible, its little tongue lapping up the water. If I shot low, I'd blast the pottery dish to pieces. If I waited for a better shot, I might never get one. The window was ajar, an open invitation. I broke the barrel, inserted an 8.44-grain pellet into the chamber, and snapped it shut. I nestled the stock against my cheek. The front sight obscured the lower half of the rat's head. I squeezed the trigger.

Recoil lifted the sight, blocking my view. When I looked, the rat was gone. Missed, I thought, but then saw it thrashing in the flowers. It disappeared beneath the porch.

Part of me felt relieved that my aim had been true; another part went into mourning. Is this the best I can do to solve wildlife problems, to kill them? I felt morally reprehensible.

When the second, unwounded, wood rat showed itself several days later my mourning period ended. Vanished in a split-second was any sense of remorse, replaced by an urge to complete the task.

And so I stand in the chair to afford a better field of fire, fully cognizant of my hypocrisy. Maybe Jim Harrison says it best: "Either do it or don't. You're going to regret it both ways." Pragmatism as moral compass. The grass waves and bends, a furry back and wormlike tail appear. I lift the rifle, set the cool stock to my cheek and touch the trigger.

# KNOWING WHAT TO LOOK FOR

I'm normally fairly observant though that doesn't mean I always understand what I'm looking at. I was following a small orange and black butterfly across the backyard a few days ago and thought it to be a pearl crescent, but then changed my identification to silvery checkerspot. Did I detect black submarginal spots surrounded by orange on its hindwing upperparts or was it orange with black reticulations? Since the creature would sit still only long enough to find it in the binoculars this wasn't the easiest thing to decipher. I always get those two mixed up anyway. A mourning cloak fluttered through deep shadows and a tiny eastern tailed blue perched on the rim of the water dish. I saw the season's first tree swallow, listened to the songs of both meadowlark species and glimpsed the elusive skink that lives under our porch, but I utterly missed the obvious at the bank last week.

This was embarrassingly pointed out to me when I asked the teller what day it was. It wasn't clear whether my quotidian lapse was due to a senior moment or a defective brain. All I knew was that I was writing a check for cash and drew a blank on the date. Rather than giving me a straight answer she waved her hand toward her blouse, directing my gaze lower than seemed seemly. "Blue shirt," she said.

I could see that it was indeed blue, though I hadn't noticed before. I could see the bank's logo embroidered above her, um, heart. I could see—well, suffice to say that I tore my gaze away, no doubt with a really stupid expression on my face. "It's Friday," she said slowly, as if talking to a child or a goggle-eyed lunatic. "We wear blue shirts on Fridays."

Since I rarely do transactions with the bank on Fridays (Mondays being my accustomed day), I hope my inobservance can be forgiven. It's not like I wander around scrutinizing what outfits women wear, unless of course there's not much outfit being worn. In such cases there's less scrutiny and more memorization, if you get my drift. But I do not want it known that I, a writer of the natural world, am lax at paying attention to details. I look, I listen, I observe. I make notes, some mental, some written. I write my account number on the back of the checks I deposit.

This simple act, once so necessary in my life, never fails to surprise the tellers. They assure me I'm the only one who does it, implying that people from the Big City act a certain way, or possess mannerisms that set them apart from the locals. (As we've been doing this for five years now, one would think this no longer worthy of astonishment. But I digress.) To me, writing the account number on a deposit constitutes careful observance because the tellers are going to ask for the number anyway. Why not make it easier on them and save everybody time?

People around here don't know how good they have it. Where we banked in Denver there were signs at the entrance to the lobby reminding customers to have all deposits ready for the tellers, with every "t" crossed and every "i" dotted, their account number on everything. Additional signs, for those who might have slipped past the warnings without reading them, were stationed at the kiosk where banking forms were available and at each window. They meant business, too. If a customer failed to heed the warnings, the teller would summarily dismiss the fool and call the next person in line. And there was always a line.

I don't know if they wore a certain color of shirt on a certain day of the week but I do know they were dead serious about proper banking practices. It was based on the assembly line process, funneling customers (and their money) in and spitting them (minus their money) out as rapidly as possible. In order to do that customers must have their papers in order and tellers must be coldly efficient, almost robotic. Banks had all the charisma and warmth of the motor vehicle department.

It's certainly more laid back here. Customers aren't faceless accounts, they're friends and have real names. Deposit slips, once crucial to a successful banking venture, are not only unnecessary, they're unwanted. The tellers will gladly fill them out for you. But it wasn't until it came time to buy a new car that we fully understood the quantum difference between urban and rural banking.

At the time, a few years back, I was working as a full-time journalist for part-time wages—below poverty level wages, actually, something the Social Security Administration was quick to observe. They sent me a letter asking if someone had stolen my identity, and included a graph charting my income from the time I first started working in 1971 to the present. It looked remarkably like Longs Peak, the tallest mountain on Colorado's Front Range—a fairly steady incline crowning to a high summit and falling off precipitously, if not vertically. My meager income weighed heavily on my mind when I approached the banker for a loan.

I told him we had found a car we wanted. "Okay," he said. I told him how much money we needed to borrow. "Okay," he said. "But I don't make much money," I added, squirming uncomfortably in my seat. He shrugged. "Go get the car and have the dealer call me," he said. There was no paper work to fill out, no reams of forms to sign, no credit checks, no DNA samplings. We shook hands over the deal.

I appreciate that kind of service. All the little details, like the tellers calling you by name and filling out your deposit slips, or even wearing weekday-specific clothing, mean so much. And now that I know what to look for, I think I'll start banking on Fridays.

# MISNAMES AND MISDEEDS

A little notoriety never hurt anyone though it can make getting dates difficult for young men of a certain age. I speak from experience but refuse to elaborate for fear of self-incrimination. The father of the girl I fell in love with had issues concerning my past, unfortunately all perfectly justified, though in retrospect I wouldn't change a thing. A leopard without its spots is still a leopard or, in the words of a birder who advised me last week that what we thought might be an errant tri-colored blackbird was in fact no such thing: "You can put lipstick on a pig but it's still a pig," Indeed. But to paraphrase Mark Twain, reports of my arrest are greatly exaggerated.

While I am no longer amazed at how fast word travels in a small town, this one took me by surprise. It also illustrated the care with which people examine the criminal and civil cases reported in the county newspaper. Listed therein are our sins and omissions, splayed in black and white for all the world to see. We have so few secrets, yet this borders on scandal. Write a hot check and there you are. Nudge up your speed and there you are. Beat your wife, pick your nose in public, kick your neighbor's dog, whatever you do—and get caught—is fodder for the gossip column. I'm convinced that such a section in the newspaper is solely used to increase sales. The public does have a right to know but the morality of it seems questionable. When I read a name uncannily similar to mine in last week's issue I was not only dismayed but knew it would haunt me.

Haunt me it has. Yes, I have skeletons in my closet that rattle around but they shall remain hidden. No, I have not been a perfect angel and have several transgressions to someday account for. This time, however, it was not me. No and no again. No. Not me.

The gossip column, or community tabloid as it's called, is one of those things that absolutely stuns newcomers. When we moved here from Colorado we knew we'd no longer be dining at fine restaurants, attending Broadway shows ( I'm making this up), or visiting spacious bookstores like the four-story Tattered Cover. An understandable amount of culture shock was guaranteed. The weekly newspapers, both local and county, provided us with what amounted to the worst shock of all.

I was used to a daily newspaper. Each morning began with a copy of the *Rocky Mountain News*, starting with the comics and then the headlines. Here, the first thing I learned was that the local newspapers don't bother with national or international news. Their content is solely the providence of Marshall County, and to me that just seemed silly. What about the world outside our borders? Doesn't that matter?

But most scandalous was the county community tabloid. To find that everything from speeding tickets to pot smoking was enumerated seemed the lowest form of journalism. That it was so wildly, wickedly popular was horrific.

Oh, sure, we could buy a copy of the *Kansas City Star* or the *Topeka Capitol-Journal*, but most of the news therein had no bearing on our county. It didn't take long to figure out that it was a trade-off, the price you pay for living in a rural area. National and international news could easily be found on CNN or any of the news magazines (themselves weeklies, interestingly enough).

It took awhile for the shock to wear off. I subscribed

to Newsweek magazine and local papers and kept an eye on Internet news sites. I read the local papers even though I didn't have a clue whom anyone was. Everything was a mystery but also a learning experience. And slowly the circle came around. Part of it began to make sense.

Now that I'm involved with journalism I have a better perspective of what constitutes important news in rural communities. The county newspaper has neither the time, resources, or money to include national or international news. Nor do people expect it to. Rural residents are every bit as informed as their metropolitan counterparts, possibly more so. At least here we know who's been naughty or nice.

I'd like to say that I'm above reading the tabloid section, that my personal mores don't allow the voyeuristic study of those unfortunate enough to find themselves on the wrong side of the law, but I can't. Part of acclimation is learning to live like the natives. Every Thursday, when the county newspaper arrives in the mail, the community tabloid is the first thing I read. Far better than the comics in the Rocky Mountain News, I find it indispensable. It's the real news of the county, the bread and butter.

# PESKY QUESTIONS ABOUT BLACK SQUIRRELS

I don't think the squirrel darting across the road as we passed Marysville's city park was purposely trying to see how close it could get without being flattened by several tons of steel, but you never know. Marysville touts itself as the Home of the Black Squirrels, hosts an annual Black Squirrel Night, and adorns its official flag with a black squirrel. Such fawning publicity is enough to make anyone a mite snooty, and squirrels are not known for their humility. For all I know, the critter was daring me to hit it.

Black squirrels are safeguarded in Marysville, that much I knew. When we first moved here I was astonished to learn that causing their demise carries a fine. Imagine—squirrel police!

This squirrel, though, was neither black nor red but a combination of the two. Its body was midnight black, its bushy tail chestnut. Such inbreeding between species isn't uncommon but it makes for colorful specimens. What it does for their self-esteem is unknown.

My curiosity being slightly askew, I wondered had I squashed the beast if the fine would be lowered on account of its mixed heritage. And if so, what fine would be levied?

Accordingly, I phoned the Marysville Police Department and spoke to the dispatcher.

"Did you run one over?" were her first words once I started asking about squirrels playing chicken with cars.

"No, no," I assured her. She seemed a little too eager to determine my guilt, I thought. Wondering if she had caller ID, I made a mental note to use a pay phone next time I research squirrels in Marysville.

"Is there really a fine for killing a black squirrel?" I asked.

"Let me ask the police chief," she answered, putting me on hold. A minute later she returned, telling me that they levy a $500 fine if caught intentionally destroying the town's mascot.

"Personally," she added, "I don't care if you run over all of them."

Talk about mixed signals. Knowing I was treading dangerous ground, I asked if the city prorates the fine for the amount of black in the squirrel.

"If the squirrel is half black, is the fine only $250? If its body is black and its tail is red and the tail is longer than the body, is the fine even less?" My serious question was met with loud guffaws.

"You just made my day," she gasped through what sounded like tears. At least she has a sense of humor, I thought. "I'll ask the chief."

There was another wait, longer this time.

When she returned, she briskly replied, "He won't go there."

I wanted to ask if a person would still be fined were a squirrel to commit suicide beneath their car's tires, but decided not to pursue it. There was that matter of caller ID to consider. I thanked her and carefully set the phone in its cradle.

Two cities in the United States bill themselves as black squirrel havens: Marysville and Council Bluffs, Iowa. Hobbs, New Mexico, once thought to get in on the act by "borrowing" several of the coal-black furballs from Marysville. With much fanfare and hullabaloo they were turned loose in the public parks, the idea being that they would breed and establish a colony to entice visitors to shell out money to see them. What they didn't count on was a bunch of miffed fox squirrels who clearly saw the interlopers as a threat. The fox squirrels took matters in their own hands, forming vigilante squads that soon eradicated the newcomers from the Land of Enchantment. It's not known if there was a penalty imposed or if any were brought to justice, but everybody knows how squirrels stash their savings. Had a fine been levied it's doubtful the rodent would have been able to locate its stash to pay it.

It's worth noting that Hobbs's fox squirrel population had been imported (i.e. "borrowed") from Sadler, Texas, earlier in the century.

Squirrels are renowned as being intelligent, fearless, conniving, cunning, voracious, pestiferous, and a few other things that can't be mentioned in a family newspaper. Anybody who feeds birds knows them to be all that and more. The furry rodents consider birdfeeders their private domain, and the more elaborate, the more squirrel-proof the feeder (as if such a thing can be), the more they consider it a challenge to be overcome.

Last year we had a problem with our local fox squirrel, whom we named Hairy Houdini after Richard Mallery's wanted poster of a squirrel that was his personal nemesis. Hairy would steal suet cakes from a feeder I had placed in a large maple in our front yard. Nothing I did could keep him out. I was losing a suet cake every other day to the rat, growing more desperate with each theft.

One morning Hairy sat on a bare limb outside our front window, placidly munching on a pilfered suet cake. I was incensed, steam whistling from my ears, my eyes crossed in rage. He only shifted position to keep an eye on me when I opened the front door. I slid the barrel of the pellet gun through a small hole in the screen and lined him up in the sights. His little beady eyes stared back, as if daring me to shoot.

I sucked in a deep breath, exhaled, and—put the rifle away. Hairy hasn't bothered the suet since. We seem to have an understanding: he can steal suet anytime, anywhere, and I can kill him if he crosses the line. For now we're coexisting in relative harmony. I actually like the guy now.

Which leads to another question I would love to ask the Marysville police chief: is it policy, official or unofficial, to follow vehicles with New Mexico license plates to make sure they don't try to squirrelnap more of the creatures? But I bet he won't go there, either.

# AN EXTRA LEG TO STAND ON

The first time I used them in Kansas I was soundly ridiculed, and that by members of my wife's extended family. I had just dragged my bedraggled carcass from the dense woods surrounding Perry Lake, my clothes grimy with blood and squished bugs and mud and sweat, emerging from the gloom of the under-canopy into the bright light of a perfect summer day. Her relatives, looking fresh in their T-shirts, shorts, and sandals, gawked at me as if I had just dropped out of the sky from a silver saucer. They were just biding their time, I think, until I did something truly outlandish, like pull out a pair of trekking poles and head back to the woods.

A few of the more otiose catcalled and jeered, mocking, "It's too hot for skiing," and "Where's the snow?" I paid them no mind. Once I was as obtuse as them, but I learned from experience that proper tools make the journey more pleasurable. The question was whether a person could use those selfsame tools in the Midwest without being considered suspect, like a liberal or an escapee from a mental asylum. Not that there's anything wrong with liberals, mind you. Or crazy people.

It was on the craggy slopes of Wolf Mountain, with Mount Evans rising snowbound over the western ridge, that I first saw the poles. My new hiking partner, a friend from work named John Daly, pulled out a pair and slipped each hand through a strap. I had seen people using one stick, usually a tall wooden staff, but this was a whole different animal.

"That is the dumbest thing I've ever seen," I said.

"Fine," he replied, and left it at that.

A few thousand feet higher, hunched under the weight of the pack, lungs laboring in the thin air, I was tired enough to borrow them when he kindly offered. Not long after, he had to threaten me with bodily harm for their return.

When I returned home, exhilarated after bagging the peak and having to scramble down several thousand feet of rocky tundra to escape a sudden electrical storm, I found an online dealer and ordered a pair.

They were real beauties, black and bronze, collapsible, with ergonomic grips made of a cork-and-rubber composite that molded to each hand, made in Germany by LEKI, the premier trekking pole company. I couldn't wait to break them in.

When my wife saw them she snickered and asked, "Going skiing?" On our next hiking trip together, while traversing a steep, rocky incline, I replicated John's generosity and loaned her the poles for a test drive. I never got them back. A second pair soon arrived in our mailbox, these more compact and colorful, black and neon sage. My wife claimed them for herself.

Sometimes we all need an extra leg to stand on, and the poles provided them. The benefits were not only enormous but instantaneous. They reduce stress on knees and lower back, add stability (especially on descents and when crossing streams and uneven terrain), and shift some of the weight of the pack to your arms, reducing fatigue. Tests have shown that using the poles reduces the amount of pressure on your legs and feet by several tons over the course of a day's hike. And, as I discovered in Kansas, there are other, more esoteric benefits as well. Benefits that won't be advertised in company brochures, I'll warrant.

It's a far cry from the snowfields above Lake Isabelle in the Indian Peaks Wilderness of the Colorado Front Range to the eastern deciduous forest bordering the Big Blue River in Marshall County, Kansas, but not so far that parallels can't be drawn.

There, we had to traverse a wide segment of Isabelle Glacier while angling for Pawnee Peak, the half-frozen lake several hundred yards below us, the open water viscous, emerald with depth. Our guidebook promised that were we to slip and fall into the lake, its precipitous sides and frigid temperatures would spell a certain and rapid death. The poles, one shortened for the uphill side and the other lengthened for the downhill side, provided us an extra pair of legs and made crossing the glacier much safer.

There aren't many glaciers or snowfields in Kansas, though, so for the most part the trekking poles have remained packed away. What I discovered at Perry Lake was a distinctly Midwestern use for them.

Here, we have spider webs. *Big* spider webs. Enter the woods and you'll encounter them, resilient as fishing line, invisible, viscid, stretching in broad snares from tree to tree, and on them, clinging at face-level, fat as old Shelob, the orb spiders.

They aren't dangerous unless you walk into their web and one falls into your mouth, which could certainly trigger a heart attack. Since their presence is ubiquitous, what's needed is a method to clear them from your path. Ergo: trekking poles, adjusted at full length, waved like a saber to hew apart the webs. They work perfectly.

Though their usage in the state probably won't catch on until enough alpinists use them while scaling Mount Sunflower, the state's tallest peak, I remain committed to spreading the gospel of trekking poles. And if anyone wants to hike with me and thinks they're stupid, fine. They can lead the way, preferably with their mouth open. We'll see who's laughing at the end of the trail.

# HARD LESSONS ONCE LEARNED, NOW RADIANT

For all our vaunted modernity, our far-reaching space program, our self-assured position at the head of the food chain, when we are suddenly plunged into darkness the eons distancing us from our caveman ancestors grow very short indeed. Couple the loss of sight with a bump in the night and our reactions revert to our primitive mammalian natures—hair bristling on the back of our necks, hyperventilation prepping our bodies to run like hell.

Mine is the voice of experience, not the least for having been on the cusp of the wilderness in northern New Mexico when some alien creature stalked the night, caterwauling its unearthly cries, the night gone menacing and haunted. There were also the comic episodes as when I stepped out of our Chevy Carryall to relieve myself and ran full tilt into a shapeless creature I was positive was one of the two hardened criminals recently escaped from the penitentiary in Santa Fe, just over the divide. That it turned out to be a skunk gave my family much to laugh about in the succeeding decades. Regardless of their ridicule, to this day I remain impressed at the dexterity I evinced by leaping through the air and slamming the doors closed behind me, all in a blink of an eye. Superman would have been jealous.

In my twenty-six years as a burglar alarm technician I became something of an expert in "bumps in the night," those mysterious noises at the back of an unlighted warehouse that could mean a rat, a time clock, or a bad guy. When entering buildings late at night after an alarm tripped I would leave the lights turned off until I had a reasonable idea the place was clear. The last thing I wanted to become was a victim of complacency.

I vividly recall the gut-wrenching feeling of traipsing through a cavernous pawn shop in lower downtown Denver after having turned on most of the lights and acting as if I were out for a Sunday stroll, only to find a gaping hole in the wall surrounded by piles of rifles and shotguns. The discovery was followed by a very long second where I imagined a burglar standing behind me with a shotgun leveled at my back, with the concomitant possibility that I wouldn't be returning home to my loving wife. I had been in the same building three nights in a row chasing false alarms but this was the real McCoy. It's ironic that by turning on the lights I precipitated an early departure for the crooks rather than stumbling upon them. Which was the better scenario is a moot point but I've thought about it many times over the years and have never lost the creepy-crawly sensation between my shoulder blades.

Such remembrances return all too easily when I step outside on a dark night and see the tail of a striped skunk flip up, quick as the flick of a switchblade. It's not ten feet away and now facing me with both barrels cocked and locked, as they say. My first mistake was by marching out the door without pausing a few seconds to give whatever creature might be lurking outside a chance to amble off, and from the looks of things I might not get a second chance. This is one of those regrettable moments where the past comes back to remonstrate with wagging finger and ruthless tongue.

I am vastly relieved when it moves away, shuffling off at

a fast pace. It disappears into a black patch and reappears in the street, illuminated briefly by the street light, a shadowy piebald shape perfectly attuned to the piebald night.

This is not the first time I've lamented the demise of our yard light, but it's certainly the most acute. I have only myself to blame because two weeks ago I took a pair of cutters to the electrical wire snaking up the weather-beaten pole behind our house and whacked it in half. A pair of wire nuts and a few wraps of black electrical tape and the deed was done. The light, which had shined twenty-four hours a day for several weeks, was now dead as roadkill. It wasn't the finest job of repairing what was no doubt a faulty sensor but we instantly began saving on energy usage. Financial considerations are always the best method for galvanizing us into action.

Several hours later we were to learn just how dark it gets on our side of town. The setting sun took with it most of the visibility except for a small patch in front of our house illumined by a new street light. Our house is somewhat distanced from Blue Rapids proper, the road still rutted dirt, and the handful of street lights are no match for the falling of night. Seeing the Milky Way writhe across the sky is reward in itself but the new problem now facing us was the lack of light where it's needed on the short stairway leading up from the driveway. Also, trying to slide the key into the lock is a test of endurance as much as a matter of blind luck, blind being the key descriptive.

When coming home at night, our car lights sweep the yard and scare away the bogeys. Going out is always a gamble. Each weekday morning now I throw the deadbolt and look out the small window in the door but all I see is stygian darkness streaked by wan shafts of light filtering through the trees. The door shrieks when it opens, its pitch determined by the speed of the act. I could fix it but I see it as part of the charm of a century-old house, and anyway it now acts as a warning. Monsters begone, it says, and I step into the dark, toward what I cannot say.

# WAITING FOR NEW NEIGHBORS

*A bad neighbor is a misfortune, as much as a good one is a blessing.* —Hesiod

Skunk on the porch, deer in the pasture. An opossum hisses at me from below the bird feeder, baring rows of crooked yellow teeth, a rictus of anger propelling me backward. Box elder bugs orgy beneath yuccas in reddish heaps, the vanguard of thousands more to come. Gray squirrel trots down the road waving its bushy tail in farewell. Raccoon inspects the trash cans for any opening no matter how small, playing follow-the-leader with its nose. Barred Owl caterwauls from the draw, an unholy uproar that momentarily stills the already still afternoon, as if all the birds and mammals hesitate in their peregrinations to listen.

Mole carves highways across the lawn. Red fox hunts the field. Coyote, mangy-coated, parallels the road where it hooks westward, keeping to the ditch, only his ears and back visible. Bucktoothed woodchuck saunters past my lawn chair. Cottontail slurps dandelions like strands of spaghetti. Thirteen-lined ground squirrel vacuums seeds from below the feeders until its jaws distend like swollen glands and it gags with each bite, desperate to pack one more kernel into an over-stuffed maw. Bobcat screams split the night.

Such are my neighbors. For space constraints I leave out the others, praying mantis below the bay window, wheel bug beside the door, jumping spider in the mail box, milk snake coiled in the basement, collared lizard doing pushups by the grill, field mouse scampering through the kitchen, and all the many others, some good, some bad, some welcome, others targets for destruction. Such as the pale tan spider that just popped out from between a slat on my picnic table—quickly dispatched, with cold vengeance.

When we bought our house on the southwest edge of Blue Rapids we had two neighbors, the doctor and his family to the south and another family cater-corner to the southwest. The doctor's house was a big structure interrupting our view to the rounded hills bordering our valley; the other house was hidden behind trees lining the road.

To our west was an unbroken field tucking the sun into bed each evening; an old barn fashioned from railroad ties met the dawn each day, a broken-backed barbed-wire fence, a copse of young trees and a bouquet of purple phlox. North was a grassy field of four acres, summer home to a pair of barrel-chested horses.

For ex-urbanites, this was a postcard of paradise. But as the opening chapters in the Good Book tell us, all paradises have a snake lurking around somewhere. As far as I was concerned, all that open land was an invitation for others to erect their domiciles, thereby shattering the near-perfect seclusion we enjoyed. When I shared this fear to friends they downplayed it, saying that there hadn't been houses there for a hundred years so why should we expect them to pop up now. Times, however, change. Soon enough, the serpent reared its head.

First a house was carted in to block my sunset, and another replaced the old barn and fence. I was less than enthusiastic about having new neighbors, and quickly enough our relationship with them soured. *My* relationship, I should note—my wife can get along with anybody. I'll blame myself because my penchant for solitude probably makes me a poor neighbor. Plus, I hated to see any changes in a place I had grown to love.

Now, I know what it's like to have good neighbors. When we lived in Thornton, Colorado, we were among several households who were very close. Our kids were friends, we had barbecues together—in fact, we were more like an extended family. One night when my wife got very sick and needed to go to the hospital my neighbors came over and took charge, as I was beside myself with worry. I don't know what I would have done without them.

Conversely, we also had a skinhead who screamed at us whenever we went outside and whose favorite activity was to reflect the sun off a wall mirror into our windows. In the larger scheme of things, that's the kind of neighbor box elder bugs are.

When I was growing up in Albuquerque, my best friend had the kind of neighbor I always wanted. She was, as I recall, around 18 or 19, quite lovely, and she would lounge topless on her back porch. A tall fence separated their yards so it wasn't like she was openly flaunting her body, but if you were quiet, and if you snuck up to the fence in one spot where a wider gap in the slats provided an unobstructed view, you could see her there in all her glory. Her naked breasts were the first I ever saw, and the sight instilled a craving within me that is yet to be satiated. Unfortunately, I was an Independent Baptist at the time and the ensuing guilt made my life miserable.

G.K. Chesterton said, "The Bible tells us to love our neighbors, and also to love our enemies; probably because they are generally the same people." I think most people would agree with him, however grudgingly.

The doctor left a year ago. Last week my neighbor to the east packed up and left as well. Rumor on the street says I'm chasing my neighbors off. I hope that's not the case, but I'm sure enjoying the renewed serenity.

I anxiously await the new neighbors, and hope we become fast friends. Meanwhile, box elder bugs swarm the doorways and lady bugs infiltrate the house, and the skunk makes taking the trash out at night a tricky proposition. I hope it takes a long time for the two houses to be sold. I have enough neighbors for now.

# CONFESSIONS OF A CHILE RACIST

Autumn is the time of movement, of birds migrating to their wintering grounds, of crisp mornings, of fields blooming with goldenrod and sunflower, but for one bred in the Southwest it is the time of the chile harvest. Roadside stands sprout up seemingly overnight, the air filled with the pungent, heavenly scent of roasting chiles. Such is not the case in Kansas.

Midwestern cuisine favors grease and gravy, not that there's anything wrong with that. My taste buds crave the sharp bite of capsicum—indeed, enough capsicum can release endorphins to provide a "high," much like that experienced by long-distant runners. It's like reaching Nirvana with your mouth on fire. The taste and sensation are literally addictive. And with only two bags of chiles left in our freezer, I was beginning to panic. What I needed was Hatch chile, and lots of it.

Or so I thought at the time. As I cast my eyes over this great state, searching for the elusive Hatch chile, I was in the process of destroying the last vestiges of chile racism. And oh, the lesson has been bitter.

Donald Rumsfeld, our Secretary of Defense, has said there are known knowns, known unknowns and unknown unknowns. It's doubtful he was referring to chiles in his press corps briefing but his intricate and uncertain phrasing is perfect for what follows.

First off, the known knowns: Hatch chile—that's chile

with an "e," thank you—is reputed to be the finest on the planet. It's not a brand name or variety but a valley and a small town in southern New Mexico, where the local economy is based on the growing of capsicums of many varieties. New Mexico is the largest producer of chiles in the nation. There, chile is a religion, and hellfire something desirable.

The known unknown was that I didn't know where I could locate Hatch chiles in Kansas. I spent countless hours calling Mexican restaurants in the larger cities and scanning the Internet. I drew a blank. Ask your typical Kansan about Hatch chiles and you might as well be talking Swahili.

A garden center in Wichita advertised them but had sold out. A phone number in a Thrifty Nickel tabloid caught my eye; *Hatch chiles in Kansas City*, it said. I phoned the number and got a recording. The friendly voice said he was roasting chiles in downtown Kansas City and would be there all weekend. We packed our bags, flew out the door and found, where the man promised chiles, a vacant lot.

I was almost inconsolable.

A few blocks away we found the City Market, where vendors from a dozen nationalities sell produce. We found bell peppers, garlic, onions, you name it, but no Hatch chiles. We also found Barbra Flores, known to local residents as the sponsor of the Vopata Memorial Watermelon Feed at the Marshall County Fair, who, with her husband Enrique, grows chiles in Manhattan. She had crates of them, all beautiful, thick, and meaty. I stared at them with unbridled lust.

But they weren't Hatch. Lori wanted to buy some, and Barbra wanted to sell some, but I balked, promising her that if I was unable to find Hatch chiles, I'd call her.

My problem was that I was a racist. Inadvertently, I had succumbed to the basest form of discrimination known.

Though her chiles were lovely to behold, I was prejudiced by their origination. Surely Kansas can't grow chiles as good as New Mexico, I knew; the very thought was enough to have me excommunicated from chiledom.

The trail grew cold. If I wanted Hatch chiles, it would have to be through mail order. Shipping would cost upwards of $40 per bushel, and I needed about five bushels. A trip to Denver suddenly looked less expensive, but when would I find the time? Manhattan beckoned, an hour's drive away. In defeat, I called Barbra and asked if we could come down. She agreed.

We drove there one evening and spent several hours roasting the chiles. The aroma was unforgettable. Enrique pulled one smoking hot chile from the roaster, peeled off the skin, and took a bite. He handed it to me and I consumed the rest. It was delicious.

Though the chiles tasted excellent when hot from the roaster, how they compared to Hatch chiles remained to be seen. This was Rumsfeld's unknown unknown. I blindfolded myself and asked Lori to give me a bite of each, one from Hatch, one from Kansas. To my everlasting shame, I could not tell the difference.

I didn't know whether to be happy or sad over this, but I knew one thing: I needed additional proof that Kansas chiles are as good as those grown in southern New Mexico. And only one person locally would be able to make that comparison—Alan Minge.

Minge, who received his Ph.D at the University of New Mexico, is highly knowledgeable about chiles. He agreed to a taste-test provided I supplied several bags of chiles for further testing.

We met at his house in Waterville. First, I gave him a slice of Hatch chile. He chewed it thoughtfully, let it roll around on his tongue. "It's very good," he said. "It has a nice bite to it. It tastes like a Hatch chile to me."

He took longer to make a decision on the Kansas chile. "It tastes just like the chile I had in New Mexico a few weeks ago," he said. "This one is from Hatch."

"Wrong," I crowed. "That's a Kansas chile." Alan seemed surprised.

Muddle-headed beliefs die hard. Just as Kansas is the nation's best-kept secret and not "flat, boring and ugly" as most ignoramuses think, so, apparently, are Kansas chiles comparable to the best in the nation. Chileheads being what they are, however, I remain skeptical about broadcasting this. Let's just keep it to ourselves, shall we?

Meanwhile, I'll keep working on my misguided beliefs.

# TENT MEETING AT K-STATE

Though to some this may border on heresy, prior to the game between the K-State Wildcats and Texas Tech I had never heard of Nicole Ohlde, nor had I ever attended a college basketball game. That's all changed now. But if I walked into Bramlage Coliseum a rank novice, I exited a different man. I only wish I didn't have this loud echo rattling through my brain in the quiet hours of early morning, like the mournful wail of a nightbird: "Nicoooole Ooooldeeeeeeee!!!"

Lori and I were guests of the *Washington County News*, who sponsored a Nicole Ohlde celebration. Personally, I think my editor was trying to provide me with a little culture, but that's usually a losing proposition.

All my perceptions of what a K-State game was like were wrong. I expected women dribbling a ball and shooting hoops, but what I found was a tent revival, and the true believers wore purple. This wasn't just a basketball game—it was a quasi-religious experience.

The announcer set the stage. When the Wildcats strutted out, he didn't shout the girl's names as much as he howled them, a Pentecostal minister stretching each vowel like a piece of taffy. Substitute "Nicoooole Ooooldeeeee" for "Haaaalelujaaaaah" and the effect is the same. For those who have never heard this, imagine a heifer giving birth to a large calf—sideways. The noise she would emit would be very similar to his utterances, and with as much feeling.

Toward the poor Texas team there wasn't so much scorn in his voice as there was an utter dismissal, as if they were ancillary to the proceedings. His voice lowered, his inflection shortened, like the disclaimers one hears at the end of a car commercial.

It really cracked me up. In fact, it brought to mind a trip we made last summer to see our granddaughter in Denver. Somewhere in the middle of Kansas we picked up a local radio station, and after every three songs the announcer would play an advertisement for a bank. I can't recall the name of the financial institution but I can easily recall the disclaimer: after the friendly, good old boy chatter came a subdued, funereal intonation of "Member, FDIC."

It drove me batty. When I finally saw my granddaughter, whom I hadn't seen for almost a year, I looked her in the eye, smiled, and said, "Member, FDIC." She thought grandpa had lost his marbles.

Listening to the crowd was like trying to decipher a new language, some unformed, primitive tongue. Maybe their words were distorted by the acoustics, but I swore that, at least in the first part of the game, the fans grunted in unison as if they had all eaten a cowboy supper of beans and hash and had collectively passed gas. Or something.

I'm a little slow at times but I finally realized they were yelling "three" whenever the Wildcats scored a goal. It all clicked when I saw the word flashing on the huge TV monitor strung over the court. Proud of my acuity, I shouted "three" at the next goal. Unfortunately, nobody else said anything. A few people looked at me funny and then studiously ignored me. I wasn't wearing purple so that probably alienated me even further.

"You mean there's a rhyme to it?" I whispered to my wife. She nodded.

It's disconcerting to be the odd man out in so august a crowd. Realizing I needed help, I asked Lori to nudge me whenever I was supposed to yell. Either her timing was off or I was engrossed in something else (those girls in their slinky, abbreviated black outfits kept drawing my attention), but I had a hell of a time synchronizing my shout with everyone else's.

Then the fans began a funky swaying motion that swept through the coliseum in a fluid wave. I saw it coming and braced myself. It looked like the tallgrass prairie when you can see a gale coming but it hasn't reached you yet, and the grass in the distance flattens like a giant hand is caressing it, and when it finally sweeps over you it takes your breath away, and you sense that somehow life will never be the same again, that something irreversible has happened. This motion swept over us like a tidal wave, leaving me giddy.

How could the Texas team stand a chance against that crushing emotion and religious fervor? They started the game in the hole and never escaped. From the opening whistle, it was a crescendo that crested when they retired Ohlde's jersey. The crowd surged to its feet and brought the roof down even as a poster with her jersey number (three—a biblical figure of completeness) rose above the floor, spotlighted, like a vision of a resurrected Christ rising from the Mount of Olives. A spontaneous chant broke out, "Ohlde, Ohlde," and purple confetti rained down like manna from heaven.

The significance was overwhelming.

There have been some disturbing consequences in the days following the game. I have an overpowering desire to mark our house with a Power Cat stone marker. And then there are the voices that still reverberate.

I woke last night to the hooting of a great horned owl echoing in my ears. Feeling a little frisky, I put my arms around my wife and whispered "Nicooooole Oooohldeee" in her ear. The owl and I made a nice duet. My wife elbowed me in the ribs and told me to go to sleep. She must not have been as impressed with the game as I was.

# LIFE IN THE FAST LANE

In the end, Lori said it was probably for the best that it turned out the way it did. Otherwise I might want to move back to be near my mountains.

Fat chance of that.

We were on a fast weekend trip to Denver to pick up our camper and, thanks in part to making better time than planned, we found ourselves with a few hours to spare. While the rest of the weekend was scheduled like the president's workweek, Saturday morning presented itself like a celestial gift. I took it and headed to Mt. Evans.

Unfortunately, I forgot the number one problem facing the urban Front Range: too many people wanting to occupy the same space.

A sign at the bottom of the mountain warned of a bike race ahead. Fine, I thought, bikes and cars can coexist. But what the bike sponsors had in mind was to have each family sponsor tag along in a car behind the bicyclists, driving the same speed and taking up the entire lane. This caused a mile-long backup of fuming drivers, of which I was one. There were very few places where a vehicle could pass both the sponsor and the biker, which meant that a lot of near-misses were taking place all up and down the mountain.

"You can't do this," I kept snarling through clenched teeth. "They should either close the road to traffic for the duration of the race or make the bikers ride on the shoulder."

"They can't hear you," my sweet wife advised me. "But I can."

By the time we reached Echo Lake I was ready to flatten the smaller bicyclists or cut off the older ones, sending them hurling through pines and boulders to splat like bugs on the rocks below. I was in a murderous rage. I perked up when I saw that the lake was the finish line, but then whimpered to see many of the bicyclists proceeding up the incline toward the summit, several miles away. I turned into a campground and reversed course. I was defeated.

I never got back to the mountains but I did get to visit store after endless store. Denver is a shopper's paradise, and my wife was eager to see what they offered. Row after row and mile after mile of wares and still the experience was strangely a lonely one. Customers and browsers had no interaction other than stepping around each other.

"Do you notice there's never any eye contact?" my wife observed. She was right. With that many people in so small a space, it was a gathering of strangers. The only conversations taking place were on cell phones. Nobody spoke or greeted any other. It stood in soulless contrast to the personable, social event that defines shopping in rural Kansas.

Still, with all those beautiful young ladies roaming around half-dressed in revealing attire there was little eye contact on my part as well. When in Rome, do as the Romans do, is my motto.

My son, who never enters the mountains nor, I'm sure, rarely even glances their way, insisted we visit the local Krispy Kreme factory.

I stood there with my family watching the little donuts puff up as they were lifted and lowered on chain-belt elevators. The whole thing is visible behind a transparent wall. Up and down they went, getting more fluffy and full, until they were ever so gently nudged into a hot oil bath.

"I just love this part," my son's wife said.

The donuts bobbed in the oil, each one with its own little square slot. The belt drove them inexorably on to where a mechanical rod flipped them over. There was barely a ripple in the oil.

"Wow," I said in a deadpan voice.

Everyone looked at me.

"Awesome," I said.

I glanced out the window toward the mountains, now silhouetted by the setting sun. A vast cloud exploded into flame over the Indian Peaks. The colors were deep and rich, purple, navy, indigo, scarlet, peach.

The donuts were gently bumped from the oil bath onto a conveyor belt. A white streaming curtain of what looked like Elmer's glue smothered them. My family was mesmerized as the donuts, dripping with white glaze, came out the other side.

"The real show's happening out there," I said, nodding toward the sunset. I was ignored.

As the donuts made for a bend in the conveyor which would herd them into a small oven-like apparatus, my family tracked their progress. Their eyes were glazed in a kind of religious fervor.

Meanwhile, the cloud flared into a bloody-edged marvel. Rays of light streamed heavenward from behind Pawnee Pass.

The donuts made the curve and headed for the homestretch.

"Wooooow," I said. Everybody looked at me as if I was bothering them. I kept my mouth shut after that.

Life in the big city is so exciting.

It was a relief when we picked up the camper and headed toward the dawn. We left the traffic behind on I-70 and followed the grain elevators home. There were few vehicles about. As we neared Waterville other drivers began to wave at us. I recognized a few faces. I waved back. It was small-town Kansas where anonymity is impossible, where people know who you are and what you're up to. No secrets. It was quiet and peaceful and uncrowded. Just the way I like it.

We might not have the attractions a big city offers, like watching donuts cook or being lost in faceless crowds, but we have room to move and friends who care.

Sometimes the best part of leaving is the coming back.

# SPREADING THE LOWLY HEDGE APPLE
## ACROSS THE CELESTIAL SKY

One of the most incongruous sights of the autumnal Kansas countryside is that of an Osage orange stripped of leaves, its bare limbs gnarled and twisted, a litter of lime-green fruit crowded at its base like mono-colored Christmas presents. Of all living things, it stands out as a one-of-a-kind specimen, adding an unreal tint to a landscape rapidly being shorn of color. In fact, it *is* unique, a monotype, the sole member of its genus. There is nothing else like it in the world.

I first heard of *Maclura pomifera* in 1991 with the publication of *Prairy Erth*, by William Least Heat-Moon. Possibly the finest book ever written on Kansas, its 622 pages take place exclusively in Chase County and cover every facet of its history. The author devotes an entire chapter on the importance of the tree on the Midwestern frontier. Not only is *Maclura* an amazing tree, but its history is equally fascinating.

Meriwether Lewis penned the first description of the wood in 1804 and sent cuttings back to Thomas Jefferson. In 1847, Professor Jonathan Turner of Jacksonville, Illinois, proposed using the wood for hedges. Turner began advocating and selling *Maclura*, which was then known as the best wood on the planet for making bows. By the early 1870s the trees began delineating the Kansas landscape. It was the most sought-after plant in the history of the United States, and then barbed wire came along and eclipsed *Maclura's* importance.

Now, it seems nobody likes having it around. Poor *Maclura pomifera*, once so popular, now so reviled.

After reading *Prairy Erth*, I decided that someday I had to have an Osage orange growing in my yard. Since nurseries in Colorado didn't stock them, the idea languished until it all but faded away. And then we decided we had to escape the burgeoning madhouse and flee to Blue Rapids and find a measure of peace. We quit our jobs, put our house on the market, packed everything we owned into a Ryder truck and set out on our new adventure.

We were freer than we had ever been or conceived of being. It was an interlude suffused with wonder and hope and magic. Everything good and perfect graced our lives. We had new friends and neighbors and, to ex-suburbanites, unimaginable quiet. Deer grazed in our yard, and rabbits, and raccoons and skunks and a solitary woodchuck. The birds visiting the feeders were species never before seen in our old haunts.

Each day revealed some new wonder. Late summer came and leaves began falling and the skies filled with long Vs of geese heading south. Recognition dawned on me that the trees across the street were, in fact, Osage oranges. Enormous pebbled balls dragged down limbs under their weight. Their color was amazing, a lime that few other things in the world possess. *Maclura pomifera*, at last.

One afternoon, my wife and I were walking the edges of our property and enjoying the sense of freedom we had come to know. We found a battered aluminum bat under the grass. I darted across the road and retrieved several softball-sized oranges. They were much heavier than I thought they would be, and when the bat made a solid connection the shock could be felt clear through my body.

Last night I stepped outside to watch the crescent moon

hanging low in the south. A few stars were visible but the air was hazy. It was warm, with a slight breeze rustling what leaves were left. After the cold, damp weather it felt like spring again. I sucked in a deep breath and held it for a second.

With only the yard light for navigation, I walked across the road to where *Maclura* grows thickest. Mindful of the sharp drop-off from the road's shoulder and of the thorny limbs, I rooted around in the inky blackness until my fingers felt the wrinkled surface of an orange. It was smaller than most, hardball-sized, heavy. It was perfect.

I strode into the center of the road and considered my choices. I could toss it into my fallow field and hope that someday a tree would sprout, or I could take it home and set it inside the doorway as cockroach repellent. But the night felt enchanted, and a giddy carelessness swept over me. I wanted this fruit to *matter*. I wanted it to propagate and grow a million more like it.

I wound up and hurled the orange as hard as I could, aiming at the arc of the moon as it hung above the trees. It was a good throw, hard enough to make my shoulder feel dislocated. For a moment the fruit spun through the night air like a shooting star, gaining altitude, and then it passed into shadows. I listened for it to hit the ground, a dull thud in the darkness, but it never came.

Like I said, it was a good throw. It might have dropped into deep grass, or fallen among damp leaves. It might even have hit the moon for all I know. It was one of those nights where it felt like anything could happen if you only wished hard enough.

The stars wheeled overhead; the moon dropped toward the west. I like to think that on that barren, comet-pocked surface an Osage orange lies buried a few inches below the flour-soft soil, and that eventually it will sprout and grow into a tall, gnarly tree and spread across the face of the moon. The scientist in me knows it could never be, that a person cannot throw an object that far, that a tree could never grow in an airless environment. The child in me, though, believes, and that makes all the difference.

# OLD HOMES, OLD BONES

When you own an old country home it's hard to keep it warm in the winter and cool in the summer. With the temperatures in the single digits for a week and another ice storm just now coating the porch I'd just cleared the day before, and after the largest energy bill I'd ever been cursed with, I decided to inspect for places where heat leaked out like air from a punctured balloon. It didn't take long to find the first spot.

Our dining room is paneled with slats of wood, varnished into a warm cinnamon tone, and between one of the slats by the bay window I could feel a frigid draft. It was so bad that, just for grins, I held a lighter up to it to see if I was imagining it. The flame bent and flickered out from the force of the breeze. Other places around the window and between several slats were almost as bad.

After a breakfast of eggs, bacon, and hash browns smothered in a hot green chile sauce, I fished around until I found the caulk gun and several tubes of clear caulk. Owning a country home means always having a caulk gun close at hand, and any self-respecting country homeowner will have at least a half-dozen tubes of caulk lying around in both white and clear finishes. Caulking is one of those things we do and do often, and still the work never seems to be finished.

Clear caulk comes out as white as driven snow, a fact that always startles my wife. When she saw me chinking one particularly wide gap between boards, she almost shrieked with horror. I had to assure her it would turn clear within a few days. Then, when she wasn't looking, I read the inscription on the side of the tube to make sure I had the right color. I did.

I spent about an hour caulking the dining room, making the job look fairly even. A professional would have done it better but after a while a man gets the hang of laying down a tight bead and then carefully wiping the excess away while pushing the caulk deeper into the crevice. And anyway, we rural men have to fend for ourselves. One of the unsung glories of living in a small country town is that people are used to doing these things in their own amateurish way, and nobody looks askance at a job imperfectly done. Esthetics is nice but functionality is better. Few of us live in model homes, with straight-cornered walls and level floors.

We have several bookcases scattered through the living room and one in the kitchen (and many more upstairs), and none of them stand straight. Our stereo speakers lean in like trees arching over a tiny stream. A rustic cabinet in the dining room looks so tilted that you'd swear a leg was missing, but it's just the way the floor sags. I could shim it up but why bother? I think it adds a certain charm, though one you won't find the pages of *Country Home*.

The bitter weather hasn't caught me off-guard as much as it made me realize that I didn't prepare enough for a severe winter. The roll of insulation sitting unopened in the basement should have been stapled up in an upstairs storage space that leads to an unfinished cubbyhole where the roof angles down at a hard slant. The lone heater vent at the top of the stairs is totally ineffective. When we moved here we insulated the attic but never got around to insulating the crawlspace between the roof and the bedroom walls. Now we feel radiant waves of heat and cold, depending on the season.

Once I'd caulked everything to my liking, I cleaned up and put the caulk gun downstairs where I usually keep it. If I happen to be working upstairs and set the gun down, I always have a hard time remembering where I left it. I'm a real stickler for putting things back where I found them. My wife isn't so good at this. If there's one thing that causes a low-level strain in our otherwise nearly-perfect marriage it is this laxity on her part. I won't admit that I had to scout around for the caulk gun today, nor that it was my own fault for not putting it where I usually keep it. Some things just aren't worth discussing, and that's one of them.

Now, hours later, with darkness falling and the hills above town fading behind a haze of falling ice, I can feel cold air slipping under the back door and more through a section of dining room wall. There's always something that needs doing. I used to have a roll of weather stripping but I can't find it. For now I cram rugs against the door to seal the draft. And you know what? It doesn't look half-bad.

I'm making a list of chores to do when the days turn warmer. I need to insulate the second floor and around the foundation, and to replace the doors or add new weather stripping. But by then I'll be so glad to be able to be outdoors that I'll probably neglect to do any of it, figuring there's always time before next winter.

Come to think of it, old country homes are a lot like country folk. Most of us are creaky around the seams, missing a few shingles, losing steam, and not quite as plumb as we once were. Since we live in the country we don't consider those to be flaws near as much as character traits.

It would be nice, though, if we could patch our character traits with a caulk gun. Caulk's cheap, and we all have some lying around.

# LAUGHTER LIGHTENS THE LOAD

# ARE WE READY FOR TERRORISM?

Readers of this newspaper will be glad to know that I am now a trained journalist. I recently attended the Investigative Reporters and Editors (IRE) seminar in Wichita, where I learned, among other things, how to find out anything about anybody by using the Internet. It's all out there, one mouse click at a time. I think there's even a Web site Santa uses to find out who's been naughty or nice. I learned the Art of the Interview and other fascinating subjects that use a lot of capital letters.

I also learned the importance of writing about things that are on everybody's mind, because most people's attention spans last around fifteen seconds. One recurring theme today is the War on Terrorism. People want to know how they're being protected from Bad Guys.

Recently, CNN.com investigated the readiness of major cities to handle terrorism attacks. Each metropolis was asked, "How Prepared is Your City?" The results of the investigation were based on every shred of relevant data and public record that could be unearthed, plus three simple questions:

* Who does your city's emergency management director report to?

* What is the number of full-time staff dedicated solely to emergency management?

* What is the amount received by your department during the current fiscal year for terrorism planning, training and equipment?

The bottom line: no city is immune from risk and none is prepared to handle the fallout from an attack.

Feeling empowered, I returned home with the idea of capturing an important story to test my newfound skills. Armed with a recorder, pen, and notebook, I set out to investigate the terrorism preparedness of Blue Rapids and Waterville.

Thinking that the man responsible for law enforcement over both towns would be the county sheriff, I drove to Marysville and dropped in on him. He balefully stared at me as I prattled my questions in a rapid-fire flurry of words. Carefully setting his pen on his desk, he leaned back in his chair. One finger slowly unfurled from his fist, pointing to something behind me.

Aha! I thought. There, on the wall, would be an organizational chart showing how the county would work seamlessly with our cities in case of attack.

All I saw was the open door. I turned back to him, a quizzical look on my face. "Don't let it hit you in the butt on the way out," he said, though those weren't his exact words.

My next stop was at the Blue Rapids city office, where I found the city superintendent and the city clerk.

"Who does our city's emergency management director report to?" I asked, jabbing my recorder in the superintendent's face.

"What?" he asked, his face screwing into a grimace. The clerk rolled her eyes.

"How many people are solely dedicated to emergency management in case of terrorist attacks?" I breathlessly rattled.

"What terrorists?" the clerk asked, looking out the window. A car parked outside had Nebraska plates. She frowned deeply.

"It's a theoretical question," I snapped.

"Why would terrorists bother with us?" the superintendent asked.

"To spread terror!" I shouted. Good grief, how dense were these people?

They looked at each other, shaking their heads. "We're totally unprepared for terrorists," the superintendent said. "Will you leave us alone now?"

"One more question: how much money is budgeted for emergency management?"

"Less than a nickel," the clerk said grimly.

There's my story, I crowed. My beloved rural town is all but defenseless and nobody in our government cares!

Waterville, I reasoned, would be different. As a rule, its populace is more intelligent, better informed, and more cognizant of the world beyond Marshall County.

The city clerk was alone in her office, playing solitaire on her computer. She took one look at my flushed face and turned off the monitor.

"Can I help you?" she asked.

"How prepared is Waterville for a terrorist attack?" I blurted. I had forgotten the questions and was feverishly digging through my pockets looking for my cheat sheet. Did I leave it in the truck, or worse, back at Blue Rapids?

"Are you a terrorist?" she asked.

"Do I look like one?"

"You're acting a little strange," she said. Reaching over to a microphone, she whispered something into it.

"How would you classify Waterville in terms of preparedness?"

"You mean, like if terrorists did something really bad, like pollute the city wells?"

I was ecstatic—finally, an intelligent response!

"Yes!" I practically shouted.

"Well, the grocery store has a lot of beer stocked up in back, and there's always the liquor store down the street. I think the Corner Mart has plenty of beer on hand, too. I guess I'd have to say we'd make it just fine, if not a little happier for it."

I was writing as fast as I could, trying to capture every nuance in her tone. In the background, I could hear sirens approaching.

"Who would you report to in case of terrorist attack?" I asked.

"Me?" She giggled, glancing out the window. "I'd run like a scared jackrabbit."

A police car skidded in with a shriek of burning rubber. The officer stepped smartly from the vehicle, one hand on the butt of his service revolver. He glided through the front door in one fluid motion, pinning me to the wall with his steely eyes.

"What's going on?" he asked through clenched teeth.

"We have a terrorist here wanting to know how he can best destroy the area," the clerk said.

"What?" I whirled on her just as the officer's pistol cleared leather.

"He says he intends on harming Waterville's beer supply," she continued.

"Assume the position!" he snarled.

I was careful not to resist. My hands were shackled and I was led away.

I filed my report from the county jail. Just as I expected, Blue Rapids is a sitting duck. Waterville, though, is ready for anything.

# DANCING THE KANSAS TWO-STEP

I was raised an Independent Baptist, the most restrictive, arrogant, ill-tempered, and just plain mean and nasty of the Baptist denominations. Early on I was taught that God is love but He also has a mean streak and won't be trifled with, especially when good, faithful Baptists backslide into such evils as drinking, cussing, card-playing, and, what might be the worst of all, dancing. When our junior high school tried teaching square dancing to a bunch of bashful, two-left-footed boys and girls, I was excused by a note from our pastor, who declared that dancing was against the tenets of our faith. The fact that David, the King of Israel, danced in the book of Psalms was never adequately explained to me, and to this day I wonder if the pastor knew it was even there.

Oh, yeah, I forgot: that was in the Old Testament, so it could be excused. Independent Baptists relish the Old Testament because they use it for their own ends, picking out whatever suits their needs and scrapping the rest. The technical name is "hunt-and-peck theology."

I distinctly remember the first time I uttered a swear word. I was out on the mesa between our housing development and the Sandia Mountains, the cloudless sky cerulean blue, when, in a fit of spiritual orneriness that strikes even the most faithful at times, I glanced around to make certain I was totally alone and said the D-word. Aloud. (Hint—it's not darn.)

It was akin to hurling a gauntlet, a blatant act of rebellion against the Most High. I don't know what I expected to happen but I was immediately shocked witless. A bolt of lightning from the blue or the earth rending at my feet and plunging me into a chasm of fire and brimstone would not have been a surprise. That nothing happened still confuses me. The world carried on as if I were as insignificant as a dung beetle.

This was all brought to mind recently by an incident that happened in Riverside Park in Blue Rapids. City superintendent Dave Sanner and I were watching a guy from the Kansas Forest Service measure a huge cottonwood tree to see if it was a state champion. It was a typical Kansas spring day, warm and humid, with a light breeze cooling our sweat and vultures hanging motionless in the sky above. Dave was holding a tape measure, me a notebook and pen.

Unbeknownst to me, a mosquito landed on my leg and began drawing blood. I felt a tingle, looked down, caught it red-proboscised, and smashed it into a red-and-black smear.

Dave slapped his shoulder.

I brushed a gnat from my face. Slapped my leg again.

Dave squashed a mosquito on his arm.

I smacked my arm, my leg, and waved my hand in front of my face as if trying to create a draft.

Dave picked a bug out of his ear with a grimace.

I ducked as a wasp flew perilously close by.

Dave slapped a spot on his arm and flicked off the remains.

And then it came to me—we were engaged in an act my Baptist upbringing would have warned against. Dave and I, unknown to ourselves, were dancing the Kansas Two-step.

Actually, if you want to be picky, it's more than a two-step though the moniker has a certain innocent charm. We were all elbows and knees and arms and open palms and body contact as we fended off the hordes of mosquitoes and gnats and other sundry insects that decided we were lunch.

Our pastor insisted that the Lord had nothing better to do than monitor our behavior for sordid affairs such as listening to rock music and dancing, whether it be square dancing or that most invidious evil, close-dancing with a member of the opposite sex. And yet I, like Job, must raise my voice and question the truth of that far-fetched notion, for I know something our pastor apparently did not—the Kansas Two-step is a natural result of God's creation.

In New Mexico, where I grew up, there were few insects around. When God created Kansas He went a little hog-wild on bugs, apparently making up on the shortage elsewhere. Considering that we have approximately fifty species of mosquitoes—fifty!—and eye gnats that zero in on, guess what, eyeballs, plus innumerable other gnats, fleas, flies, wasps, and hornets, and that many of these pests take delight in tormenting humans, then dancing must be understood as the evolution of evasive action.

In time, somebody created music and a beat and choreographed the flailing and slapping and sidestepping into something more artistic, thereby earning the ire of Independent Baptists.

I dislike dancing in any form, not on religious grounds but because I feel I look stupid doing it. Once, at the wedding of my older brother's daughter, I actually asked my wife onto the dance floor and did a few slow numbers, but the novelty was marred by my family hooting and hollering and taking photographs of the historic occurrence. It was kind of nice, I admit, but not something I'd want to do everyday.

And yet here I am, doing the two-step whenever I step foot outside. I was starting to feel like a backsliding renegade when I noticed that our neighbors, out for a walk, were doing the same thing.

Mary Ann Spunaugle and her daughter-in-law, Cora, were coming down Gypsum Street late one afternoon with Cora's baby, Cheyenne, in the stroller. They acted normal at first, but then I saw the beginning signs of apostate behavior. The baby fluttered her hands in front of her face, and Mary Ann batted at something invisible, and Cora slapped her arms and legs and jumped sideways. Before you know it, we had a regular hoedown in front of our house. It was shameful behavior but I pretended not to notice.

# A STRANGER IN THE MIRROR

Maybe it was spring madness or just madness in general, but last week I shaved off my beard. This wasn't a spur of the moment decision but one that had been coming for a while. I think every twenty years or so a man ought to see what his face looks like. The last time I saw my chin was when my oldest son was five years old. It scared him. It scares me now.

Maybe some things are better off hidden. Chins, for one. Double chins, weak chins, appurtenances that shock and awe after two decades of concealment. There was a reason I grew a beard in the first place, I recalled, and the chin was one of them.

Those chipmunk cheeks, my Parker inheritance, were another reason, only now, after a few years of living large (as they say), they've morphed, expanded, and sagged. Not very attractive.

I looked in the mirror and a stranger stared back. Not a total stranger but someone who resembled the man I once was. I looked just like my uncle, Richard Smith, from the nose down. This is not necessarily a compliment to either of us.

I had told my wife that morning, "Today might be the day." She smiled and didn't reply. Later, I locked the bathroom door and stared hard into the mirror. Most visible was a white patch in my beard that makes me look like a skunk's back, or the dividing stripe on the highway. A patch that glows with an inner luminosity in all photographs. A patch that whispers, *old*. My right hand held the clippers, my left, white-knuckled, gripped the sink rim.

*Do it and be done with it or walk away and forget it*, I said. *Screw it up and you can get a column out of it.*

Is that it? I'm a column whore.

I thought of those old photographs of me beardless. I looked good—handsome even. I also looked younger. Not that that had anything to do with it. There's not a vain molecule in my body. Honest.

There's a moment when time slows to a crawl, when your life is a cinematic loop with beginning and end—the end being the present moment, the moment that precedes the grand finale by a whisker of time—and this was it. I knew it. I could walk away and forever wonder, or I could take those clippers and see what I looked like. If I did that, I knew, I was committed.

I took one last look at what I'd come to identify as me, and slid the clippers from gullet to lip. White hair fell like snow.

There was my chin, the one I'd purposely concealed.

Too late for crying in my beer, I thought, and grimly trimmed off the last of it. After wondering how short to make my sideburns, I realized that I'd forgotten proper grooming. I had to train myself all over. When I had trimmed the whiskers as close to my skin as possible, I lathered up with shaving cream and sat back to wait a few minutes. I rechecked the door to make sure it was locked.

I drew a razor across my cheek, the blade catching on grizzle. Do I draw it down, sideways, or upwards? I had no idea. All I knew was I had to get it done.

When my face was naked as a baby's butt—and about as attractive—I threw open the door and marched into the living room. No half measures here, no skulking around to see if she noticed. She noticed, all right.

Lori—my precious wife, the woman I've devoted twenty-nine years of my life to—exploded into giggles. She laughed until tears sprang from her eyes. She looked away, glanced back, and looked away again.

"I'm sorry," she gasped. "I just can't look at you right now."

And: "I don't know who you are."

And: "You have to go away for a while."

I wondered for how long, a day, a week, a few minutes? I marched back into the bathroom and stared at the stranger. Oh it was me all right, a little chubbier, a bit worse for wear. I hated what I'd done.

I wished for an outbreak of SARS (severe acute respiratory syndrome) so I could hide behind one of those fashionable face masks. Maybe nobody would notice my suddenly naked face.

Going public was the next hurdle. I swore that if everybody reacted like my wife I'd sequester myself until my beard grew back. At least my rabbit, Mr. Bun, didn't care what I looked like.

As I walked out of the house I noticed something new. My face felt cooler, almost sensual. The breeze caressed my now-exposed flesh. If it wasn't for that chin, I thought, I could enjoy this.

Friends greeted me as if nothing had changed. They were either being polite or unobservant, I reckoned. They said I looked younger when I mentioned that I'd shaved. I went home and stared at myself again, and sure enough, I'd shed a few years by getting rid of the damn thing. Not that it mattered, really. It was just an observance.

And yet I simply could not resign myself to this new face.

Nor could my wife. If I wanted to see my uncle whenever I looked in the mirror I'd paste his picture there. Since I can't very well glue my whiskers back on, and since my beard doesn't grow very fast, I need some help. I wonder if Miracle Grow works on facial hair.

# THE MYSTERIES OF WOMEN FINALLY REVEALED

Women think they have a monopoly on indecisiveness. As far as they're concerned their birthright allows them the luxury of waffling, wavering, and vacillating over the tiniest details, often at the expense of a man's patience. What's worse is they actually consider this an asset rather than a liability. If a man has the temerity to change his mind, or can't make up his mind, women scorn him as somehow less masculine, an uncouth troglodyte. This is blatant discrimination.

A few decades back men were told to get in touch with their feminine side. Most men didn't have a clue what this meant, but that's nothing new in the dialogue between the sexes. What women meant wasn't that men should suddenly act like total goofs when it came time to decide on whether to buy, say, the Dockers in baby blue or pastel pink, but that men should be attuned to their sensitive nature. Otherwise, women still wanted men to be men.

The idea of masculinity, as it is of femininity, constantly evolves. In many circles it's no longer unfashionable for women to be the breadwinners and men to be stay-at-home dads. Nor is it uncommon for women to hold high positions as accountants, lawyers, or CEOs. There are women astronauts, car mechanics, salesmen (er, saleswomen), politicians, scientists, and policemen (damn it, there I go again). That women have risen to positions traditionally reserved for men proves they've learned to get in touch with their masculine side, which facilitates decisive thinking.

Men have, in fact, allowed women the freedom to be and do anything they desire. Men are like that—caring, compassionate, understanding. Men love women and will do anything for them.

Men are suckers.

Women reciprocated by turning vicious. An entire cottage industry now exists to humiliate men. It's called television. Modern commercials, no doubt produced by women, indicate men are not only incapable of making up their minds but also have the IQ of a rock. Women appear in control, able to grasp complex issues (like which breakfast cereal to buy or what telecommunications firm is the best bargain), while men languish in utter and hopeless stupidity. *Can't make up your mind?* the commercials not-so-subtly suggest, *You're a loser!*

Not that we earn any sympathy for it. We're meant to feel like failures.

Can you imagine the howls of outrage that would ensue if men made commercials showing women in the same light? Men would be branded as sexist, discriminating, vengeful lowlifes. We'd go to bed alone at night. Suppers would be cold and silent. Our children would turn against us.

Men know the deck is stacked against them.

And yet, much as it pains me to admit, perhaps women are partially correct. There's something decidedly bizarre about a man who can't make up his mind. It goes against the grain, it hurls the universe out of whack. Geese migrate south in the spring and rivers run uphill. But if Mother Nature herself slinks away in disgust, it's nothing compared to the emotions a man feels when he's trapped inside the mind of a woman.

As part of an ongoing investigation into the decision-making process of women (or the lack thereof), I recently determined that the only way to understand women would be to put myself in their shoes, or as much as any man can. And the best way to do that would be to shake my very foundation, to rattle my self-esteem so much that I would be forced to see myself with new eyes. I wouldn't wear mascara or false eyelashes, or saunter down the street in fish-net nylons and mini-skirt (thank God). No, I'd do a complete make-over.

I marched into the bathroom, took a long last look at the face I knew so well, and shaved off my beard.

As near as my investigation can tell, women do this not because it's fun but because it restores their confidence to its original level of uncertainty. It's a genesis, filled with all the bedeviling questions that nag and howl. *Does my hair look good? Should I use a different nail color? Should I go shopping for a new outfit?* A make-over is the very foundation of foundationlessness.

Believe me, it works.

The male part of me immediately decided I didn't like it. I'd grow it back starting right away.

But then a strange emotion crept in, taking me completely by surprise: vanity.

Women stopped me on the street and said they liked me without a beard. I shaved the stubble off.

My wife couldn't look at me without laughing hysterically. I stopped shaving.

People said I looked younger. I shaved once again.

Inadvertently, I'd stumbled upon the very essence of womanhood, the ultimate source of conflict and irresolution. Vanity is the driving force behind a woman's inability to make decisions. Vanity is the destroyer of stability. Of all emotional states a human is capable of, only jealousy is as destructive. It's no wonder that the author of Ecclesiastes concludes that vanity leads to "a vexation of spirit."

It also can really screw up a man's thinking. My spirit was sorely vexed.

I begged my wife for help. *Please*, I implored, *tell me how you prefer me.* But do you think she could make up her mind? No.

It's been a struggle but I think I'm back on track. I've given up on getting in touch with my feminine side. My beard is growing back and with it my self-confidence. I no longer have trouble deciding what shoes to wear or which color of socks matches my jeans. In fact, I no longer care. I'm even considering changing my long-distance phone provider!

I am man. Hear me roar.

# BRAVE NEW (DISCOUNTED) WORLD

Turning fifty beats the alternative but that's not to say I welcome its arrival. When you reach a certain age you're entitled to luxuries unknown in your youth. While some facets of your life might be spinning out of your control, in others you have shattered the fetters of age-restricted restraint and can now be as crotchety as you want. In a word, you've reached an age where you can *reinvent* yourself.

I remember the day I hit forty. I no sooner arrived at work and sat down to read a book for a half-hour when one of my co-workers, a noxious idiot named John, stuck his head in the room. John was incapable of understanding that I wished to read, not chat. I always showed up early in order to beat traffic, and he showed up to yak. Talk talk talk, my God, that man could talk, and never say a thing worth hearing. But I was forty now, and as I glared over the rim of my book I realized I had attained that magic age where I didn't need to be polite if I didn't want to. "Beat it," I snarled.

For a second John looked like he'd swallowed a particularly sour lemon. I don't believe anyone had ever told him to go away, that his presence was insufferable. He made a little choking sound and disappeared. I went back to reading.

John kept his distance afterward but he never was good at keeping his mouth shut. A self-styled expert on any subject, he made the mistake of telling a linebacker-sized gorilla that he didn't know how to play darts. The hulk, who might have turned forty that very day considering his reaction, promptly dragged John from the bar and rearranged his facial features.

I danced around the idea of adding one more decade to my lifeline, wary of what it meant. Fifty seemed old to me, not merely as an esoteric number but as the wrinkled face staring back from the mirror. This graying shadow couldn't be me, could it? Like it or not, it was.

Omens preceded my birthday. Mars crept closer to earth than ever in recorded history, eminent in the night sky. I tried seeing significance in the advent but astronomers blamed it on the planet's orbit. Others in our community succumbed to the half-century mark, preceding me in such numbers that I wondered if there was a contagion loose in the land. That they were still standing and breathing days and weeks later was reassuring. And then, on the heralded anniversary of my birth, a white bird descended on our yard.

I like to think the ancient Aztecs would have had plenty to marvel at with the concurrence of a flaring star and a monochrome bird. Surely something new and auspicious was taking place. Portents in the heavens, signs on earth! Any symbolism could easily be rationalized, but I wanted to make something of them, to claim them as my birthright.

The bird was a juvenile house sparrow and perfectly, utterly albinistic. It hung around with a group of ten or more sparrows coming en masse to feast on seeds fallen from the platform feeder. Where normally I consider a house sparrow as welcome as a toothache, this bird was special. White as new sheets, it glowed in sunlight, and in flight resembled a smaller version of an egret or gull. It stuck out of the crowd whether flying or hiding in the shrubs. It was different, unique. It was also, alas, a target.

The problem with being colorless is that you can't hide

except on freshly-fallen snow. Typically, mammals or birds lacking pigmentation have short lives. I'd decided this bird was a special treat, sort of a cosmic birthday present, when a Cooper's hawk entered the yard at great speed. Mourning doves, house sparrows, and finches erupted in panic. Most of the sparrows took shelter in the forsythia but the hawk burrowed in after them. The air was filled with plaintive cries and chirps. It was the last time I saw the albino.

It's difficult to stabilize yourself once your vaunted omen has turned into raptor bait. It's just as difficult to take your plight seriously when your birthday cake is graced with a plastic vulture, a special touch added by Tom Hays of Three Suns Restaurant. All that's left to do is lift your flagging spirits by their bootstraps and march on, head held high.

Turning fifty should be a time for reassessing your life. I've had some trouble doing this because I'm constantly being interrupted by my wife, who is delighted to have a half-centenarian for a husband. She wants me to join AARP, the American Association of Retired People, whose doors are opened to those—dare I say—as young as me. She wants me to buy *Unbelievably Good Deals and Great Adventures That You Absolutely Can't Get Unless You're Over Fifty*, a book by Joan Rattner Heilman. She wants me to maximize my place in society. She wants me to cash in.

Apparently, I've reached an age where I'm entitled to more than petty surliness. Now, discounts are allotted. I can get reduced rates at motels and some restaurants. I even noticed a "senior citizen discount" listed on a recent receipt from the Marysville IGA, and while I relished the savings, the idea of being considering an old person temporarily lashed me to a froth.

As usual, my wife is right. As I enter my fifties I

must be prepared to grab every discount, every favor, every perquisite I can get. After all, I'm not getting old, I'm earning entitlements.

# DEFINING NEED AND WANT—A MAN'S GUIDE TO SHOPPING

I bought a new knife last week. While that's not a stop-the-presses type of event, it's rare enough for me that after the fact I started thinking about weaponry, toys for men, and the differences between men and women. Mostly, though, I was taken aback at the enormous pleasure I felt during the selection process and, better yet, when the package arrived and I slipped the new knife from its box and flicked it open.

I'm fully cognizant that the following details will mean absolutely nothing to my female readers, but bear with me. My knife, a Lightfoot M1 tactical folder made by Columbia River Knife of Oregon, has a "unique blade grind, asymmetrical contoured frame, deeply textured scales and a Mako Flipper blade guard," as the brochure says. "The blade is a refined Tanto shape with a custom-style hollow grind, slight belly and recurve and a hint of a drop point," made from premium AUS 8 stainless steel with black titanium nitride non-reflective coating for superior corrosion resistance, and combination razor-sharp edges.

I don't know about you, but that sets my mouth drooling.

But wait—there's more! Aggressive friction grooves gnarl the thumb ramp and flipper, which acts as a blade guard when open. It's assembled with black stainless steel spacers and Torx fasteners, Teflon bearings at the blade pivot, and the patented

Lake and Walker Knife Safety locking mechanism that makes the folder a virtual fixed blade when actuated.

In other words, it's a real beauty.

It's not that I really needed a new knife, though my old folder was getting dull and its serrated edges made it impossible for me to sharpen. "Need," for a man, is of lesser importance than "want." It's critical that women understand this. The car *needs* an oil change. The plumbing *needs* to be fixed. To say we *need* a new knife (or rifle, or shotgun, or whatever) is really our way of saying we want something new.

Men are suckers for advertising that appeals to their masculinity. A while back I went shopping for a new cheese grater, and found the "ultimate" grater on the Internet. Based on the principle of a wood rasp, it sported a razor-sharp stainless steel blade with large grating area and non-clogging teeth. "Maximum flavor, minimum effort," the ad said. Lori thought I was nuts, and, indeed, it turned out to be a real dog. Someday I'm going to unload it as a bridal gift.

It's been a long time since I indulged myself in the purchase of a toy. I buy lots of books, and computer equipment for my job, and a few months ago I ordered a new coffee maker when the old one crapped out, but with the exception of books there hasn't been a whole lot of heart-pounding excitement in the shopping. I guess you could say I "needed" the coffee pot and the PC stuff, which certainly dampens some of the euphoria.

Though I hadn't intended on buying a new knife, the idea blossomed when I received a credit card rebate from REI, a recreational outfitter. Each year we use the rebate to buy socks—good socks, the kind that lasts for years. Since they're basically free, the price is affordable. But this year I started thinking that since we already have six unopened pairs, perhaps I could shop for some technical equipment. I didn't need a headlamp or hiking staffs or gaiters, so I checked the knife section. Within seconds I was comparing products and prices and features, and, well, the next thing was the ordering process and the waiting.

When I told Lori about it she asked about socks. "We got socks," I said. "I *need* a new knife." Which was sort of true.

Knives have always fascinated me. As a young boy I read every Tarzan book published, and I reveled in Tarzan's generous use of his knife when dismembering lions, gorillas, snakes, and commies. My first blade was a machete, somewhat larger than his model, but it served the purpose when fricasseeing weeds and an occasional slow lizard.

Sometimes this interest led to impractical items. After two Dobermans chased me down the banks of the St. Vrain River in Lyons, Colorado, and whose pursuit was shaken only by my wading across an irrigation canal posted with signs promising certain death if entered, I decided I needed something to defend myself in the unlikely event it happened again. I mulled over my choices and decided upon a huge, Bowie-style knife. I had this moronic idea of hanging it inside my fishing vest and whipping it out like a sword when confronted by teeth-baring canines. That it was unwieldy, obtrusive and heavy became evident on my first outing. The knife went into a drawer and never came out.

Even women have to admit that mistakes do occur. Other than the cost of the object, it's no big deal. We live and learn and move on.

My M1 arrived in the mail a few days ago and I've been happily carrying it since. Now and then I open the knife and inspect it, my eyes caressing the curvature of the blade, the snug grip. When I showed it to Lori I knew I was wasting my time. I prattled on about the steel and the fasteners and the shape but I might as well have been saying the governor is a Martian.

It doesn't take much to make men happy, being the simple creatures they are. I feel the weight of the knife in my pocket and I'm unreasonably content. Surely that alone was reason enough for its purchase. You know, I think I really needed a new knife.

# IGNORING THE VOICE OF REASON

Give me my computer, my Internet connection, my NOAA Web site with Doppler radio. Give me my TV and the Weather Channel. Give me my weather radio with its obnoxious but strangely comforting siren and its announcer's voice that retains its digital poise even while advising those in the listening area that they're soon to be whisked away to Oz. If nothing else, give me a beer. Please, give me a beer.

Stuck as I was in a large cooler in a HyVee store in Lincoln, Nebraska, I missed my high-tech gizmos that allow me to track incoming thunderstorms from an almost divine perspective. I was also getting cold and tried hiding the trembling in my hands that jostled the cup of punch I held. It wasn't fear, though my wife called me a chicken in front of the hastily and altogether unplanned assembly of shoppers and white-shirted employees. *You* stand in a refrigerated cooler for an hour and see how you fare. This old desert dog was out of his element and needed more clothes and more information.

It's strange how helpless we feel when deprived of our senses. In this case I'm including the technological senses our modern age provides, the gadgets that are normally within easy reach. Yet even without them we usually have our five senses to inform us. Here, surrounded by four aluminum-sheathed plywood walls and ceiling, stacks of boxed vegetables, two dozen solemn people, a bank of humming fans circulating the crisp air, and outside our narrow enclosure a tall cinderblock wall and high ceiling of latticed steel, I was bereft of vision, hearing, and, since I'd been fighting a cold, smell.

That left taste and touch, both to which I put to good use when the store manager brought in punch and several boxes of fresh-baked cookies. I didn't want to die on an empty stomach.

We all have a sixth sense: a hunch, a gut feeling, common sense. Since it's mental rather than physical it's impossible to verify its worthiness, but most of us will agree that at times our bacon has been saved by heeding this mystical voice. That I was sharing this cooler with these nice people was, to my dismay, precisely because I ignored that voice.

Nor did technology help me. All the way here I had watched the storm approach while listening to the radio herald its vanguard. I told my wife we were nuts to head into the teeth of the storm just so we could buy a new sewing machine, and yet we had postponed the purchase for weeks and now we needed one badly for a quilting class my wife was taking. Now, I realized, I might pay the price for my obtusity.

Clouds were just blanketing the sun when we arrived in Lincoln. Rain swept the parking lot at a restaurant where we ate lunch. Thunder rattled the windows. A waitress was telling a fellow employee how during the last storm customers were ushered into the coolers until they were packed like sardines. I listened haphazardly but the import didn't sink in until later, when we duplicated the act.

After Lori found a sewing machine she liked, she had to visit the other specialty stores in the strip mall, where cloyingly helpful employees suggested that we proceed farther into the city to shop at yet more stores. My wife was more than willing. I elected to run for home.

My vote was discounted. Black clouds hemmed the horizon by the time my wife tired of spending money. A tornado was reported near a small town south of Lincoln; upon locating it on the map, I realized that our paths would converge were we to leave. We were stuck. An eerie dusk settled in, punctuated by sonorous peals of thunder and fulminant bolts of lightning.

An uncomfortable realization set in that we were just like the beetles, crickets, and millipedes that venture into the building where I clean. Why they do so is a mystery, but what happens to them is fairly certain. If they encounter someone who wishes them well, they may be swept back outside, with only their dignity harmed. If they linger, though, or the wrong person comes along, they're squashed. I hoped Nebraska wouldn't be that way for us.

Always being one who looks for the silver lining, Lori decided we needed to hit the grocery store to give the storm time to move past. A deluge hit just as we walked through the door.

We were almost on the last aisle when the manager advised everyone to head to the coolers. "Leave your carts where they are," he said. People were moving to the rear of the store, so we followed. I thought of the new sewing machine in the car and wondered if we'd ever get to use it.

From news reports heard later, a violent storm swept through the southern part of town while we waited it out like ostriches with our heads buried in the sand. Sirens wailed, winds toppled signs and at least one building, torrential rain brought flooding, and a vast rotation spun the clouds like a witch's cauldron. We saw and heard nothing, divorced from reality, shivering in the cold, waiting for the all-clear or the walls to implode.

After an hour of this we were released. We weren't out of

the woods yet; indeed, the ride home was a daunting one, but there were lessons learned. I now know what to do if you're in a strange town and have a nasty storm bearing down on you: find a grocer, where they'll put you up in their finest cooler and feed you cookies and punch. That's Midwestern hospitality for you.

I also learned to pay attention to what my senses were trying to tell me. Next time I'm grabbing a beer before diving into the cooler. I'd hate to die thirsty.

# WHOM THE GODS WOULD DESTROY

There wasn't time for recriminations when the truck began to tilt onto its side, the howl of the wind like the shriek of a wounded jackrabbit. I was a little busy at the time, eyes straining through the downpour, the entire universe in motion and yet me seemingly at a standstill, my foot stomping the gas pedal to the floor, the windshield wipers vainly beating back the flood, the green air filled with vegetal matter. It was only afterward, when my heart calmed to a steady thrum and my breath returned in uneven gasps, that I recalled my fateful words.

I'm no fan of George W. Bush, let me make that clear. I consider him a dangerous man when he acts like Clint Eastwood in a cheap spaghetti western, blowing smoke from the barrel of his Colt .45. When he taunted the Iraqis with a "Bring 'em on" several months ago I knew what the outcome would be. They'd bring it on, and they did. The result was an endless string of body bags. So why did I emulate him? What prompted me to step outside and square off against the dark clouds marching in from the west and dare them to, yes, "Bring it on"?

Insanity. That's my excuse and I'm sticking to it.

I have a little help here from a Greek playwright, and believe me, I'll take whatever help I can get. Euripides wrote, "Whom the gods would destroy, they first make mad." His statement is both harrowing and vivid, and wise, too, as if his was the voice of experience. As if he had once challenged the gods, gone toe-to-toe with them, and they had responded in kind.

It was an early form of "Don't try this at home, for professionals only," but we humans exit the womb swinging, testing our bounds from an early age. Many of us have never evolved past the two-year-old stage, when a resounding "No!" was our favored expression and our usual temperament was pouty. I'm as guilty as the next man.

But to accost the storm gods so blatantly is not a rational act. In my defense, I was pushed to it after watching several promising rainstorms tease us with their moisture-laden clouds, only to bypass us and drop their precious load on others less deserving than us. The gods' willfulness sent me over the edge. And when another storm rose up, let fly a few drops, and then whisked dust on top of them—a New Mexican rainstorm—I was *pissed*. Prior to leaving for Waterville to attend a dedication ceremony for the new ambulance building, I faced into the clouds and hurled the gauntlet. I sneered; I cajoled; I laughed a bitter laugh. "What are you going to do about it?" I shouted.

A bolt of lightning sizzled overhead.

Rain caught me at the Fawn Creek bridge. At first it wasn't bad, a fairly typical storm, but things deteriorated rapidly. Just past the high school cutoff it hit harder, threatening to overpower the wipers. The wind hit like a hurricane, ripping water off the streets like ocean spray. And then it really turned ugly.

On all sides of me, everything began moving, trees swirling around, leaves and limbs pelting the truck like hailstones, rain slashing across the windows and whipping in sheets across the road, the clouds skirling and riotous with a pale sun tinting the maelstrom with a golden luminescence. But I seem to be standing still, encapsulated within walls of steel and glass. Everything in violent motion but me.

Or so it seemed. The truck was taking a beating, rocking and swaying with the gusts, the gale blasting at an angle. As a curve approached, I realized that when I got there the wind would broadside me.

And there was a roar, though whether from the wind or my madly beating heart was impossible to say.

Several things happened at once. The curve opened to my right and the truck tracked into it. A terrible force slammed the vehicle. It yawed. Rain obliterated my view. Clenching the wheel, I muttered "Don't roll, don't roll, don't roll," but it felt for a second as if the left tires were leaving the ground. The truck teetered as the roar intensified to a scream. Seeing saw the turnoff to the golf course through a wall of water, I spun the wheel heedless that I might cartwheel and ran up against the leeward side of the maintenance building.

Silence was like an explosion.

After the violence, the stillness was surreal. Trees and shrubs on the golf course jitterbugged as if being electrocuted; the air was a green amalgam consisting of leaves and bark and grass and milo and cornstalks; the distant hills above the river were veiled by rain. My heart pounded. My hands shook. I was surprised I was yet in one piece.

Once the wind calmed to a roar, I left the shelter of the building. I was reluctant to do so but I had a meeting to attend, though I suspected that the meeting had now been overruled by more pressing matters. Two power poles had snapped like twigs and now dangled from the tension of the lines. Tree limbs foliated the streets of Waterville. Lightning still stabbed downward, heavy bolts lingering on the ground like a lover's caress.

The dedication being cancelled, I returned home. I felt drained of life, weary beyond words. Hugging my wife as we watched the storm move to the east, I recalled my words. And I could have sworn I heard a soft chuckle in the growling thunder of the retreating storm. Euripides, or the storm gods? All I know is next time I'm keeping my mouth shut.

# THE DEVIL IN THE DETAILS

The NOAA weather radio is one of the greatest inventions ever made. It's like having your own National Weather Service satellite hovering over your house keeping a personal eye out for everything happening within hundreds of miles. Nothing can escape its purview, not tornadoes, dust storms, hurricanes, tsunamis, child abductions, cattle rustlings, dirty-bomb attacks, UFO sightings, or incidents of Dick Cheney being seen in public. Weather radios are technological guardian angels. I hate them.

Living as we do in Tornado Alley, I finally broke down and bought a weather radio to keep us safe. Call it our own Department of Homeland Security. Since many of our severe storms strike at night when visibility is nil and we're fast asleep (or trying to), I felt any warning it bleated would give us ample time to reach shelter in the basement.

What I failed to realize was that most of our severe storms strike at night when visibility is nil and we're fast asleep (or trying to), and the weather radio would bray like a deranged jackass—over and over and over. This is the Midwest, after all.

I put it off for years after hearing bad things about them. Older models, while effective, would give alerts whenever one was issued within the continental United States and Puerto Rico, the U.S. Virgin Islands, and the U.S. Pacific territories. It didn't matter if the skies were clear where you lived; if a tropical storm was coming ashore in Hawaii, the weather radio would warn you of it. Naturally, this caused more than a little consternation and sleeplessness among weather radio owners.

Coincidentally, the U.S. Fish and Game Department reported that the number of game birds being harvested increased in the early 1960s as the first generation of weather radios were made available to the public. At first attributed to better firearms and ammunition, it was later determined to be the result of hunters using the radios for wingshooting practice.

However, technological advances have made them much more reliable. Newer models can be programmed to accept only localized alerts using SAME technology. That stands for Sanity Aggravating Messaging Encoding.

For rocket scientists or those with IQs in the high double-digits, the radios can be programmed to restrict alerts to specific counties. For the rest of us, the weather radio can be programmed as an alarm clock or function as an AM-FM radio. The reception is fantastic.

Weather radio goes back much farther than most people realize. The first functioning weather radio was God. Noah was sitting on his porch thinking about firing up his grill when a voice from Heaven startled him.

"Noah. This is God."

"Yessir!"

"Noah, it's going to rain."

"Looks pretty clear to me, Lord."

"Noah, trust me on this."

"Okay, I won't start the grill, I'll cook inside."

"Noah, shut up and listen."

The weather service, while hampered somewhat by possessing less-than-omnipotent powers, issues two types of alerts: watches and warnings. It's important to distinguish between the two of them.

A watch is issued when conditions are favorable for a thunderstorm, tornado, or _____ (add your favorite catastrophe). Forecasters at the National Oceanic and Atmospheric Administration crank these out when they see the potential for a storm (or whatever) developing at some point in the immediate future. Watches usually have an expiration time, as in "The National Weather Service in Topeka has issued a severe thunderstorm watch for Washington and Marshall counties effective until 10 p.m. A watch means that conditions are favorable. We'll be at the bar keeping a close eye on the situation as it develops."

A warning means that a storm (or whatever) has now progressed from a theoretical state to an actual presence. Conditions are no longer favorable, they're downright instigative. Your weather radio will emit a fearsome siren guaranteed to stop your heart, followed by an announcement such as "The National Weather Service in Topeka has issued a severe thunderstorm warning, effective until one a.m. A strong cell has been detected near Linn. This storm has a history of producing calf-sized hail, biblical floods, electronic-destroying lightning, and hurricane winds. It also has a history of doing little more than grumbling around the edges, like a cranky old school teacher. You just never know! It's tracking northeast at a speed of ten miles an hour. Stay tuned for additional updates."

This is actually a joke. The weather radio is programmable only so far. One is able to remove weather watches, but not warnings. There's never a reason to stay tuned for updates because the weather service will make damn certain that you're kept apprised of the latest developments. They're inescapable.

According to the NOAA, only the most imminent life- and property-threatening hazards are broadcast, "where the public has to take immediate action to protect themselves. An operational guideline is that messages are alerted only for hazards urgent enough to warrant waking people up in the middle of the night."

Recently I was forced to take immediate action to protect myself in the middle of the night. A wave of violent thunderstorms moved through Washington County, triggering the first of innumerable alerts. No sooner had I silenced the alert than another jarred us awake. Storms with dizzying regularity roared through. Each time I fell back asleep, the radio would erupt with flash flood warnings, severe thunderstorm warnings, even a warning that Dick Cheney was seen driving down Highway 36 en route to his secret bunker located two hundred yards southeast of the intersection of Victory Road and 16th, right behind the small dogwood patch.

My wife threatened to shoot me if I didn't silence the radio once and for all. Even though I worried about being killed by a tornado, hers was an imminent threat. I wearily crawled from bed, unplugged the radio, yanked the standby battery, took it downstairs, and tossed it in the freezer. After that, I slept like a baby.

Yeah, weather radios are really great. The reception is so good I can finally pull in National Public Radio!

# THE FINE ART OF MAKING MOWING ENTERTAINING

I've just finished mowing my lawn, or what passes for a lawn, a rather drawn-out affair using a push mower. It strikes me that I've been less observant towards the rudiments of yard maintenance in rural Kansas than I have been toward the natural world, paying more attention to the various species of woodpeckers that frequent the suet cake hanging in the elm tree out front than in getting an education in how we try to tame our changing landscapes.

When I first purchased the little mower I raised a few eyebrows but gamely went ahead, considering thrift over function. The preponderance of lawn tractors should have been a telling clue but it went right over my head. A twenty-one-inch mower was all I ever needed back in the city and I saw no reason to switch, though our new yard was considerably larger. My ideas were rooted in a rural fantasy bred by alienation from city life and a hope for something better. No need to go big and expensive because I was planning small and intimate, crafting my own wildlife sanctuary and coexisting with nature on its own terms.

With luck we learn from our mistakes though at times I despair of ever reaching a point where I feel I'm free of being a bumbling idiot at least on occasion. Sitting here in the shade of a hackberry while a cool breeze dries my sweat-soaked shirt, I can't help but compare my mower to the behemoth my neighbor pilots. A quick calculation of blade width and horsepower leads me to believe I could mow my yard in a quarter of the time were I to invest in such a machine. If the adage that time is money holds true then I'm going broke in a hurry.

And yet there's more to it than simple economics, as if time spent outdoors, whether wandering afield or cutting swathes through one's yard, can be measured against notion of time management we humans are so fond of. I might be slow as a turtle but it gives me pause for reflection as well as the ability to study my yard up close.

People are also devoted to putting a spin on things, an all too familiar trend in politics, using it to further their ends and justify their means, or to simply defy common sense or whatever odds they might perceive to be stacked against them. With that in mind I have no problem with lauding my dinky mower as an inexpensive form of aerobic fitness, a sad but all too true take on the subject. Too bad that the beer I consume afterwards negates any health benefit gained from the exercise.

It's ironic how things turn out. My lofty goal of having a viable tallgrass preserve is rapidly deflated after finding the first tick imbedded in my anatomy, leading me to cast a jaded eye on what seems such a fine wild area. There's a method to what I once considered madness in the local habit of manicuring yards, an act based upon experience and knowledge. As a newcomer I feel slightly silly but also adaptable, trying not only to learn from my mistakes but also to conform, whenever it suits me, to my new surroundings and the community at large.

There might come a day when you see me blithely cruising around on a monstrous yard tractor, drink in hand, waving at passersby with a smile, relishing the horsepower and cutting width, making short work of the weeds and grasses that share this small plot of Kansas soil, but until then I'll keep plugging away by the sweat of my brow, step by step, row by row, while the sun drops in the west and shadows grow long and lanky and the ghosts of our ducks snap up the last few insects before retiring to their refuge beneath the stairs. Over the roar of the engine I'll note the chimney swifts arcing overhead, the wildflowers blooming along the fence, the loamy path of the mole as it burrows across the yard leaving a wake, and I'll sweat by the bucketful as I toil and grind. And never, ever, will I complain.

***

Considering that it takes me over three hours to mow my yard, I consider myself somewhat of an expert on the art. Mowing grass in Kansas is different than in Colorado and it took some adjustment to refine the dos and don'ts. Just in case there are any newcomers out there, I present my observations on how best to enjoy what is admittedly everybody's least favorite activity.

*Mow with your mouth shut.* This is the voice of experience talking, though thankfully it was a smaller insect that choked me and not a three-inch long katydid.

*Think of the cold beer that's waiting for you.*

*Get in touch with your inner child, the spoiled one that throws a fit when asked to mow, the one you wish you could be and get away with.*

*Mentally practice wingshooting starlings as they fly by.*

*Calculate the number of bugs the swallows and swifts overhead are removing from the atmosphere.* Cheer them on.

*Try to identify the weeds and different grass species growing where your lawn should be.* Most folks don't have a major problem with this but I'm blessed—or cursed—with a veritable botanist's nightmare. In fact, I live in fear of having broad-leaf weed killer being accidentally sprayed on our yard. If such an unforeseen event should occur I'd be left with a desolate, lifeless moonscape.

But most of all, *keep your sense of humor*. We're the only species in the known universe that spends inordinate sums of time trying to cut back what nature clearly intends on rising up.

# TO THE STARS THROUGH GRASSHOPPERS

It may have been dizziness caused by a lack of oxygen, but then I've been prone in the past to see things that were not there, or might have been there but unseen by anybody else. Years ago though still fresh in my memory was when I saw a half-jackrabbit, half-man at the Tom Frost wildlife area across the street from our home in Broomfield, Colorado. I was out on one of my walks when I glimpsed this creature stalking across the grass near the edge of the perennial pond, once a watering hole for cattle and now relegated to disuse by the encroachment of development. It was a strange apparition that mixed the physical traits of man and black-tailed jack, walking into the setting sun, highlighted against the washed-out tan of the prairie dog colony to the north. What was surprising was that there was no surprise—it seemed as normal as the magic of the curlew flying by on a storm-wracked afternoon or the gusts of air fanning off a low-flying pack of pelicans. It was, I surmised, the spirit of the field, and I so named it.

Afterwards I could sense its presence at odd times, though I never saw it again. I would be sitting near the pond, studying a family of pied-billed grebes, the young birds monotone ragamuffins, when suddenly I'd hear a rustle in the grass beside me and sense something there. Some inexplicable being. I took it as an act of faith that this was a holy place.

This was different, though, far from Colorado, in vastly different circumstances. I was mowing the yard, tight-lipped against the plague of grasshoppers that boiled from the grass before the mower, eyes squinted against the setting sun and the rain of debris blasting out of the broken discharge chute. Those grasshoppers that survived being run over made half-hearted jumps that often brought them within reach of my feet. I stomped as many as I could, doing my best to finish off what the lawnmower had not. I found myself mowing a lot slower than I wished but my kill rate was astronomical.

I was lost in a weird reverie, wondering what it must be like from the grasshopper's perspective to have a lawnmower run over you. Sort of like getting sucked up in a black tornado that just destroyed a sheet-metal factory, all deafening roar and whirling blades of death, I guess. And then I saw him.

He was peering at me from behind the shed. My first impression was of long black hair, fierce dark eyes and fawn-colored tunic. He resembled, in fact, the Kansa Native American Ad Astra, whose likeness was being hoisted atop the Kansas capitol dome.

I pulled up short, releasing the throttle. The mower sputtered to a stop. Silence descended. The man ducked behind the shed.

Now what? I wondered. My first concern was of safety—should I get the shotgun and investigate, or call the police? Then again, I hate to act inhospitable if it's a new neighbor. Deciding to brave it out, I walked over and peeked behind the building.

There was nothing there but a stack of rotting boards, a hackberry growing much too close to the shed, and knee-high grass. A five-acre field stands behind our property but I couldn't see how he could have crossed it without being seen. It gave me the willies, that.

I yanked the cord on the mower and started up again,

casting nervous glances about. Grasshoppers went under the blades, leaped aside, jumped on my bare legs, ricocheted off my face, and threatened to poke me in the eye.

I worked another fifteen minutes when I saw the man again. This time he was trying to hide behind the apple tree and having a hard time doing so. What immediately struck me was the disconcerting fact that the last rays of the evening sun shone right through him as if he were as insubstantial as dust motes. Our eyes met, mine red-rimmed and weepy from allergies, his dark and deep as night. We were forty feet apart, separated by the overgrown patch of a once-promising garden, now left to the weeds, crickets, katydids, and grasshoppers.

My fingers slipped off the throttle. The roar of the engine was replaced by the incessant singing of insects.

We studied each other for a moment that lasted for ages.

He straightened up and stepped from concealment. He began walking toward me. My first thought was to run like crazy, but then I figured if he was half-invisible then he could in no way harm me.

When ten feet separated us he stopped, feet slightly apart, hands dangling at his sides. He bent to study the ground where the lawnmower had grooved a path, passing a hand over the stubble. Those depthless eyes took in the machine and then cut to me. I stood like a stone, frozen in place. And did I detect a twinkle in that darkness, a faint smile upturning the thin edges of his lips?

He leaped into motion, making me jump. Stooped over, he scooted across the lawn as if pushing the mower, whipped around at the fence and started back, but this time he went slower, making exaggerated movements that I first didn't understand. He twisted and sidestepped and shortstepped and pounced, all while acting as if guiding the mower. Then it dawned on me—he was imitating my stepping on those grasshoppers that had escaped.

He pulled up within arm's reach, a broad smile splitting his face. One finger reached out and lightly touched my chest.

"Dances With Grasshoppers," he said.

The sun flared like a torch as it balanced on the rim of the world and in that sudden luminance the man disappeared.

# IS TEXAS FULL OF IT?

Much has been made in the media about the newly-released study by Texas State University students Mark Fonstad and William Pugatch, and Arizona State University student Brandon Vogt. First published in the obscure journal *Annals of Improbable Research*, the study gained notoriety when it was picked up by Reuters, the international news agency.

To some people it proves what they've suspected all along. To others, such as Lee Allison, director of the Kansas Geological Survey, it's a "cheap shot."

Fonstad and his colleagues set out to determine whether Kansas was, indeed, as flat as a pancake. Using a well-cooked flapjack from the International House of Pancakes, they first took digital images of a cross-section using a ruler for scale calibration. Then they made a topographic profile from the sample using a confocal laser microscope. The transect diagram looked like a butte—steep sides, pocked surface—about what you'd expect to find.

Using digital elevation model data from the U.S. Geological Survey, they made a second transect, this one of the topography of Kansas. The diagram was also what you'd expect if you were at all familiar with the elevation decline from west to east: a slanting horizontal line.

Using a complex mathematical formula, the fledgling scientists determined that the flatness of the pancake measured

0.957 and Kansas measured 0.9997, out of a value of 1.000. Their conclusion: Kansas is not only flatter than a pancake, it's "damn flat."

I'm not a scientist by training so I turned to Professor Bill Nutso from the Department of Soil Analysis and Dubious Theories at Kansas State University. He at first seemed hesitant when I explained what I wanted to do, but then his scientific mind kicked in and he started firing questions at me. He had all the equipment needed for an analysis, he said, but he needed a sample of Texas soil. How could we get that on such short notice?

Luckily, I had gathered several jars of Texas dirt during my recent travels there. One was taken from the Davis Mountains in the western part of the state, another from near the Brazos River in the north, and another from the coast near Corpus Christi.

Nutso met me at the lab.

"Do you have what we need?" he asked. I showed him the soil samples and a small box containing a fresh cow pie.

Nutso scooped out a small glop of the manure and set it in a glass tube. The tube went into a large metal contraption festooned with gauges and digital displays. "This is a Barton System (B.S.) Digitometer," he said. "It uses spectrographic analysis to break down the chemical components of the specimen."

While the digitometer was humming away, he sat down at his computer and began tapping the keys. "Texas has the largest number of free-range cattle in the United States," he said. "In fact, three to four times as much as any other state. That makes for a massive amount of excrement. Texas is also the largest producer of sheep in the nation."

The digitometer gave a little beep. Nutso removed the

manure sample and placed all three jars of dirt on a revolving tray. The machine began humming again.

"Texas also has a huge population," he continued. "With Mexican food and barbecue so popular, a vast amount of beans are consumed daily. It also doesn't help that it's predominantly a Republican state. Studies have shown that Republicans are famous for slinging the, well, you know what."

The digitometer beeped again. The results of the analysis spit out on a silver tape.

"You were right," Nutso said, reading the figures. "The dirt samples show an unusually high concentration of fecal matter. For instance, Kansas measures 0.000025 on a national mean average of 1.000. These samples measure 9,934,979. That's incredible! There is so much dung in this soil that you can flatly state that Texas is full of it."

Nutso paused, his brow wrinkling. "All those windstorms, hurricanes, tornadoes, and traffic must really keep manure particulates concentrated in the atmosphere. Humans would naturally ingest them through breathing. It might be possible to do a DNA analysis of a Texan's blood to determine if not only the state is full of it, but if the people are, too."

His eyes locked mine. "But where would we find a Texan?" he asked.

Though I was loath to admit it, I held my arm out. "Take my blood," I said. "I was born in Texas."

For a long moment he didn't move. His eyes bore into mine like drills. "Are you sure you want to do this?" he asked. I nodded.

Nutso drew a blood sample and placed it in the digitometer. While it was being analyzed, he re-read the figures from the soil samples.

"If I publish this I'll be hunted down and killed," he muttered.

There was another beep. He read the silver tape, his eyes lit by a weird glow.

"Your blood has elevated levels of waste matter," he said. On his computer, he punched up a series of charts. He pointed to a long twirling string. "The DNA doesn't match that of a sheep or pig," he said. "What's odd is that it's an almost perfect match for a cow, but not just any cow. The DNA is nearly identical to that of a male of the species."

Professor Nutso turned to me. "The B.S. Digitometer proves that both Texas and Texans are full of bull shit," he said. "Damn full, I'd say."

Though repeated efforts were made, the editors of the *Annals of Improbable Research* as well as the student geologists refused to return our phone calls. A spokesman for Reuters said that they had no intention on publishing our findings because the results were common knowledge.

# NO CHANCE OF SUCCESS: MEN SHOPPING FOR WOMEN

Tis the season for giving, and at no other time does a man most sense his shortcomings.

Gary North puts it this way: "Men don't like to shop for Christmas…or anytime, for that matter, except for the few items they really love. It's the thought that counts, and they hate to think. 'What does she want most this year?' This question reminds us of the grim reality: we don't have any idea, and we never have. The feminine retort, 'You should have known,' haunts us from the day we get married until the day we reach room temperature."

Women want it that way. It keeps men on the defensive. It makes men feel caddish and ignorant and unworthy of their love. And when we feel that way, we tend to lavish them with even more gifts.

Me, I like to shop, with certain exceptions. While it's true I vehemently dislike visiting Walgreens, Dollar General, or Hobby Lobby, it's not due to their products or services but because the idiots who lay out the aisles have no idea how to group things dynamically. This might be a man thing but I see a female touch in the design. Women are perfectly happy to aimlessly roam every aisle, to pick up all the frilly and useless junk cluttering the shelves, not because they're interested in buying them but because it satisfies their feminine nature.

"Oh, look, honey," they coo at us, showing us some little

plastic gizmo that would bore the greediest two-year-old to tears. The smart man will never utter the words he most wants to ("Is that what we came here for?") and instead will do his best to look interested. Rolling eyes and deep sighing are not recommended. For their part, women try to ignore our body language, which by this time is screaming, "Someone please shoot me."

Men want order. Men want reason. Men want to be able to march into a store, find what they want, pay for it, and get the hell out. This leaves more time for creative shopping, like at stores selling sporting goods or booze.

By implication this means they're shopping for themselves, with a firm idea of what they want, where to find it, and how much they're willing to spend. It's only when they shop for women that their world spins out of control.

Buying a birthday gift for a woman is sheer torture. Since women think we're supposed to know what they want, they feel above responding to our pleas for suggestions. We're put in a hopeless position. If we buy the wrong thing, they think we're cretins. If we buy the right thing, they think we should have bought something else to go with it. We can't win.

Christmas shopping, though, is birthday shopping on steroids. It's not just one gift we're looking for but a host of them. And they must be exactly what she wants, even if she refuses to tell us what that might be. No wonder liquor sales spike during the holiday season.

This year, like every one of the past thirty years, I've asked my wife what she'd like for Christmas. I'd have as much response were I to ask our new rabbit what she wants. My wife promises to tell me and then never does.

So I did something I've never done before. Swearing off wheedling and pleading, I instead eavesdropped when she spoke to her friends. She wanted a floor loom, I deduced. Feeling very clever, I hit the Internet and started researching looms. After suffering heart palpitations over their prices, I contacted various manufacturers, called her friends, spoke at length with shop owners, and read online reviews. This is what a man does best—research, decide, buy. No wandering aisles like drunken sailors.

I ordered the model I thought she'd like best. I could afford it if I didn't get anything for myself or the kids for the next two decades. Wanting complete secrecy, I arranged to have shipping details sent to a friend, who promised to let me know when the package was en route.

It remained to go through the motions, of asking her what she wanted, begging for information, etc. When she ignored my requests, I didn't sweat it. I felt pretty cocky.

Four days later I heard her talking to the shop owner I'd purchased the item from. She was asking about looms, and each question brought a stab of fear to my heart. Maneuvered into the room, I made a big show of rubbing our rabbit. I acted innocent and felt miserable. How was I supposed to stop her without spilling the beans? My elaborate scheme was unraveling like a snagged seam.

When she told the owner she had to get my opinion first I almost collapsed with relief. But I wasn't out of the woods yet. My mind raced feverishly to come up with a ruse.

"Is that what you really want?" I asked like a clueless husband.

It was. I suggested the price was perhaps a tad too lofty, and instantly saw a shadow pass over her face. The damage done, I cringed when she started harping how she rarely spends money on herself, etc. etc. (Husbands, fill in the blanks here.) I was screwed and knew it.

So I went on the offensive. "I already bought you a loom," I said.

That shut her up. She stared blankly at me, took her glasses off, rubbed her eyes, carefully set them back in place, and stared some more.

"What kind?" she asked.

I refused to divulge details. I had the high ground and meant to capitalize on it.

Yet I had lost the element of surprise. Bitterly, I realized on some primal level that men are never allowed to hold the high ground, that our actions are controlled as if we were simple marionettes dangling on a string, at a woman's whim or mercy. No matter how hard we try to outwit them, we're doomed.

I hate Christmas shopping.

# THE WORLD THIS TIME

# THE EIGHTH DAY OF CREATION

The red sun is just lifting above the horizon when I pull off the road and park.

Eskridge, population five hundred counting the cats and dogs, lies a mile off, slumbering in its blanket of elms and maples, tucked in a fold of the land. Near me is an old cattle chute, now fallen into disuse, filled with curly dock going to seed. A nighthawk rests atop one crossbeam, eyes slitted, studying me with a lazy insouciance. All around me the land falls away in broad sweeps, green and lush and splashed with wildflowers.

I cut the engine and rub my eyes. Time for another cup of coffee, but first I want to stretch my legs. I open the door and the world rushes in.

An otherworldly singing fills the air. It comes from everywhere, as if the atmosphere itself is suffused with it. Accompanying it are the songs of meadowlarks and dickcissels and cowbirds, but the main theme is something entirely different. Something primitive and wraithlike. It slowly rises and falls, a whistling tune stretched out, elongated, strident. At first I think it's a curlew, but there are no curlews here. *Sandpiper,* I realize. Upland sandpiper, the shorebird of the tallgrass prairie. Dozens and dozens of them, in the air with their stiff-winged flight, on the fence posts, scurrying along the ground. All of them, apparently, singing.

In the beginning God created the heavens and the earth, I was told during my youth. It took Him seven days, our pastor said, and he repeated the timeline like a mantra throughout my childhood and into the early stages of adulthood, as if repetition it made it true. The world was made in *seven* days, he stressed, beating on the pulpit like a roofer driving nails. He excoriated Darwinists and geologists. When the Bible said seven days, he shouted, it meant seven twenty-four-hour days. One week. *Period.*

It was a favorite topic of his, as was the book of Revelation, the beginning and the end, and truthfully it was a welcome respite from his usual fire-and-damnation sermons. By re-entering the Garden of Eden and pacing backwards to the hanging of the stars in the firmament we could dwell for a short while in perfection. Cosmology as refuge. The world then was ideal, he said, every living creature in harmony. Bugs didn't bite, the lion lay down with the lamb, men and women got along, and there was only the Baptist religion.

After the Garden everything went to pot, of course, that wicked, faithless woman and the wily serpent throwing a wrench in the works. Since I grew up in rattlesnake territory I always wondered about that snake part. But his belief about how nature turned against man, how evil and wicked it all became, ran full-tilt into something within me that said otherwise. But who was I to gainsay him? I was a skinny little redhead who found the world frightening.

How his view of the biblical creation conflicted with the geological record troubles me. I've heard theories that the seven days represent epochs, large chunks of timeless time, that the fossils of dinosaurs and evolutionary images of reptiles morphing into feathered birds were "experiments," or dead-ends, that the Almighty was merely whiling away His time. Nothing I've ever heard or learned or studied has fully appeased me. Perhaps like the pastor I simply yearn for the world as it once was, perfect and guiltless.

Such ruminations seem odd while standing weary and red-eyed beside the road but the remembrance comes unbidden. A shorebird seems an unlikely bird for the inland grasslands but this once was a sea, and once covered with ice. Change is all around me. These Flint Hills could soon be the repository of wind generators spinning energy from the restless air, clean energy, renewable energy, but energy exacting a price on the natural world that we may someday regret. These sandpipers singing up the sun are declining in numbers, possibly on a one-way march to oblivion. Rural towns like Eskridge, sleeping in its little hollow, also face extinction. The momentum is relentless.

At the moment of creation, when light threw back the darkness, change was set into motion. That much I know, no matter the method of emergence. For six days God fashioned the natural world, and then He rested. And on that seventh day, if such a day really existed, I like to imagine God sitting back in His chair and taking measure of what He's done. He pops a cold beer, looks out on the Flint Hills. All around him upland sandpipers are singing. The sun is peering over the rim of the world. It's perfect. So perfect, in fact, that He doesn't want it to end. So He does what only He could do—He stops time, holds it fast in its tracks, for the length of the seventh day.

I mean no disrespect, no sacrilege. By imbuing the Creator with my own foibles I am better able to imagine the concept of divinity. Given the chance, given the ability, knowing what was sure to come, I would have relished that last day, made it last, memorized its every second to play back when times were hard.

Did the sandpipers evolve or did they spring fully-formed on the fifth day of creation? Standing there immersed in their haunting songs it seems a moot point, one approached only by a faith I no longer possess. For me, there is only the here and now, and I'm tired and need a cup of coffee.

I realize that time has briefly stopped, and now it begins again. For the moment all is calm, the air cool and moist, the sun lifting above the horizon. There is no shadow on the Flint Hills, no indication of the demise of the prairie sandpiper. It is dawn on the eighth day of creation, and all the world is singing.

# SOMETHING BUGGY THIS WAY COMES

The insect that stung me in the eye died for its sin but it was little consolation. At least it died quickly while I was left to dance in circles using language that would make a bartender blush, clutching my face and wondering just why in blazes it had run into me. I mean, couldn't it see me? Or was it an insidious plot to harm me, an act of revenge for the slaughter of its fellows? I tend not to be a conspiracy nut but sometimes paranoia is both healthy and justified.

Kansas is rife with bugs. It's amusing that when we moved here our friends in Denver shook their heads in dismay over our trading mountainous Colorado for a state that's "flat, boring, and ugly," not to mention lethal in tornadoes. Ignorance about our corner of the state is unfortunately common and they got it wrong on almost all accounts, and Denver, by the by, was where we almost lost our house to a twister. Can't say that about here, or not yet at any rate. If they wanted to stop us from moving, they should have mentioned the bugs.

Good grief, we have bugs here. According to *Insects in Kansas*, a field guide by Glenn Salsbury and Stephan White, we have an estimated fifteen thousand to twenty thousand insect species within our borders. Several thousand of these remain unnamed and unknown. The book is a veritable Who's Who of nasty, bloodsucking, crop-damaging, stinging, biting, chewing, clawing, and just plain ugly critters that gives me the willies just looking through it. I bought it so I could identify the various forms of grasshoppers that were razing my garden, thinking to make myself more rounded and informative about the local avifauna. Birds are my specialty, true, but I'm branching out into butterflies, dragonflies, and wildflowers. Insects, seeing as we have such abundance, were a natural progression.

A man can only take so much, though, before his mind shatters and his passions are unleashed. Rather than retrieving the field guide from the house and running out to the garden every time I saw a new insect, it became far easier and more rewarding just to smash it to a pulp. Our squash was annihilated by squash bugs, our tomatoes stripped by hornworms and grasshoppers, and so many weird-looking bugs infested our corn that I gave up on it. Sitting outside on a warm summer evening was a torment of mosquitoes, biting gnats, and huge flying wood roaches that resemble dirigibles with wings. Hiking, of course, covered us with ticks and chiggers. I am deathly afraid of hornets and wasps, and I was shocked to find how many we have in Marshall County, some as large as Volkswagens.

But the insect I declared war on is the lowly box elder bug. Also known as democrat or pop-bugs, the red-and-black devils proliferate by the thousands around our house. Stepping outside is an invitation to have them fly into our eyes, mouth, ears, or ricochet off our heads. The field guide labels them as "nuisances" but not overly harmful, except possibly to strawberries. They tend to invade houses in fall and winter, carrying on their summertime tradition of, well, bugging you.

Which they did an admirable job of the first year we were here. They crawled under the door and into every nook and cranny they could find, flew through the house, landed in our food, and in general raised havoc. I loathed them, and went to the Internet to find a solution.

The first Web site I found sold a special box elder bug spray that was sure to wipe them out. It was safe on upholstery and carpet, didn't require a hazmat suit, but also quite expensive. I was contemplating financial ruin when I came across another Web site that said common dish soap and water were lethal.

I liked the sound of that. I dumped out a spray bottle of glass cleaner and added a few tablespoons of dish soap and filled it with water. The first box elder bug I found was my guinea pig. One spray and it fell to the ground, its little legs writhing for a few seconds, and then it lay still. I felt like a god.

That fall I slaughtered them by the thousands, spending far too much time in the process. It became something of an obsession for me, hunting them out and eradicating them. I wanted—and got—a box-elder-bug-free house for the winter. But if I entertained thoughts of having won the war, I was a fool.

This spring they returned in even greater numbers. They were everywhere, and my little spray bottle was no match for their masses. A search of the yard found them congregating in leaf litter, red knots of procreating bugs.

I brought out the heavy artillery, a sprayer that attached to the hose. Dumping an entire bottle of soap into the reservoir, I moved through the yard leaving a foamy wake. I killed them in the leaves, in the grass, under the deck, in the gravel, in the cracks of the cement. Some I even knocked out of the sky in aerial combat.

The next day I went outside and rummaged through the leaves. There was no sign of bugs anywhere.

A week later they were back. I drove to Wal-Mart and bought a commercial sprayer, with brass wand and nozzle, three-gallon pressurized tank, shoulder strap, and several bottles of dish soap. I named it Mr. Death. Once more, I ventured forth and smote them.

And then the bug nailed me in the eye. I've talked to a number of people, all of whom say they've never heard of such a thing. Thumbing through the field guide I came across an assassin bug, and it got me thinking. What if? Nah, it couldn't be. Bugs aren't that intelligent, that resourceful, that vindictive. Are they?

# AN UNCOMMON AFFLICTION

Birders grow accustomed to strange looks and whispered comments, no doubt from the odd places where we love to hang out, like sewage ponds or tick-infested thickets. Our sanity is often called into question but it's rare indeed that a physical malady is suspected or hinted at. But just such a thing was suggested last fall while I was serving food at the Alcove Spring barbecue.

"I thought you had a tick or something," said an upstanding member of the community, who shall remain anonymous.

The poor fellow clearly had never been around a hawkwatcher, an individual who frequents migrant traps that force raptors to funnel past geological obstacles in often stunning numbers. He watched as I repeatedly stopped what I was doing and craned my head back until I faced the cloud-studded sky. Every minute (or less) the act repeated itself, as if I had a spasm in my neck.

So far as I can tell there is no scientific term for it, but I'll admit this: it is a physical disorder, impossible to overcome, terminal, with no hope for recovery. Like allergies or flu, it's seasonal, worse in spring and fall. I'm released from its grip only during the insufferably hot summer months and winter's icy grip. It begins around the first of March, drops off in late May, only to resurface in early August; by November I'm on the rebound.

I first came down with this in 1995, when I was invited to

the Dakota Ridge raptor monitoring site southwest of Denver. For three months each spring volunteers would perch on a knife-edge of upthrust rock called a flatiron and count raptors moving north. I rapidly grew addicted to it. Regardless of the weather, we remained at our posts. We broiled, we froze; only violent weather forced us off the ridge.

When we moved to Blue Rapids I thought my hawkwatching days were over. After all, we have no huge lakes or mountain ranges to force hawks into narrow channels, nor are there any raptor monitoring sites anywhere in the Midwestern states of Oklahoma, Kansas, Nebraska, or the Dakotas. But one spring day while I was out working in the yard I happened to look up and see a northbound hawk, and then another right on its tail feathers. The hawks came off a low hill to the south and angled over on a perfect northern flight. I quickly set up my spotting scope and began scanning the skies. I counted several red-tails, a few falcons, small accipiters (Cooper's and sharp-shinned hawks), an osprey, plus chevroned formations of pelicans, cormorants, and geese. For the rest of the day I was good for nothing, the yard neglected and forgotten.

In the following days the flight grew heavier. Through great good fortune I had discovered a raptor flyway, and it was directly over our house.

Whether it was a fluke or not remained to be seen. As summer turned to autumn I kept a sharp watch, and I found the hawks returning. Sometimes they passed directly overhead and sometimes I would spot them a mile or more to the west. But they were there.

Last Wednesday a lone harrier flew over our house, heading north. I'd been outside enjoying the warm weather and admiring the blue sky streaked with thin cirrus clouds, and the sight sent a shock through me. This early? It didn't seem possible.

I'm afraid that since then my peculiar affliction has flared up. I've grown restless and crave the outdoors, where I find my neck tensing until my head follows the pull of my eyes upwards to rove in unfettered release across the heavens.

They're coming, I tell you. I can feel it.

So if you meet me and I can't seem to keep my eyes at ground level, if I act distracted or stare off into the distance, or refuse to meet your look, please pay me no mind. There's nothing you can do to help me. It is utterly and gloriously hopeless.

# (ALMOST) DOWN AND OUT IN BLUE RAPIDS

Well, they did it again. If they think for one second this will slow me down, they're dead wrong.

Actually, they're dead right, because they did slow me down. In fact, they almost laid me out. Shortly after mowing my yard my left foot started swelling. It puffed up like a frightened blowfish, with an angry red mark the size of a silver dollar just behind my toes.

Spider, I figured. I'd worn a pair of boots I normally don't use, and though I shook them out beforehand that doesn't mean squat to a spider. No big deal, pop a few Benadryl's, take pain killers, soak it, and all would be well.

Out of spite, I took Mr. Death, my industrial-strength green pressure sprayer, out for a stroll through the yard, killing every box elder bug in sight. I even sprayed a few bees just for grins, and normally I like bees. At this point, I'm mad at the entire insect world, all fifty bazillion of 'em.

Overnight, my foot ballooned. The red mark enlarged. The top of my foot took on a waxy, scarlet blush. Walking was more than painful, and slipping into shoes to go to work was pure hell.

I researched spider bites on the Internet, in the process finding out all sorts of other nasty critters that can drive a man to his knees. How about kissing bugs? I don't see them listed in *Insects in Kansas*, the definitive field guide by Stephan White and Glenn Salsbury, and I hope they're not here. That isn't to say they might not be imported, brought in for a quick hit—you never know. A kissing bug sounds like a cross between the worst aspects of a tick, a chigger, a brown recluse, and Godzilla. That Kansas doesn't have them amazes me. We have everything else except for fire ants and killer bees, and the latter are on the way.

I let a day go by without too much concern. No need to panic, you know. And anyway, a man dislikes too much fuss and will do anything within his power before capitulating and going to the doctor. "It'll pass," I said sagely.

It didn't. It got worse. The good people around me consoled me with tales of infections being lanced only to have baby spiders spill out like the creature in *Alien*, of amputations, of huge holes being rotted into flesh by that most dreaded of arachnids, the brown recluse. Under their tender care my panic took on a life of its own, mounting even as the skin on my foot stretched tighter and tighter, the red spreading up to my ankle.

My editors went so far as to insert a special report in the newspaper on how to avoid insect bites, though it was a little late to be any good. Brenda Helmerichs, the Waterville postmaster, brought me a small moonshine jug of spider bite medicine, bless her heart.

All to no avail. On the third day, with no reduction in swelling or pain, I yielded to the inevitable and went to see the doctor.

It was about what I expected, which is why I rarely seek medical attention. The young doctor looked at my foot, prodded it, and did what no doctor should ever do—he frowned.

"Does it hurt here?" he asked, jabbing it with a finger. Once I stopped screaming I was able to reply that indeed it did, a little.

"It looks like a bite of some sort," he said.

With that kind of deduction, I silently snarled, I could be a physician and get paid a heck of a lot more than a journalist.

He prescribed steroids, antibiotics, and no-drowse allergy pills, seeing as how I was going away on a trip for a few days and would be far from knowledgeable doctors such as himself. My plan was to represent Marshall County at the Kansas Sampler Festival in Independence, but more important was to spend a few hours on foot in the woods around Elk City Lake searching for southern birds that never make it to our northern tier of counties. Birds like red-shouldered hawk, Carolina chickadee, and Acadian flycatcher. I was practically foaming at the mouth in anticipation.

I arrived home with medication and a burning desire to kill something. After dumping half a bottle of liquid dish soap into Mr. Death, I hobbled outside, wincing at the pain. There were clusters of box elder bugs in the wood chips around the yuccas, many of them locked in passionate lust, and though they tried fleeing from me, some airborne, others scampering cowardly beneath the patio stairs, I laid waste to their numbers. In an ironic reversal, I visited upon them like a biblical plague.

Two small black beetles strolled across the porch as if they owned it. On any other day I would have left them alone, but today was not a good day to be so brazen about it. For good measure I stomped them with my left foot. Shafts of pain lanced up my leg but the crunch of their exoskeletons lightened my heart.

I pried my boot off with a gasp, slipped off the sock, and looked at my foot. It was not a pleasant sight. As if that weren't enough, the area just behind my jawbone on the left side began throbbing. Touching it was excruciating.

After ingesting enough pills to choke a horse, I reclined

with my foot up and wondered where this was heading. First I get stung in the eye, and now this. It reminded me of the Palestinians and Israelis, tit for tat, a war of escalation with only losers left standing.

Too, spring has just begun and we've not yet seen the huge numbers of insects that are sure to follow—possibly even ambush bugs, assassin bugs, even those weird-looking kissing bugs. I might be armed with brains and a three-gallon sprayer named Mr. Death, but I'm grievously outnumbered.

Far be it from me to suggest a truce, and even were I to consider it, I haven't a clue who to appeal to.

# MESSAGE FROM THE BUGS: WE CAN HURT YOU

Winston Churchill said nothing is more exciting than being shot at and missed, a statement I can attest. Finding yourself unventilated in the aftermath of a shooting spree gives you a fresh perspective on life as well as leaving you awash in misgivings about your present location. But however thrilling that first errant shot is, the second or third or fourth begin to chip away at your resolve until all that's left is an undercurrent of paranoia and a thirst for violence. Which is why when I saw what awaited me by our front door, I stopped as if once again looking down the barrel of a .30-06.

A casual observer would have seen something other than what I did, but you must understand my history, or at least a part of it. The gunshots I referred to took place in northern New Mexico during the early 1970s. It's peculiar how several of my friends who served in Vietnam during that same era never experienced incoming rounds, while I was the object of hostile fire in the U.S. of A. I was stationed as a guard in Las Vegas, a small town washed up like flotsam against the base of the Sangre de Christo Mountains, and on certain holidays like the Fourth of July and New Years Eve it was best to keep our heads down. Those shots were *close*. But it wasn't until we moved to Kansas that I started taking hits.

Admittedly, my new enemies weren't humans, nor armed

with high-velocity projectiles, but they were much more sophisticated than your average late-night shooter. They were also much smaller, colored red for vengeance and black for their dark demon hearts. And there were a lot more of them, too—it wasn't long before I realized I was outnumbered ten gazillion to one. Those are questionable odds at best, but supposedly we humans have enlarged brains with which to contrive new strategies for waging war. What I couldn't know was that they possess resources beyond my wildest imagination.

My new adversary on Kansas soil was a diminutive and allegedly non-injurious insect whose name reflects its favored habitat: the box elder bug. *Leptocorouos trivittatis* is a true bug, of the order *Hemiptera*, which means half-winged. Most members of this family are "good bugs," predators that feast upon other insects, but by their very name one can detect a glimmer of their potential: ambush bug, assassin bug. Real nasties. Box elder bugs do little to the trees they attack, my field guide says, but "at certain times of the year they can become a nuisance." Which is something of an understatement.

We found that in spring and autumn they swarm the south side of the house and in winter they move inside like uncouth in-laws who make themselves at home. I don't recall how long I put up with their shenanigans, but at some point I snapped. Raving like a madman, I smashed them with whatever was near at hand. But what I needed was something to retaliate on a massive scale.

Soap and water were lethal, one Web site promised. After filling a small spray bottle with the stuff, I ventured out into a scarlet cloud of box elder bugs. One pull of the trigger and a dozen fell writhing to the ground. A mean, malevolent laugh escaped me. Now, I realized, sheer numbers were no longer a problem. I held the equivalent of a nuclear device.

The spray bottle was far too small to combat the numbers I faced, so I switched to a green three-gallon commercial sprayer I named Mr. Death. Together, we smote them high and low.

They smote back. One afternoon while hiking at the old Irving town site, a bee flew into my eye and stung me. The pain was excruciating, and the warning was registered loud and clear: Desist or face your peril.

Once I could see clearly, I attacked with renewed vigor. I attached a spray bottle to my garden hose, filled it with soap, and left a sudsy wake that obliterated them in the billions. More returned the next week.

So did a brown recluse, patiently waiting in my boot. By afternoon my foot swelled to daunting proportions. I was out of commission.

Last autumn we had a tentative truce. This spring, however, they're back, and I've taken an extreme dislike to them flying in my eyes and landing in my food. I prepped the sprayer and hunted the box elder bugs in their hiding places, leaving a trail of corpses.

And now I stand on my porch looking at what awaits me. Next to the door handle is a very large brown recluse spider. We stare at each other, saying nothing. My foot throbs to remind me of the pain I suffered last year. The spider is coldly expressionless, like a hit man measuring his mark. We are caught in a moment of time surrounded by a multitude of box elder bugs who watch the showdown from the wings.

I refuse to back down, though I may be wounded grievously. Retreating to a different door, I slip through the house and take up Mr. Death. The war continues. Who will be left standing is anyone's guess.

# A NEW BREED OF DEVILRY

After my dubious record of dealing with insects this year, I was somewhat taken aback at seeing a mosquito fastened to my leg. I was sitting on our front porch minding my own business, late evening settling down about me, the katydids and crickets ratcheting up for their incessant nocturnal chorus, the first nighthawks materializing to swoop and soar like feathered butterflies and all of them making a beeline for the south, when I felt a burning on my calf. I glanced past the book in my lap and saw it there, feasting on my blood.

It's one thing to write about West Nile Virus and spout statistics about the improbability of being infected and another to stare down the proboscis of a blasted thing that may or may not be disease-ridden. I was reminded of the time my gaze was directed down the barrel of a 12-gauge riot shotgun a police officer had pointed at my face; on one level I figured he probably wouldn't squeeze the trigger (though I wouldn't know it if he did), while another part of my brain was wondering if I should utter a clever last word, or at least request that he remove his finger from the trigger.

It was a Mexican standoff, a few terribly long, surreal moments when time ceased to be and there was only the gaping bore and a crimped shell bearing my name and a skull and crossbones twenty inches down the black barrel, and my life was dependant upon the reflexes of a trained law enforcement officer looking at a man standing in a doorway with a large stainless steel revolver in his hand. And lest anyone question my background, I was there in the performance of my duties as a burglar alarm technician who had responded to a silent alarm. The two of us met quite by accident and quite by surprise. He had the upper hand, obviously, as he got the drop on me. I'm still smarting over it.

This time was much the same only of shorter duration. My right hand left off holding the edge of the book and, faster than lightning, smashed the mosquito into a black smear. But the question hangs in the air like fog—yes, no, maybe?

The world as we know it has entered a new stage, has suddenly taken on a darker, more malevolent hue, and we are left to both understand it and to find our place within it.

For years I took garlic as a supplement, a hefty dose that was reputed to make me healthier, reduce cholesterol, improve circulation, and possibly even make me better looking. I can't vouch for any of those but it did have one interesting side effect that no documentation mentioned: mosquito bites no longer had any effect on me other than a mild tingling sensation as they sucked my blood. For a few seconds the bite might itch, but then it went away and I was good as new.

It was like possessing a magic pill, allowing me a measure of freedom rivaling that of Superman. I could enter the most mosquito-infested thicket or swamp and laugh at their antics, move freely and without hindrance through veritable clouds of the nasty vampires, let them suck until they had their fill, and not worry one whit. I felt invincible.

I suspect all that's changed, at least for the time being. West Nile Virus, running unchecked across the state, is one more disease added to the arsenal of the insect world. As if ticks and chiggers weren't enough, or stinging wasps and snarly hornets, or grasshoppers eating our window screens and siding, or spiders taking offense at my toes, now there's this to worry about. Too bad we don't all have vast amounts of stock in insect repellent manufacturers, possibly the only ones in the world who greet such news with delight.

Don't be alarmed, though, for technology is coming to the rescue with the amazing Mosquito Magnet, a new device that not only attracts and slays mosquitoes, gnats, and no-see-ums but also provides the satisfying pleasure of being able to view their corpses.

The contraption looks like a propane gas grill with a huge green and white blender on top. By emitting a warm puff of carbon dioxide, it mimics human (and cow and horse) breath, luring bloodsucking insects. About the time they're licking their lips, or what passes as lips, a fan snatches them up and sucks them against a screen, where they while away the last few miserable days of their lives. A window on the side of the blender lets you count the thousands of bugs that won't be bothering you anymore.

At $495, it's hardly as inexpensive as a can of Off, but think how spiffy your yard would look sporting one of these hummers. Your neighbors would revere you. Be the first on your block to own one!

I'm undecided over how I intend on handling this new menace. In the past, while in the tropics and birding in swampy areas, I've always worn long pants and long-sleeved shirts, and relied on insect repellents as little as possible. My fancy new birding pack, made specifically for birders to tote their field guides and other items, has a water bottle pocket that's just right for a can of bug spray. I guess I'll be joining the estimated thirty percent of other Americans who use the stinky stuff, though I wish they'd come up with a new fragrance. How about vanilla, or roasted green chiles?

Our neighbor might have summed it up best when he said, "That perfume I'm wearing is called DEET." Indeed. It's all the rage, very tres chic.

# LA LLORONA STALKS THE NIGHT

In the end, I decided it must have been a bobcat calling from the darkness across the road, violating the still night and orchestrating the voices of every dog in town. I found a Web site with vocalizations of the wildcat and listened to it repeatedly, trying to recall the timbre of what I'd heard. The recordings were similar but not exact, so I can't be positive. I was left with the lingering question of whether it had been a mammal or a ghost, La Llorona, calling for her lost children.

It had been uneasy night from the time the sun disappeared into a thin cloudbank to the west. An owl began hooting as dusk settled in. Dogs barked restlessly. I stood outside for a moment feeling a sense of heaviness in the winter air, as if a storm was approaching. My wife was expected home late, increasing the nervousness I felt. I'm as superstitious as the next guy, maybe even more so, but I felt something in the air, a menace, a change, some inexplicable thing just beyond the limits of my senses.

Night was complete when Lori arrived. I met her outside, heard the dogs howling.

"Something sure stirred them up," Lori said.

Once inside, we bolted the door as pioneers must have done to keep the wolves at bay. Lights threw back the darkness and the sense of unease. We were safe.

The wail split the night and made the four walls invisible. It pinned us to our positions, Lori in the recliner, me on the floor. Our Angora rabbit, Mr. Bun, leaped upright, ears erect, eyes wide. The three of us froze.

"What was that?" Lori choked.

I had no idea. Either a mammal or a woman being dismembered. The sound came from across the street somewhere close by. I grabbed a million-candlepower spotlight I use for owling and cautiously opened the door. Mr. Bun, finding himself alone in the living room, skittered across the kitchen floor in search of his cage.

The spotlight turned night to day, each tree precise and stark against the darker background of coal-black shadows. I swept it down the road, through the trees and across the grassy field between us and the grain elevator. Nothing.

When the wail came again I jumped a few inches, goosebumps erupting on my skin. This time there was no wall between me and the sound. I slammed the door and threw the deadbolt.

"It has to be a bobcat," I stuttered.

Several nights later we heard it again. Just back from Milford, where we'd spent half the day in search of birds only to find a paltry two new species—pelican and swamp sparrow—we were unpacking the car when the caterwaul rose from the trees lining the perennial creek. Short wails, almost snarls, repeated several times, as if awaiting a response that never came. Someone had to walk down the driveway and cross the street to retrieve the mail, and it wasn't going to be my wife.

Feeling far less brave than I acted, I marched across the road to the mailbox. The wail surged again, one of the most primitive, eerie, and unsettling sounds I've ever heard. The ex-city dweller in me thrilled at having it so close while every instinct within me urged me to run like hell.

When I worked in Las Vegas, New Mexico, in the early 1970s, one of the first things I was taught was to listen for vehicles approaching the plant with their headlights extinguished. Another was a warning to stay clear of La Llorona. This last was from a slender, unassuming man whom acquaintances described as a *brujo*, or witch. He said that La Llorona, dressed in flowing white robes, roamed the Gallinas Valley on stormy nights searching for her drowned children. If her voice was heard, all was lost. I shrugged it off as nonsense but then one electrifying night when every thunderbolt in the world was directed upon our generator plant, he placed a ball of aluminum foil, wet with his saliva, on my wrist. It glowed with a blue fire and scorched a hole in my flesh. After that, I didn't know what to believe, for northern New Mexico is not like any other place. I never saw or heard La Llorona while I worked there, but I quickly learned to listen for vehicles.

Even farther back, when I was growing up, my family was camped in the Holy Ghost Campground in the Pecos Mountains above Santa Fe. One summer we were visited by a strange apparition whose bloodcurdling cry terrorized us. Nights found us locked inside our camper, afraid to venture out. One evening my father went outside for a moment and returned white as a ghost.

"Something just crossed between us and the river," he said. The river was a scant fifty feet away.

We were hiking in broad daylight when we heard what sounded like children in a playground approaching. Laughter, cries, a cacophony of voices, but something wasn't right, whether a sense of foreboding or otherness. My father had us huddle together, us boys wielding tree limbs as cudgels, our mother in the middle. The sound stopped just within the border of trees surrounding the small meadow, as if something was watching us. My father investigated but found nothing.

My father, I should note, was an outdoorsman and hunter who had a level head and a courageous heart. This was something beyond his experience, beyond all of ours.

Cries in the night. At heart we are little removed from our caveman ancestors, the fear of night-cries an integral part of our genes. For a moment I paused beside the mailbox with the creature calling a stone's throw away and thought of La Llorona wailing for her children, and then I broke for the house.

It had to be a bobcat. Didn't it?

# DOWN AND DIRTY BIRDING

There's been good-natured competition between Linn and Blue Rapids over the quality of our respective sewage ponds ever since a red-necked phalarope showed up in May 2001. Basically a bird of the oceans, it arrived in BR without fanfare, though I happened to be at the ponds looking for such things. It was only the second time I'd seen one, and I knew it was a good find. I notified the Kansas Ornithological Society as soon as I got home, and then called Dan Thalmann, editor of the *Washington County News*, a birding friend.

It was the spring red-necked phalaropes showed up all over Kansas, even, sad to say, in Linn. To make a long story short, Dan and I had a brief Internet war on the listserv, a discussion group for birders, over which town harbored the most phalaropes. Blue Rapids lost. I think the final tally was Linn, eight, BR, five.

Dan's reasoning was at least refreshing: "I do believe that I will continue to get superior birds here in the Linn sewage ponds. Us Washington Countians are real, down home folks and the quality of our sewage reflects that. Marshall Countians, on the other hand, are just a bit high-falootin' and the arrogant sewage can only be consumed by shorebirds for so long before they come lookin' for a home-cooked sewage meal."

Our two ponds couldn't be more different. Blue Rapids has three moderate-sized pools, Linn two huge ones plus a third dugout of about two acres that's apparently used only when

Washington Countians have had too much home cooking. Ours is lined with riprap, theirs are cement slabs that slope gradually into the goo.

The year the phalaropes came, two of our pools were lowered to mudflats—at least, we liked to call them mudflats—creating ideal shorebird habitat. During a month-long period I was able to add about thirty species to the Marshall County checklist, birds not seen or recorded here before.

This year our ponds are filled, reducing their attraction to migrants. I've found a few black terns, two spotted sandpipers bobbing among the rocks, but that's all. Dull as toast. (In the future I need to somehow convince our city superintendent to drain one pond for birding opportunities in spring and fall, but I have no idea how to do that so that it makes sense. Maybe I need to work tourism into it, somehow. What an idea! I'll get the Marshall County Development Corporation working on it.)

Over Labor Day weekend my wife and I stopped at the Linn sewage ponds for a quick look after visiting the Washington County Museum. While my wife read a book I crawled through the fence, crept a few yards along the base of the raised dike, and eased my head above the grass to peer along the shore.

A few small shorebirds were nearby but the one that caught my eye was larger than the others, its plumage overall a warm rich brown. I didn't need a field guide to figure out what it was though I'd never laid eyes on one before—a buff-breasted sandpiper, a bird that has eluded me for over a decade. I studied it for a while and then made a mad dash to the convenience store, where I unsuccessfully tried notifying Dan.

When we rolled into our beautiful Blue Rapids, I tried again. He answered on the second ring.

"Dan," I said, "there's a buff-breasted sandpiper at your sewage ponds."

"No there's not." Dan's been a journalist so long he doesn't believe anything unless he sees it himself.

I convinced him that indeed there was and he rushed over to look. The bird was nowhere to be found. For his trouble, though, he found a flock of sandpiper-like birds flying in a circle above the ponds as if trying to decide whether to land. He watched them through his binoculars as they wheeled overhead, gathering impressions and details, and, when they disappeared to the south, thumbed through his field guide for answers. By their color and the way they flew with their legs dangling behind them he determined they were piping plovers, an endangered species, and new to Washington County.

Which, I'll add, was the same for the buff-breasted sandpiper: a county record. Let's not forget that.

It pains me to say it, but Washington County netted two new birds to its checklist. I got a lifebird out of it (which alleviates some of the sting), and there's the fact that I was the one who added the buffy to the list. Unfortunately, however, Marshall County has never hoisted either a buff-breasted sandpiper or a piping plover—yet. The Linn sewage ponds worked their magic again.

I like to think that Linn is closer to the Central Flyway, that Route 66 of the skies that migrating birds follow down from the north country to winter in the south, but in reality the town is a mere handful of miles away. Considering the distance many of the birds have flown by this point, often thousands and thousands of miles, it is but a pittance. And it's no secret that Marshall County is much more lovely and inviting than our sister to the west. So what gives? What do they put in their sewage?

In other words, what ingredients go into their "home cooking"?

Whatever it is those people are eating, maybe it's best we leave it to them. It would go a long way toward explaining why Linn, with a population of 425, has such expansive sewage ponds. It's clear that the residents are kept pretty busy, and I'm not sure it's worth it for a handful of feathers passing on the wind.

# IN SEARCH OF THE WILD TIMBERDOODLE

So there we were, the four of us standing in the middle of the road at Washington State Fishing Lake as the western sky flared scarlet from an unseen sunset and the wind kicked sand in our eyes and dusk fell with a roar in the trees and a glimmer of the evening star shining through a rent in the clouds. Of our small assemblage only I had a real interest in the evening's proceedings, the others having come along for a free barbecue. We listened and watched while light faded. And then, faintly and far off, came what sounded like a nighthawk's cry. But there were no nighthawks here, not now. Was it *Scolopax minor*?

My experiences with the American woodcock have always been based on a lie, though not in the same league as when a birder spots one or two field marks on a long-sought-after bird and wrestles with his personal mores in an attempt to make his eyes see what his heart wants him to see, and what his conscience knows is false. No, it was ignorance, pure and simple.

The first time I saw what I thought was a woodcock was while flyfishing the Blue River below Dillon, Colorado. A stretch of whitewater forced me to shore, and as I crossed a lush meadow to bypass it a pair of birds exploded at my feet, leaping into the air with a shout of wings that scared the daylights out of me. They appeared to be stocky birds with long, thick bills. Woodcock, I surmised, once I got my breath back.

Unfortunately, they were no more woodcocks than limpkins. While I could easily distinguish a brook trout from a brown, or a rainbow trout from a green-backed cutthroat, I wouldn't have been able to identify a common bird if it had perched on the tip of my flyrod and whistled Dixie, much less a secretive, reclusive bird such as woodcock. It just sounded right, I guess, having seen them in hunting magazines my father used to read.

The second time I thought I saw woodcock was above Eagle, Colorado. It was my last camping trip of the season and I was alone, taking a walk as the first stars popped out in a frosty twilight. A pair of long-billed, stout birds winged by, and as I watched them disappear down the narrow valley I thought of my wife back home and the night seemed desolate. Woodcock, I said again.

And again I was wrong. What I had seen were Wilson's snipe, a cousin to the woodcock. As I discovered when I shifted from fishing to birding, woodcock are eastern birds and rarely set foot in mountainous Colorado. Since most of my birding took place in the West, I figured that the species might well be one of those that grace the pages of my field guides but never appear in my binoculars' field of view. Many are the birds that fit that pattern, and only the lucky ones among us have the financial wherewithal to seek them out one by one.

But hope is a flame illuminating the unseen. We relocate or travel and find ourselves in strange lands, as sometimes do the birds themselves. And yet even in Kansas woodcock seemed farfetched. Then Dan Thalmann found them at Washington Lake.

By any stretch of the imagination, *Scolopax minor* is an odd bird. Though technically a shorebird, it haunts upland prairies, especially where nearby woods give it refuge. It takes flight only when almost stepped upon, and then it zigzags through the woods as if pursued by a hunter's shotgun. It's been known to fly with its young clutched between its legs. When it feeds on earthworms, its favorite food, it rocks back and forth like a wind-up toy, moonwalking across the forest floor with one step back for every two or three forward. Its mating ritual involves rocketing from the ground with an explosive *peent* and soaring as high as two hundred feet before dropping in a dizzying spiral. Its wings make a high twittering sound. Its coloration is that of forest leaf litter. It's been called bog-sucker and timberdoodle.

After Dan's report, I spent several evenings walking the road where they had been seen, the nights humid and velvety and humming with mosquitoes. Always I would return home with nothing to show for it but a multitude of insect bites.

It is not in me to give up. So here we are, the four of us, night falling fast, all sounds torn away on the wind, and from the edge of the woods comes a distant *peent*. Could it be this easy? Another *peent*, this one closer. We stand there eating dust, ears straining. The sunset fades. Venus is shrouded. Darkness falls.

Were I with other birders the night would be young, but non-birders quickly lose interest in the chase. Bird noises cease. There is only the sound of the wind and the wind and the wind and it thunders like heavy surf battering a forlorn and dismal shore.

*\*\*\**

This may sound strange, and it may be something only a birder can comprehend, but sometimes the best bird is the one that got away.

Though my lifelist retains a blank spot where American

woodcock should be, the chase itself accounts for much of the exhilaration of finding a new bird. That breathless anticipation is reward enough.

This is by no means the last time I'll look for this species. There will be other evenings when I linger in the deepening gloom listening for that distinctive call. Next time it's mine. Next time the wild and elusive timberdoodle will be all mine.

# THE DARK SIDE OF CHICKADEES

I was just now watching a chickadee attack a sunflower seed. Maybe I was slightly bored and that made my staring out the window all the more languid, but I realized that a chickadee throws his whole weight into the pummeling. It grasps the seed with its feet, rears back from the tips of its toes, and slams its beak into the seed with everything it's got. POW! It's all or nothing for the little piebald bird.

A lot of people think highly of chickadees because of their diminutive stature and their charming, busybody nature. I learned the darker side of chickadees the year I banded birds south of Denver. After taking a weekend course in banding basics, we met one spring morning just as the sun was clearing the eastern horizon. We walked up a narrow valley on well-worn trails, unfurling black-stringed nets in places where birds were likeliest to fly. After a dozen or so nets were placed, we retired to the banding station to sip coffee and nibble on donuts. It was now up to the birds.

Because banding nets are very fine-threaded, almost like gossamer, a bird will jam a leg or head through the weave until it's held as fast as a fly in a spider web. It then simply flutters a bit while waiting for the next odd thing to happen. Every ten minutes we'd march off in twos and threes to the nets with one of our members holding a handful of colored cloth bags. The master bander would free the bird, carefully so as not to bend a wing or twist a neck—sometimes this took some effort if the bird had struggled—and the bird would be slipped into a bag and a draw-cord tightened. The color of each bag corresponded to the size of the bird: big, medium, small.

Being a novice bander, I was allowed to handle the robins, grosbeaks, and towhees, all medium-sized birds. We would clench them around the head with two fingers and flip them upside down so they would struggle less. But before proffering them to the bander for measurements and the silver band, we had to reach into the bag and get them out. This was when banding became a painful experience.

The bag had to be opened only enough to slip your hand in. At the bottom was a living bird, none too happy to find itself in the bag to start with and even less thrilled to find a giant's hand groping it. Robins shrieked like they were being plucked alive—Fire! Rape! Help!!—while towhees were only slightly less histrionic. The grosbeaks were silent but vengeful.

Grosbeaks possess massive bills used for crunching tough seeds. As soon as my fingers touched the feathers of a grosbeak it would whip around and clamp its beak around a finger. Hard. Then harder. A bander reaching into a sack containing a grosbeak was sure to utter words best not spoken in church on Sunday mornings or within hearing of one's pastor. Listening to a bander on such occasion would make one unfamiliar with the role think that banders didn't like birds. "You miserable son of a—OUCH!!—I'm not going to hurt you, you—OW!— let me go!"

But as bad as grosbeaks were, chickadees were the worst. So they said, those wise in their years of banding, those of the ragged fingernails and scarred fingers. A chickadee is the Torquemada of the avian world. It understands everything about the human physique. It knows exactly where each pressure point is; it can intuitively detect the most sensitive part of a person's anatomy; and, with its tiny sharp bill, it inflicts the maximum amount of pain. That point is usually the person's cuticles.

The master bander wouldn't let me retrieve the chickadees; that was a job for those she entrusted to not let agony be a catalyst for prematurely releasing the bird. I watched with fascination as a young lady wriggled her fingers into a small sack, her expression one of expectancy. It was evident when the bird found her fingers for she winced and turned pale. The lump in the bag would bob and bounce as she sought to secure the bird, but the bird was clearly giving better than it got. When she finally pulled it out, blood speckled the bird's feathers. It was hers.

Since that time I have great respect for chickadees.

Sitting here watching the chickadee split open the seed, you'd never know such a nice-looking little bird could be so vicious. But it's probably just paying you back for interrupting its busy schedule. Chickadees are always in a hurry to get somewhere, and being trapped in a net, stuffed in a dark sack, and ignominiously manhandled is just too much for them. "I'll show you," it says. And then it does.

I never banded after that first season. For one thing, the schedule was just too hard. And though I understood the validity of banding, I just didn't feel right putting the birds through such hassle. Still, it was a good experience and I'm glad I did it once in my life. However, if I ever get the urge to join my friends down at Fort Riley for banding, I think instead I'll just put my finger in a pair of pliers and squeeze hard. The pain's the same and there's less driving involved.

# THE LONELINESS OF THE LONG-
# DISTANCE HAWKWATCHER

There was nothing in that vast blue field, nothing that moved, no cloud, no winged form, nothing my eyes could trace or linger upon. Only when I lowered the binoculars to scan the horizon did anything swim into focus, and so sudden did the distant trees and stony ridges leap into view that it startled me, brought me back to earth as if I had fallen from a great height or regained my sight after a long blindness. Abruptly grounded, I let the binoculars drop to my lap. The Big Blue River glinted in the sun, visible through the cottonwoods below. I was alone atop a grassy knoll. Mostly, I was lonely.

I had come to this place in the hopes of seeing migrating hawks. They pass through northeastern Kansas each spring and fall, northward or southward depending on the tilt of the planet, but much of it depends on factors I have not yet learned. Nor, apparently, has anyone else. Across the nation are dozens of sites that by dint of topography funnel raptors into narrow corridors where they can be seen by the thousands. No such place exists in the Great Plains. Once the migrants leave the borderlands, they vanish into the great middle section of the nation.

My wife vanished, too, gone to Phillipsburg for a fiber convention. Only for a few days, she said. I said, I'll be okay. But it was a lie, because I'm never okay when she leaves.

Empty sky. Empty house. Empty me.

Early in my birding years I was invited to watch migrating hawks from a knife-edged ridge south of Golden, Colorado. A few dedicated birders took me under their wing and gave me an education I can never repay. They taught me how to tell a Cooper's hawk from a sharp-shinned, and how to identify a northern goshawk at a distance of nearly a mile. They taught me to recognize a head-on raptor by its dihedral, the way it holds its wings in a soar. They taught me how to study an empty sky and find something moving within it. They taught me how to see.

They were dear friends and companions, and I left them there one spring and moved to Kansas, where I thought my hawkwatching days were forever gone.

Aloneness and loneliness are not the same. The first is physical, a reduction of numbers to its lowest denomination. The second is spiritual. I've never minded being alone, indeed I've found solace in being removed from the masses of humanity that crowd our planet, but loneliness is branded on me like a psychological scar, an old wound that never fully heals. I know loneliness, and I fear it.

Old history, sad tales, we've all got them. Mine was a divorce and a career involving a series of rough New Mexican towns. I wasn't a birder then, but I was watching. I was scanning my horizons, looking for options. Love is also a form of watching, and then I found it.

I also found hawks in the skies above our prairie home. Seasonally they come through by the hundreds, sometimes high, mere specks against the clouds, and sometimes low, barely clearing the trees. Weather, temperature, cold fronts, all play a part they understand and I do not. Finding them requires patience and a backdrop of clouds. Against an empty sky they slip past the limits of our vision.

As this sky was empty, and yet not. I knew they were up there, I just couldn't see them. For another hour I stood vigil before leaving. This was no longer alone, this was lonely.

Clouds rolled in, night fell. The gibbous moon flitted through rents in the clouds, brushing the yard with quicksilver light that faded and brightened and faded. Venus glowed like a beacon for one fleeting moment and vanished. I realized I was looking west, toward Phillipsburg. It was no coincidence.

I busied myself the next day, keeping an eye on the sky. The weather was unstable, with dark clouds to the south and west. No hawks were flying now, probably grounded due to storms. Doppler radar showed a line of thunderstorms moving through the area where my wife was. Afternoon lengthened and we were hit with our own fierce storm. I wondered if she was on the road then and experiencing the same winds, the same downpour.

Night was as dark as that earlier blue sky was empty. I kept watch, peering through the window blinds, listening for the crunch of tires on the gravel road. Nothing. For the little I could see, I might as well been blindfolded.

And yet there are other ways of seeing. When all else fails there's always the heart.

I left our Angora rabbit, whom I had been brushing, and stared out the north window. A vehicle was approaching. I didn't have binoculars to enhance my vision, nor, this time, did I need them. My heart *knew*. I was out the door by the time her headlights swept the yard.

The hawks will come, eventually, and if the light is right and if the wind is from the right direction and if there are clouds to highlight them, I will look up and see them there, riding the thermals, soaring on outstretched wings across our narrow river valley. Theirs is the imperative driving them to the breeding grounds, but it is not theirs alone. Our imperative is to watch, whether for a hawk, for love, for a friend. Our needs and desires are one and the same. We are all part of the great migration. We are all looking for home.

# THE WILDERNESS OF NIGHT

Not having seen any carpenter ants during the day, once the sun set and darkness fell and stars peppered the sky and lightning bugs flickered in the field, I gathered a flashlight and a can of ant killer and searched the stairway. Nothing moved. But I knew they were coming. I wanted to follow them back to their nest and kill them.

I have nothing against carpenter ants except when they invade our home. And nightly, for a week, they had been raiding the trash can in our kitchen, their numbers steadily increasing.

I opened the door and stepped into a velvet night so thick with humidity it felt like a sauna. Innumerable ants scurried across the patio. A Woodhouse's toad, looking like a lump of left-over modeling clay, studied me. Wood roaches scampered away from the light. Pillbugs and carnivorous crickets, both large, black-bodied ones and smaller, tan, almost translucent ones, hunted their prey.

At the base of the house and wrapping around past the yucca and four o'clocks was a thin trail of carpenter ants, winding under the deck toward the lawn. The trail entered the grass and became harder to find, especially with my flashlight batteries fading. There were so many insects that I felt like an alien, that I had stepped across an invisible boundary and entered another world. The trail curved and twisted like the writhing body of a snake, having little form or reason, though I was looking down through the blades of grass that must appear like redwoods to them. Bent over like an old man, I swept the light around until I picked up movement, suddenly realizing where they were taking me.

A highway of ants was surging up and down the rough trunk of the elm tree. I could see them as far as my light would reach, rising into the highest branches. There was no ant hill to inscribe on a mental map to return to with gasoline or carbide crystals when the sun was out, but a trail with no beginning and no end. I stood there in the dark with my flashlight dimming, feeling helpless, engulfed within a world I could not fathom. Crickets fiddled their cadence, mosquitoes buzzed in my ear, lightning bugs flashed in the darkness, moths fluttered around my light, and the eyes of spiders hidden in the grass glowed with internal fire.

I am outnumbered, I thought, and all but hopeless with the gaps around that ill-fitting door. This is why we humans want tight houses, to insulate ourselves from the denizens of the night.

Out of spite, I laid down a thick foam of ant killer at the base of the door, wiping out a dozen ants—a mere drop in a very large ocean, but if nothing else it made me feel as if I had some say in their fate and mine.

But the night kept me enthralled. An entire universe was taking place around me, all on a miniature scale. For the most part, it took no notice of me; I was inconsequential. And I could not bear to leave.

The night has an allure we have forgotten. Perhaps it's why we enjoy camping so much, not because it's a break from routine but because we teeter on the edge of experiencing the nighttime on a more intimate level.

There was only one time in my life when I experienced

a full night on its own terms. We were thirty miles south of Playa del Carmen on the Yucatan Peninsula on a night much like this, only infinitely darker. The only lights were distant, those of Playa and Tulum, a small Mexican village whose Mayan ruins stand sentinel on the rocky headlands looming from the turquoise waters of the Caribbean. Stars were muted behind a thick vapor of humidity. Waves crashed ashore, insects droned in rhythms like cicadas—the darkness was anything but quiet. We were searching for sea turtles coming ashore to lay their eggs, and the guide instructed us not to use our flashlights. Until dawn we would be walking the shoreline and crisscrossing through coastal scrub around a treacherous rocky outcrop, handicapped by sightlessness. We were the least of the creatures of the dark.

While the sun rules the heavens we are the alpha species, but when the sun slips behind the rim of the world we become merely a sideshow, an oddity. A raccoon scolded us, bats and owls and nightjars zoomed past, and spider eyes glowed around us like green phosphorous. We stumbled through thick grass and across boulder-strewn sand as the constellations wheeled across the skies. Time lost all meaning. It seemed like ages before we found heavy scrape marks leading from the surf to a high dune; while the guide cautiously investigated, we collapsed in the sand. Waves hissed across the beach. We were soaked in sweat, rank, exhausted.

The guide appeared like an apparition, telling us we'd have to wait about thirty minutes, or until the turtle, a loggerhead, was well into its egg-laying cycle. There was little conversation, only the night sounds of a strange land. And then he led us over the dune and showed us a huge depression that the turtle had dug, and within it an ancient, leathery tortoise wheezing from the effort of birth. She looked weary beyond words, her eyes mere slits. We held the eggs, the size and shape of ping pong balls, and felt something larger than ourselves, the tug of the moon on the tides, the genesis of life on an antediluvian shore.

The night world exists without our acquiescence or desire. It is complete and perfect in itself. Steeped in mystery and wonder, it waits just beyond our closed doors, our curtained windows, our comfortable and snug lives.

It is a wilderness I am increasing drawn to.

# GODS AMONG US

There are gods among us. The lookie-loos driving down our street are looking in all the wrong places. They slow to a crawl, heads craned, eyes goggling at the new house being built across from us. What do they see that's so fascinating that they return day after day? Four walls, a roof, doors. An ugly scrape of bare dirt where once stood a small copse of trees, purple phlox nodding in a springtime breeze, a rustic fence, Queen Anne's lace. A barn built of creosote-soaked railroad ties once stood there, and each year a pair of phoebes raised their young within the dark, cool walls. All gone. But I'm thinking of divinity as revealed in a scarab, and loss is a minor note when compared to seeing the face of God.

Or not. These distinctions can be difficult to make unless one is prepared to loosen the Judeo-Christian roots that bind us. For a moment, though, suspend that belief. Go with me on a journey.

The dirt road leading west from Stella's Meadow at Alcove Spring is an unlikely place for what followed. After tramping through the deep woods and carefully stepping along the meandering creeks in search of migrant birds, the road seems a letdown. It's too open, too formless. And then something comes along that changes everything. In my case, it was a beetle.

When we think of beetles, if we think of them at all, it's of black, hard-shelled insects, or of lady bugs clad in red and black. Farmers are acquainted with more beetles than most for the family contains some of the world's most destructive, as well as numerous, creatures. One-third of all insect species in Kansas is a beetle; worldwide, that number is one-fifth, comprising almost three hundred thousand distinct species. When an English cleric asked the evolutionist J.B.S. Haldane what could be discerned about God from the works of nature, Haldane replied, "An inordinate fondness for beetles."

That's the Judeo-Christian mindset. Step back a few thousand years and the question loses meaning, for God *was* a beetle, a dung beetle to be precise, of the family *Scarabeidae*. In the age of polytheism, this particular god's role was to roll the sun across the sky. The scarab beetle was held sacred by the Egyptians, who believed it spontaneously came into being from balls of dung. It became a symbol of rebirth and eternal life, and amulets in the shape of scarabs were placed on the breast of the deceased. As far back in time as one can go, to the very first recorded writings on slabs of clay, the scarab was revered as the creator and sustainer of life.

Quite a lineage for the insect that darted past me at on the road to Stella's Meadow. My eyes caught a rainbow of color and followed it as it settled on a dried twist of coyote scat. When I focused my binoculars on it, a new universe opened for me.

The inch-long scarab with long curving black horn and iridescent body was *Phanaeus vindex*, or splendid dung beetle. Its wing covers were a brilliant luminous emerald, gilded in brightest gold along its sides, with a deep coppery red triangle on its back. Two golden globes dangled from short black antennae. True to its nature, it set about attacking the dung.

It wasn't until I got home and identified the insect that the true (or untrue) scope of my find was revealed.

I learned that most primitive religions revered the scarab

as a giver of life. Dung beetles live on fecal matter and are a critical component in the removal of waste. (In parts of Texas, they remove eighty percent of cattle droppings.) There are rollers, tunnelers, and dwellers, the rollers being the most famous, for they form perfect spheres of dung and roll them to a suitable spot, dig a hole beneath them, and let the ball drop inside. Their eggs are laid in the dung. Tunnelers share human traits in that the females arrange the tunnels while the males gather the dung. The single horn on the male is used for fighting and defense. Their life expectancy ranges from three to five years. And, in the first chapter of the book of Ezekiel, God revealed himself to the prophet in a fashion strikingly similar to the depictions of the sacred scarab.

This imagery surprised me. In a thesis entitled, *God is, Forsooth, a Scarab*, Brett Ratcliffe, professor of entomology at the University of Nebraska, theorizes that the four creatures within the vision were representations of scarabs. Each had "wheels," which could signify dung balls, and above them shone the "firmament," represented in religious paintings as rays of light emanating from the heads of saints or divinity, which would correlate to the clypeal serrations on the scarab's head. Each had two wings, and when the wings moved the sound was fearsome, common to the induced airflow of large beetles. Their wings were raised, seeming to hold aloft a sapphire. Compared to the image of the sacred scarab, the similarities are remarkable.

Now, I'm not saying that a bug is anything other than a bug, but clearly this particular bug has sparked the imaginations of people the world over. From the beginning of time the scarab has played a role in man's search for divine truths. To think that the beetle on the road to Stella's Meadow carried such weight lends it a charm far greater than its stature.

These things go on around us all the time though we rarely pay attention. We're busy looking elsewhere, trying to see the Big Picture and missing it entirely. There are unexplored universes at our feet. Somehow, we need to learn to see the divine, even if it's in the form of a diminutive beetle that once pushed the sun across the heavens.

# A PLACE TO CALL HOME

Last Chance, Colorado, was named more for the traveler heading east than west. As a sign once cautioned, this was your last chance to buy gas or food for X-number of miles, the Great American Desert yawning ominously at your front bumper. The sign has long since fallen but the town remains, or what's left of it, a handful of houses and a restaurant. It's not much to look at nor does the modern traveler see much of it. The town lies in a trough of a swell, the Great Plains undulating in long, slow waves rolling out from the foothills of the Front Range. There's a weathered sign advertising the restaurant, quickly overtaken at sixty-five miles per hour, and then the traveler crests the wave, drops into a narrow declivity, blasts through an intersection, and tops the opposite crest almost before realizing a town even exists in that desolate wasteland. But the birds know, because the town is an oasis.

When we think of an oasis the image that immediately pops into mind is that of a palm-shaded, green haven in the midst of a barren desert, with perhaps a Bedouin or two resting their camels beside a limpid pool. But an oasis can be much more, and in more places, than one supposes. On the shortgrass prairies of eastern Colorado, in the arid scrublands of southeast Arizona, even in the tallgrass hills around Blue Rapids, oases exist. Some are perennial, ephemeral, and others remain a permanent fixture. Last Chance is one of the latter.

In the rain shadow of the Rockies life is pared to the bare

minimum. Grasses are stunted and huddle close to the thin soil. Trees are few and far between, mostly clustered tightly around farmhouses and ranches. Birds that have adapted to the harsh conditions flourish there—the longspurs, sparrows, meadowlarks, and buntings. Add a little water, some vegetation, and the scale of diversity becomes immeasurable. Birders call these places "migrant traps," areas where migrating birds are forced to seek in order to survive their long journeys to and from their breeding grounds, but they're really more than that. They're an oasis in the middle of a desert, and just as they attract birds, they also attract birders.

Most migrant traps are as lovely as the ideal oasis. One of the better-known ones to Colorado birders is Crow Creek, a green ribbon meandering through cactus-studded prairie northeast of Greeley. It has a nice campground where one can camp in the shade of trees, and the birds one finds are guaranteed to amaze. The only fall-out I've ever witnessed was there one spring morning, when I found thrushes by the thousands, a veritable carpet of the songbirds. There were robins and hermits and clay-cheeked and Swainson's, so thick that walking was tricky. Many of the rare birds on my Colorado list were found there. It's a spot you could stay at forever and never get weary of.

Last Chance fails the scenic test, however. By any measurable means it's a dump. At the intersection of Highway 36 and Colorado 71, the Lions Club erected a small pull-off with an outhouse and picnic table. Two Dumpsters collect the trash of wayfarers and are always overflowing. The air reeks of raw sewage. The outhouse is horrific, and only desperate travelers crack that door and enter. The town itself is depressing, more skeletal than alive. And yet it has something that nowhere else within fifty miles possesses—water and vegetation. Not much water but enough to form a seasonal pool beneath the tall cottonwoods lining the creek behind the outhouse.

We were returning from an impromptu two-day haul to Denver and I was one of those desperate travelers. The Mexican food I had thought so tasty was now a live thing arguing in my guts. This is not an indictment of Mexican food so much as a condemnation of the particular restaurant we had patronized. Last Chance offered me a refuge of sorts, and I took it.

Birdsong was a jarring dissonance. I could distinguish the songs of dozens of doves and grackles, the one melodious, the other like a rusty gate-hinge, with the burbling trill of western kingbirds adding to the din. By consciously drowning out the others I could faintly hear a thin whistle of a western wood-pewee, a bird I'd not heard in many years. I grabbed my binoculars, skirted the chain-link fence separating the park from the creek, and took up a position where I could peer through the heavy vegetation into a shallow puddle of water.

The concentration of birds was staggering. A bandit-masked yellowthroat scrounged in the weeds, and yellow warblers sang from high in the tree tops. I saw orioles and blackbirds and jays, and an empid flew to perch on a bare branch nearby. (Empids—*empidonax*, Latin for "a bird whose similarity to others of its kind makes it almost impossible to identify so it's best not even to try"—are a birder's bane, safely identified only by voice or in hand.) I hoped for a snatch of song or a call note, but the bird remained mute. It was the only silent one of hundreds of birds who had discovered this oasis and called it home.

Home. The thought tugged at me like the incessant pressure in my unhappy bowels. Lori was asleep in the truck, her head lolled to the side, hair spilling across the seat like a fan. I studied her for a minute, studied her as I would an empid, and I thought, *there's my oasis*. For an oasis is only a refuge, is only an island. There are fancy words for these micro-habitats, scientific jargon that twists the tongue but loses all melody. Home is a word I understood. At the end of a chain-link fence in Last Chance, Colorado, with a halo of kingbirds chittering above me, I capped the lenses of my binoculars and headed for home.

# SUMMER DOLDRUMS AND RANDOM ENCOUNTERS

Birders naturally are happy as pigs in slop when migration is taking place. With millions of birds surging out of the tropics, opportunities abound for seeing species one normally wouldn't see, and there's always that rare bird that strays wildly from its path and ends up in a place as odd to it as the surface of the moon. This is the bird that makes us drop whatever we're doing and hit the road, taking our chances at finding it before it either flies the coop or becomes victim to an inhospitable environment.

Such a bird was the long-tailed jaeger that showed up in Washington County on September 8, 2000. My friend Dan Thalmann called to say it was hanging around a junction of two dirt roads, far from its usual offshore haunts. My wife and I threw the spotting scope in the car and took off like escaping bank robbers.

Jaegers resemble gulls except for their chocolaty plumage, but to compare them is like saying a kitten is similar to a cheetah because they're both felines. Jaegers are fierce predators, the avian equivalent to an inner-city thug. Normally found on the high seas, this one had turned left instead of right and ended up in the middle of Kansas.

But that bird was nearby, only a few miles away, whereas the roseate spoonbills that appeared near Garden City were a bit farther. So far, in fact, that I refused go after them. I just didn't feel like taking the gamble. It's part of an inherent character flaw I'm loathe to admit: I am a lazy birder.

Where once I would have blasted off in the car to drive halfway across a state, now I seem to bide my time. Living in Denver, we had to traverse great distances to find birds who were confused enough to enter the wrong geographical area but smart enough to keep away from the big cities. Now, many good birds flow though our yard and finding them there gives me such a deep sense of pleasure that I spend more and more of my time hanging out at home. I'd rather be here than anywhere else.

Once summer comes, though, my birding enters a slow phase. Birds are nesting and raising their young, I'm gardening and mowing the weeds. On hot, muggy days I prefer being inside with air conditioning and a good book, watching the world go by outside the window.

Once birds have nested and the young fledged, there comes a curious phase in their lives called post-breeding dispersal. Dispersal is poorly understood but the theory is that birds are looking for future nesting sites or, as in the case of young chickadees, searching for a different flock to overwinter with. Young birds tend to move farther distances than adults though anything is possible. In migration an observant birder can see species rarely seen in the neighborhood.

That's the theory, anyway. Where once scientists commonly imbued wildlife with human traits, a term called anthropomorphism, nowadays they go to excruciating extremes to distance themselves from the slightest taint. Me, I don't lose sleep over it. I consider dispersal as the logical outcome of empty-nesters who have worked like dogs all spring and half the summer to raise a family and now it's time to see the sights before heading back to Mexico or Central or South America.

But I think my lazy spell is about to expire. Reports are coming in that shorebirds are already on the move. In my yard I've seen several kingbirds, a Bewick's wren and flocks of tree swallows, birds not seen for several months. Things are heating up.

On the morning after the Fourth of July bombardment I stood outside feeling as if I had a hangover, my head still resounding with explosions. The three-part cooing of a collared-dove filtered through the trees. It sounded so lonesome, the call of a single bird in a strange land, calling out for others of its race. And then, faintly, coming to my ears almost as an echo, was the call of a second dove. Grabbing my binoculars, I bolted down the road.

We hardly have time to take a breath, exhale, and we're back in the game.

\*\*\*

Whenever I unfold my deck chair I first inspect it for jumping spiders or other interesting surprises before sitting down. This time there was a two-inch frog staring back at me.

It wasn't quite what I expected but then the very best gifts rarely are. After I retrieved my field guide to Kansas amphibians, I knelt down and inspected the frog. It was mottled overall, a pale tan color, almost perfectly matching that of the fabric, with long toes and enlarged finger pads. According to the book, it was a Cope's gray tree frog, and Marshall County is the westernmost limit of its range. Along with the nearly identical eastern gray tree frog, the two species constitute the only amphibians in the state that change colors to match their surroundings, chameleon-like.

Much of our life consists of random encounters, lucky or

not-so-lucky happenstances, simply being in the right place at the right time. Birding is that way, as is almost sitting on a frog that I had never before seen. And so, occasionally, are relationships.

Twenty-nine years ago I was lucky enough to cross paths with a young girl in New Mexico. It was her eyes that stopped me dead in my tracks, almond-shaped, pale blue like alpine columbines. Within five seconds, maybe less, I was head over heels in love. We married seven months later.

A lot of things go through my mind when I open my chair and find a tree frog—wonder at a place that holds such mystery and pleasure, gratitude for a woman who never let her dream die and who brought me here. What a place. What a woman.

# SPEAKING IN TONGUES AS GRASSHOPPER MANAGEMENT

By my conservative estimate there were approximately 394,975,201 grasshoppers in my yard when I mowed it a few days ago. Most were very small, less than a quarter-inch in length, so my estimation might be slightly off. I would have had a better count but gnats kept flying into my eyes and up my nose, and two I swallowed, so I was a bit distracted. Still, you get the idea: there were an awful lot of grasshoppers.

I was hoping many of them would be sucked through the blades and fricasseed into mulch, but an inspection afterward showed barely a dint in population. It was a vast and terrible army, voracious in its appetite, eating everything in sight.

As we celebrate Independence Day and summer settles in, even a short walk through the yard is enough to illustrate the abundant fruits of July: *Orthoptera*. This order of insects is one of the most melodious, and the gentle susurration of crickets and the pulsing rhythms of katydids form an inescapable backdrop to summer every bit as evocative as hot days and sultry nights. Being a student of nature I try to see the beauty in everything, and the order *Orthoptera* includes some truly wonderful specimens. The problem is trying to get past grasshoppers.

According to the Kansas Department of Agriculture, there are approximately 118 species of grasshoppers in Kansas, of which only around fifteen cause significant economic damage.

The rest are, I suppose, mere nuisances. This subtle form of discrimination doesn't surprise me, coming as it does from an agricultural bureaucracy. In their eyes the world consists of farmers and non-farmers. Grasshoppers not considered destructive are those that eat the flowers, ornamental shrubs, window screens, and gardens of non-farmers, but leave farmers' crops alone. Taken literally, it means that unless you are a farmer, you and your possessions are of no economical worth to the state of Kansas. This does not mean you can stop paying taxes.

Insecticides are one way to control grasshoppers, but they must be applied during the third and fourth nymphal stage, which corresponds to early July. Once grasshoppers reach adult stage only a nuclear device can stop them.

That doesn't stop my older brother from spraying, though. A devout Baptist, he believes that pesticides and herbicides were ordained by God for use in an eternal battle that began in the Garden of Eden. Weeds and grasshoppers have been our burden since Eve ate the apple, and only through immoderate applications of toxins may the world be redeemed.

I shy away from such lethality. Insecticides like Furadan, Sevin, and the improbably named Warrior, Scout, and Mustang are nondiscriminatory (unlike the KDA), eliminating the good with the bad. Using them is like throwing out the baby with the bath. Imagine a silent July evening, no hum of crickets, no murmur of katydids, no electric zing of cicadas. I'd rather have a few grasshoppers.

Of course, my yard contains considerably more than a few, leaving my choices for control to either creating an ecological wasteland or trying to coexist with the order *Orthoptera*, warts and all. But since they ate the paint off my porch and munched holes in my window screens last year, I feel some control is necessary. But without the use of pesticides, what hope do I have? Not a prayer.

Or—maybe I do.

A recent foray into cyberspace came up just the miracle I needed. I was Googling for information on natural grasshopper controls when I found a Web site devoted to the patron saint of grasshopper management. Not that I knew such a saint existed, but that's the beauty of the Internet. Seek and ye shall find.

Centuries ago, a grasshopper infestation threatened the wild grapes of Finland, I learned. At the last minute, a simple man stepped forward and shouted a series of words that sent the bugs packing. That man was Saint Urho. A fifteen-foot-tall statue of him can be seen in Menahga, Minnesota. He's depicted wearing a simple frock and carrying a rustic wooden pitchfork with a giant grasshopper impaled on the tines. Nice touch.

If it worked for him, it should work for me. Kansas, Finland, it's all the same. After practicing a few times to stop my tongue from tripping over the vowels, I marched outside and, after determining that none of my neighbors were home, I stood on the porch and outstretched my arms like Charlton Heston parting the Red Sea and shouted, "Heinasirkka, heinasirkka, mene taalta hiiteen!" Which means, in Finnish, "grasshopper, grasshopper, go away!"

Nothing happened.

I tried again, using more conviction. My words had no effect. I marched through the yard, thinking that maybe they were hard of hearing. I raised my voice in a holy convocation. I shouted, I railed. Nothing.

Further research led to the embarrassing discovery that Saint Urho was a hoax. Apparently I hadn't read that far. My hopes were burned to ash.

Fledgling birds molt into juvenile plumage. Bluebirds raise a second brood. Sunflowers track the sun's progress through the heavens. I sit outside enjoying the hum of crickets, the murmur of katydids, the zing of cicadas. Sweat rolls off me, slickening my trigger finger as I raise the pellet rifle to my shoulder and center the crosshairs on a big green grasshopper. The hopper slowly creeps along the porch railing, intent on the window screen. I take up the slack in the trigger.

"Heinasirkka, mene taalta hiiteen," I whisper. The grasshopper nudges an inch forward, oblivious to the magic words. With the snap of the spring it disappears.

I'm no Saint Urho, no Pied Piper leading grasshoppers to, say, Nebraska, and the pitchfork I own is old and rusted. Better by far is a fine pellet rifle. Though the process is much slower than uttering a few unutterable words, I'm taking back my yard one *Orthoptera* at a time. After all, it's July. Let freedom ring!

# BIRDS AT DAWN, A SUMMONS TO THE JOURNEY

Did you feel the change last Thursday? Or maybe it really happened before that, a week or two prior, though that might be stretching the timeline back too far. Give it a week, no more. A week of sunlight falling softer, draped at a different angle, shadows dappling where they had not dappled before, the blue of the sky pallid, washed out, mornings crisp against bare skin. One day the clouds welled up, backdrop to increasing numbers of swifts and swallows and dragonflies, tugging so hard at me that I felt as light as a strand of milkweed silk, teetering precariously on the rim of the planet before gravity released me from its hold to freefall endlessly into the empty blue spaces between the clouds, spinning, purling, plummeting starward. And then surprised to find my feet rooted to the prairie grasses tinged with autumn's first bleached tones. Shaken and stirred, hawks on my mind.

But why Thursday? What was so portentous about that day? It began like any other, dawn a fiery stratum on the eastern horizon, fog in the wooded draws eroding into Elm Creek drainage, clouds roiling the sky. I had just left my morning job, tired, in need of another cup of coffee, when a small flock of Canada geese banked to my left and circled above a tranquil pond, their wild cries shattering the silence. My pulse quickened. *It's starting*, I thought. Everything changes now.

One group of migrant birds does not delimit summer and autumn; that I understand. But the signs of movement and change are all around us, and the pace is quickening. The first monarchs are moving through, vanguards of a larger horde soon to paint our lands orange and black. Shorebird migration is in full swing. Near at hand are birds not seen for months, those shifting locations in an act of restlessness between breeding and departure.

Our flicker arrives, hammering away at a dead snag across our field. Though flickers are common in our area, we never see them in the summer months. It reminded me of a pair I'd watched by the Linn sewage ponds a few weeks ago. One, a female, lay dead in the road, victim of a car collision. The male circled her, pausing to nudge her body, and then settled down beside her, acting all the world as if he were mourning. When cars approached he would flutter aside, though just barely. Twice cars almost crushed him beneath their tires. A truck roared past, and this time the male stood its ground. There was only enough time to gasp in shock. Feathers drifted on the wind, the two bodies separated by only a few feet. Surely we are not alone in the ability to feel loss.

Nature intrudes by its very fecundity. Investigating a rustling emanating from the basement, I find a chimney swift hurling itself against a window. I creep up and grab it, careful to entrap its wings. When I take it outside and open my hand, it rests on my palm for a long moment, its black eyes taking the measure of the open sky and the clouds flaring in first light. A flick of its wings and it's gone. A second swift bears in from the east and joins it, chittering in greeting.

Days pass. I scan the skies for movement, conscious of the tilt of the planet and the cold fronts sliding down from the north, of southbound hawks flowing like a feathered current.

One hot afternoon I sit outside at the picnic table, binoculars in hand, the sun like molten lava on my skin, but I know that were I to slip under the trees the temperature would be much more moderate, the land holding the heat with less insistence. The coolness of the shadows tells the true tale despite the sun's assertion of its dominance.

With a turn of the focus ring I reduce my world to the narrow field of view seen through the twin magnesium-alloy tubes of my Swarovski's. A half-dozen skippers cavort among the purple blossoms of the Russian sage, small, moth-like, mostly dark, their distinguishing marks subtle at best. Where once I would have skimmed over them, relegating them to those impossible-to-identify butterfly species, today I scrutinize each one. I'm feeling lucky, or at least intent on indulging in as much of this late-season opulence as I can.

The darkest skipper is a common sootywing, and I recognize both checkered and Zabulon skippers, but the others are new for me. I alternate between binos and field guides. They're not as hard to ID as I thought: tawny-edged skipper and sachem. Adding new species to my checklist is tantamount to a cosmic upheaval. I rock back on the bench, momentarily dizzy.

Each new day is bittersweet. My mood slips into a slow adagio half-sorrowful, half-joyous, a melancholic state destined to last until winter binds me to its bitter presence. Desperate to account for each moment, I'm suddenly fearful that I have squandered the summer.

I pull into the driveway as the sun spills over the horizon, remaining in the truck as a doe leads two white-speckled fawns past our porch. One dutifully follows its parent while the other lollygags, more interested in me than its journey.

And then it comes to me why Thursday was so important.

My steps had been faltering, hesitant, more absorbed in being successful than in connecting to the natural world. Something realigned itself within me when I saw the geese by dawn's early light. My feet are back on the path I must take.

"Ending is a journey," Basho said, "and the journey itself is home." As I step from the truck, the fawns bound away. It is dawn of a new day. I am home.

# BLIND SNAKES AND HOT SPOTS

If there's ever a book written on the birding hot spots of Marshall County, Lake Idlewild, lying just north of Waterville, surely must take top honors. It has the most varied habitat of any public place in the county, with open water, cattail marsh, hardwood forest, upland prairie, and a lovely outlet stepping down a series of rock shelves to meld with the Little Blue River a quarter-mile away. And yet I often bypass it in favor of other, lesser places.

When I do go there, as I did last week, I'm often surprised by its avian bounty and boundless beauty. Invariably, I ask myself why I don't spend more time there. And then I remember: snakes.

When we first moved here, people warned us that it was infested with copperheads. They were so thick that locals tended to avoid the place, we were told. And copperheads were a surly lot, ill-tempered, quick to strike, and venomous.

But a birder can never refrain from a place as lovely as Lake Idlewild, so I returned, usually during spring and fall migration. True to warnings, it was only a matter of time before my wife and I ran into a copperhead.

My naive experiment to see if rumors of their irascibility were true was not, as Lori insists, a matter of self-defense for the serpent. It was only a small pebble I rolled at it, not a boulder, and the velocity of the pebble was so slight that it barely managed to cover the ten feet separating us. Personally,

I believe the snake's instant rage was totally without conscience. Copperheads are, I deduced, a belligerent lot.

This subject was renewed recently by an offhanded statement by Lori's uncle. He said copperheads were heading to their dens now and were blind, making them a real menace. They'll repeatedly strike at anything that gets near them, he said. What makes them blind? I asked. From what little I could gather it was associated with them shedding their skin.

And so, after two days of strong south winds and one of early season cold, I found myself drawn to Lake Idlewild. I roamed the drainage outlet and through the rocky shelves, pacing gingerly, searching the ground before me. I imagined myself being assaulted by blind and vengeful copperheads, of being filled with venom until I fell writhing like a bug. Though the birding was superb—I found the first mourning warbler ever recorded in the county—I was relieved when I stepped into the truck, my hide intact.

I was curious whether the story of blindness was true. Thirty minutes of Googling brought me a wealth of information about copperheads, some good, some not so good, but the real question eluded me. I needed an expert.

I found him in Paul Sievert, Department of Biological Services at Emporia State University and president of the Kansas Herpetological Society. I asked him about seasonal blindness.

"That's not quite true," he reassured me. Blindness, or being in the "blue stage," is caused by a milky substance that comes between the old and the new eye caps when a snake sheds its skin. The substance acts as a lubricant to slip the old skin off faster. "They look like they have cataracts," he said. During the blue stage, which lasts from three to five days, snakes have difficulty seeing, and that makes them irritable.

As for copperheads molting simultaneously, that's not true. "Only one or two out of ten sheds at the same time," he said. Shedding is dependant on diet; some snakes shed four or five times a year, while others only once or twice, he said. And when they're in the blue stage, they tend to hide rather than to move.

Traipsing through Idlewild didn't seem so menacing to me now. I asked him if I should be worried about hiking in areas where copperheads are known to congregate.

Copperheads prefer flight over fight, he said. Given the opportunity, they'll hide when approached, he said.

I liked the sound of that.

"But," he continued, "copperheads are responsible for more bites than any other venomous snake in North America." Where rattlesnakes will coil and rattle and cottonmouths will gape to expose the white lining in their mouths, copperheads will provide only the barest warning before striking.

Oh.

"However," Sievert went on, "they rarely use much venom in their strikes. In fact, if you were bitten by a copperhead, chances are you'd sit in the waiting room at the hospital without being admitted. If you're a healthy adult and not allergic to things like bee stings, you probably won't have many effects from a copperhead bite."

My image of dying a horrible death by blind and bellicose copperheads vanished. If I was bitten, I could leisurely meander down to the clinic and let them treat me. Super.

Copperheads live on mice and small mammals, Sievert said. If you're fixing to step on them, they can see that you're much larger than their normal prey, and thus won't waste valuable venom on you. Unless, of course, they're milked over, in which case they'll let you have it with both barrels.

There's that thought again.

"The bite is extremely painful," he added.

I felt myself deflate. "What's it feel like?" I asked nervously.

"It feels a lot like a hornet sting, over and over," he said.

I thought about that.

"Over and over and over."

I think I got his drift.

I'm not sure whether I felt better or worse after talking to Sievert. I suppose that copperheads are just another reminder that the world is not arranged to fit our concerns. But if the threat of copperheads, real or imagined, keeps people away, I'll have the best birding spot in the county all to my tense, jumpy, apprehensive self.

# NOT JUST A SONG FOR DRAGONS

When I was a kid I would sometimes lie on my back, hands behind my head, and lose myself in the blue sky. I don't know if kids still do that or if their days are stuffed with electronic games or TV or just hanging out. I suspect that watching the sky isn't high on their A-list, though.

It's been years since I last felt like prostrating myself outside and it hasn't become any easier. Such an act seems childish and undignified. I didn't realize that all I needed was an example and a theme song.

One day when we were manning the hawkwatch station in Denver, hawks were flying very high directly above us. Seeing them necessitated craning our necks at an awkward angle, and it wasn't long before we were all suffering from the strain. One guy chose to sprawl on a flat boulder, resting his head on a pack. It seemed to work, just as it seemed to attract vultures. Maybe it was our collective stink from perching on a naked rock for hours in the hot sun; either way, it was disconcerting, and he soon quit.

This was brought to mind by a variety of factors associated with the approach of autumn. Monarchs, birds, and dragonflies are moving south and this combination has given me a blinding neck-ache from looking up.

Migration is a herky-jerky affair. Cold fronts push birds, butterflies, and dragonflies in huge masses before them, while others ride on their tailwinds. For the most part we know where different bird species migrate to, and the wintering grounds of monarchs are well documented. What remains a mystery is the destination of dragonflies. Where they go, what species are migratory, and, the million dollar question, how to find out, are part of the fun in watching them zip past.

I wasn't aware that dragonflies migrated until two years ago, when we had a spectacular monarch flight. The butterflies were everywhere, in the skies, in the trees, landing on me as I stood watching, but I noticed that whenever there were big flights there would also be incredible numbers of dragonflies with them.

I was researching dragonfly migration recently when I came across a photograph of a scientist studying monarchs in the Sierra Madres of Mexico. He was lying flat on his back, and it was impossible to tell if he was dozing, counting butterflies, or murdered by bandits. What the image revealed was that adults can, and possibly should, revert to a prone position when counting migrating bugs. It's like being a kid again, but with a purpose. If he could do it, I thought, I could do it.

I remained hesitant to hurl myself on the ground during a flight of dragons and monarchs last week, preferring to sit at the picnic table and get a sore neck. The sky was deep blue, marbled with fissures of cirrus and speckled with monarchs drifting by on a stiff north breeze. Above them, hundreds of dragonflies were winging their way southward. It was a rapturous moment, which might account for the song that popped into my head.

Our brains are amazing machines, having files stored away in forgotten drawers, collecting dust, only to be one day pulled out, cleaned up, and returned to the light of day. Which might explain why an unfamiliar song suddenly gained such prevalence. I found myself grinning, humming the chorus, of which I knew only a few words: *show me heaven*, it went, *leave me breathless*. I was certainly breathless over the spectacle before me, so the song fit the moment.

When I told my wife about the song, which happens to be on an album of hers by Jessica Andrews, she said that it was about making whoopee, not watching dragonflies. Oh. I ruminated on that for a few minutes and then decided it's not up to me to judge the fine points of a song, only to accept its inclusion in whatever act that fulfills me. Plus, if that's the case, then lying down seems to be warranted. Rather than craning my neck, I'll join the scientist in the grass and hum along.

I was pleased as punch as I moved to the backyard and found a suitable spot away from prying eyes. It wouldn't do to have someone drive by and see me there. They'd probably call an ambulance, or screech to a stop and rush over to see what's wrong. There I would be, spread out like a dead man, my binoculars strapped to my chest, lost in a trance. I'd be embarrassed, and they'd be embarrassed, and we'd all get a chuckle out of it, and they'd go off to tell their friends about that weird guy on Gypsum Street, and maybe they'd even warn their children to stay away from that end of the block.

I lay down, aware of the ridiculousness of my position. Grass tickled my neck. The north wind ruffled my hair and sent a tempest of swallows past. Between us, big orange butterflies relentlessly flew south, and above them, so high that the naked eye was useless, were the dragons. In my mind, a female vocalist belted out my theme song.

*Show me heaven*, I sang along, raising my binoculars. *Leave me breathless*.

For some inexplicable reason, I found myself getting curiously excited.

# A LESSON FOR THE LIVING

I watched a sparrow die today.

It was just a house sparrow, *Passer domesticus*, the ubiquitous bird of cities and farms, reviled by most people who feed birds, a "trash" bird, as birders call them. She lay beneath the platform feeder, cushioned in grass, her breath coming hard, beak gaping to catch one more lungful, her eyes closed in weariness.

Normally this wouldn't touch me on quite the level it did, but she was unique. She was an albino, a survivor of marauding hunters, and for several weeks she brightened our yard with her pale, ghostly presence.

Now she was dying.

She took no notice of her surroundings, nor of me as I stood beside her. I had stepped outside to look for migrating hawks and found her instead. She seemed so small and pitiful that I decided to keep vigil with her. I sat down heavily beside her in the grass, my binoculars draped around my neck. Nobody should have to die alone.

There was no reason for me to categorize her as a female. All I can say with certainty is that it was a fledgling, that it hung around with fifteen or twenty other young sparrows, some molting their juvenile plumage to reveal darker feathers on the breast. Most were nondescript, "little brown jobs" in birder slang. This one glowed. When she flew it was like a miniature comet, or a winged snowball. And she loved to take baths in the water dish.

The fact that she was dying was not remarkable. Albinos usually have short lives, whether from a genetic defect or, in the wild, from being a target. Lately we've had numerous raptors hunting the yard, plucking sparrows from the feeders or chasing them across the field to snatch them with a puff of feathers. That she had survived this long was a minor miracle.

Overhead, fat clouds dragged their dark heavy bottoms across the sky. The cool breeze shifted from west to north and strengthened. Conditions were ideal for migrants to catch a free ride south, and soon I saw them, high up, some mere specks, others lower. Two Vs of pelicans soared by, wings outstretched; cormorants, also called sea crows, lumbered by in long serrated formations. An occasional hawk passed by very fast.

On the ground, below the feeder, all was in motion too, except for the albino sparrow and me. Beetles wove like drunks through the seeds, box-elder bugs mated at the fringes of the grass, ants meandered, and grasshoppers clattered by. The sparrow gasped for air. I picked her up, cupping her in my hand, hoping my warmth would comfort her.

She was still, her heart a thin pulse beating with mine. Occasionally she would gag, opening her eyes and looking around in panic. During one bout she seemed to notice me, and she struggled to escape my hand. I opened my fingers. She lurched away, five inches, ten inches, a mad wobbly scramble that ended at a clump of grass. She collapsed, gasping hard.

"I'm still here," I assured her. Why this mattered was neither an act of reason nor of mercy.

The sound of wing-beats roused her. Other sparrows, nervous at my presence, had flooded the feeder. They watched me and I watched them and she watched them, and then they flew away.

The sparrow closed her eyes.

Had she heard their wings? Did she remember the sensation of flight, perhaps even of her first, when she left the nest and gathered the sky to her, made it her very own? When she saw that which is invisible to us—sky currents, sky rivers, sky doldrums, sky freedom? Did she remember the feel of air in her wings? I wondered what it must be like to die in an open field, under a sky filled with birds, and never be able to join them having once tasted flight.

Surely it is different for us, grounded as we are to this earth. We can become airborne any number of ways, from jets to planes to parachutes and hang gliders, but it's not the same. It's not flight by our own volition or ability. It's not being woven into the fabric of the sky, of soaring like the most pure and perfect adagio.

It took her a while to die. The clouds broke apart and drifted away and the sun beat down fiercely on my unprotected head. Her only sign of life was an almost imperceptible rise and fall of her flanks, a slight bob of her tail. I felt my skin burning but I would not leave. She panted, eyes closed. Her movements were like a clock slowly unwinding.

At the end she jerked to her feet, cocked her head to the side and collapsed. Her tail was stiff. Her flanks no longer moved.

I sat there a while longer, wondering if her last movement was a death-constriction or a longing to see the sky once more, to die with it in her eyes. I prefer the latter. It has music in it.

I buried her in the garden, digging deep. For a moment she lay at the bottom of the hole, a pale shell of herself, a soulless husk, one eye open to the sky in a forever-look. For oration there were crickets and false-katydids and the wind in the hackberries. The first shovel of dirt dimmed her pearly luminescence. The second obscured it.

They say His eye is on the sparrow. Though I'm not a religious man, I take comfort in that. If any conclusions can be drawn from this, let it be that sometimes—who knows?—we are never as alone as we think.

# A HOUSE OF SPIDERS

I wouldn't wish this on my worst enemy.

When I shook out a pair of jeans I hadn't worn in a while, a big spider tumbled out. It plummeted like a brown rocket and disappeared into the cuff of my pants, which I'd rolled up to shorten. My wife, who was standing beside me, jumped back. I froze.

It was a *big* spider. Not as big as the wolf spider that had boldly strode across the floor in the bathroom last week, leaving my wife in a lather, but big. Big enough that I didn't want it in my pants.

Unfortunately, formal education is remiss in teaching people how to extricate themselves from such situations. What's needed is real-world advice on how to deal with a spider in your britches.

I stared at my pant leg, hoping it would crawl out, and then dreaded it crawling out because of my sandaled feet and exposed flesh. I attacked the cuff with fists and palms. Lori stepped back farther.

When I paused, the spider darted out and slipped up my pant leg.

"He went up your leg," my wife observed.

This is what's meant by the phrase, "Going from bad to worse."

I thought of taking my pants off but decided instead to bombard them in wholesale terror. Once I was through beating my leg black and blue, I slid my cupped hands down my leg, hoping to force out anything that might be alive, dead, or wishing it was dead. The spider, very much squished, fell out.

Normally I'm not too concerned with spiders, though I've been leery of them since the bite last year that sent me to the doctor with a swollen foot and golf-ball-sized depression that flamed and turned purple. The wolf spider gave me the creeps. This spider reinforced the sensation. What I found next was even worse.

On the bathroom wall, serenely climbing toward the closet door, was a brown recluse.

This was the first recluse I'd ever seen. I studied it under a magnifying glass. There was the miniature fiddle on its cephalothorax, the six eyes, that unmistakable outline. What surprised me was its diminutive size. For so destructive a package, I expected something larger, like Godzilla. After identifying it, I smashed it. It seemed almost a pity, but there you have it.

It's one thing to host an errant wolf spider and quite another to host one of the most poisonous spiders in North America. As the saying goes, where there's smoke there's fire. The question was, how much fire?

For answers, I turned to the Recluse Community Project, a Web site hosted by Jamel Sandidge, Department of Ecology and Evolutionary Biology at the University of Kansas. Sandidge has assembled what can only be described as the preeminent source of knowledge about this troublesome spider.

A study of a house in Lenexa turned up over two thousand recluses in a six-month period, I learned. Three hundred were caught in a Texas home. A sticky trap placed under a couch in Memphis, Tennessee, collected forty-four recluses in one day. Where one is found, more are sure to follow. The question lies in finding them.

Recluses, I learned, are nocturnal. It helps to think of them as zombies in *Night of the Living Dead,* which assuredly instills a sense of dread for the gloaming. An hour or two after dark, Sandidge said, get a flashlight and inspect around the furnace and hot water heater, unoccupied or rarely-used rooms, under stairs and behind furniture. "Recluses move around primarily by walking against structures, such a baseboards, cabinets or walls," he said. So I did.

As darkness filled the house, I turned on a few lights and tried to quell the creepy-crawly sensation that night brought. I imagined spiders stirring, like vampire bats or half-rotted corpses. Trading sandals for boots and arming myself with a long-handled wooden spoon and a flashlight, I crept into the bathroom. A recluse was just emerging from the base of the closet door.

I dispatched it using the spoon, as I did nine others in the bedroom. Sandidge said that glue boards are highly effective for recluse control, so I located a package of them we'd bought when we had a snake loose in the basement. I was on my knees in the bathroom in the process of cutting the board in half when the biggest, baddest brown recluse I'd ever seen sauntered into the room.

The spider stopped three feet away from me, as if sizing me up. I would have fled the room screaming except that there was no outlet; my wife, who was in the hall, backtracked with some speed. After controlling a sudden onslaught of arachnophobia, I dropped the glue board on top of the spider. I almost missed, but the board caught it across its body. It measured over two inches across.

In the basement I found a legion of spiders of various species. More recluses were in the stairwell. What I had thought to be our home was, in fact, theirs. Ours was a house of spiders.

Sleep eluded us that night. The next morning I decided to fight back. I filled Mr. Death, my three-gallon sprayer, with a liberal mixture of soap and water—lethal to spiders, Sandidge assured me. I placed glue boards everywhere. I assaulted the spider stronghold in the basement with a shop-vac and Mr. Death. I vacuumed webs and spiders from one end of the house to the other, upending furniture to get them in their hideouts, emptying drawers and boxes, seeking them out and destroying them. I caulked cracks in the walls and floors. By the time the sun dropped below the horizon, I felt like the house was ours again.

After dark, a thorough search turned up nothing.

The next morning we found a recluse caught in the trap by the bed.

# THE LAST DAYS OF OCTOBER

If we had the freedom of birds, would we leave this place, trading it for the warmth of the Caribbean or the swampy lowlands of the Pantanal, or would we hunker down and face the oncoming winter with grim acceptance? Many birds made their choice when the cold front blew through last Friday. The great-tailed grackles that had delighted and entranced so many people in Blue Rapids were gone, plunging the town square into an eerie silence.

Hundreds of the birds had paused in their southward journey to provide musical entertainment—if you can call it that—to the residents. For over a month the birds had congregated in the trees in Fountain Park or had wandered the streets, a noisy and restless cavalcade. Their endless whistles, whoops, clacks, and shrieks were something few people had heard before, and certainly not in this profusion. For possibly the first time, great-tailed grackles had staged an extended visit to Blue Rapids and appeared to be in no hurry to move on.

They were first seen in Kansas in 1963, harbingers of a southern invasion. Now breeding in the central and southern parts of the state, the grackles are usually found in our area only in spring and fall. They're members of the *Icterid* family, collectively known as blackbirds but whose family includes orioles, oropendolas, caciques, and meadowlarks. With one possible but unproven exception, there are no records of the bird nesting in Marshall County.

I thought that would change last spring, when a pair moved into the cattails at Lake Idlewild. The male would preen and pose, fanning his huge tail, while the female fawned and acted like she was impressed. His unmelodious cry grated off the low hills. They finally abandoned a half-completed nest and disappeared.

Describing their vocalizations might be the biggest obstacle to a modern field guide author. How does one translate grackle into English? Though they gamely give it a whack, the end result is often more entertaining than the song itself.

David Sibley, author of the superb *Sibley's Guide to Birds*, describes it as "a series of loud, rather unpleasant noises, mechanical rattles *kikikiki* or *ke ke ke ke teep*; sliding, tinny whistles *whoit whoit*; harsh, rustling sounds like thrashing or flushing toilet; loud, hard *keek keek* or *kidi kidi*. Common call of male a low, hard *chuk* or *kuk*; female call a softer, husky *whidlik* or *whid*." Got that?

Alvaro Jaramillo and Peter Burke, authors of *New World Blackbirds: The Icterids*, play it safer with their comment, "The repertoire of noises that this species can produce is substantial." Indeed it is, and they should have stopped there. But no, they made a stab at it, too. The song of the male, they wrote, "begins with harsh notes similar to the breaking of twigs, followed by an undulating *chewechewe*, then an abbreviated version of the twig-breaking notes, and finally several loud, two-syllable *cha-wee* calls."

I've paid particular interest in the vocalizations of the great-tailed grackle in several states and along the Texas coast, where the grackles join their even larger cousins, the boat-tailed grackle, but I never heard anything remotely sounding like the flushing of a toilet or the snapping of twigs. Maybe I haven't been listening hard enough.

I had hoped they would remain until my upcoming Christmas Bird Count, still months away, but they apparently hopped on the strong wind accompanying the front and departed. Interestingly enough, people along the Texas coast despise the birds, finding them, in their millions, a bit too garrulous.

As the front passed through I found a half-mile-long serpent of blackbirds near the Big Blue River. The flock contained several hundred thousand *icterids* of various species; I spotted brown-headed cowbirds, red-winged blackbirds, common grackles, Brewer's blackbirds, and maybe one or two rusty blackbirds, but no great-taileds. When that seething mass took flight I watched them swirl in a tornadic column, a roiling, noisy mass of black feathers and baleful yellow eyes.

A cold front can change everything as October fades to November. Some birds leave for good, riding the strong tail winds to conserve energy; others appear as if by magic. I had gone out to welcome them, finding the season's first Harris's sparrows and dark-eyed juncos. The sky was filled with the last of the Franklin's gulls. A golden thread of fallen leaves stitched the river to the shore. As I stood at the base of a hill, the towering gray ruin of the old gypsum mine appearing in the gloom like the gates to the underworld, I listened to the wind in the trees and counted kinglets flitting in the brush.

The season's first hard frost whitened the ground on Sunday morning. I was inside our bedroom painting when leaves began to fall. It seemed as if the maples were shedding, that each leaf had waited until this one moment to let go en masse, drifting down lazily to carpet the grass.

Stepping outside, I heard the soft susurration of the leaves as they fell. There is nothing stopping me from getting in my truck and following the birds, I thought—nothing except that

I love this place, that I call it home. I looked toward the south and thought of those long lonely miles, of the risks involved, the dangers. And then I went back inside and returned to my painting.

Life presents us a multitude of opportunities, leaving us the unenviable task of choosing the right one for ourselves. My choice is to wait out the winter, bitter and long though it may be. I'll be here next spring when the birds return.

# ZOOTIES IN RETREAT, THE TARNISHED MAGIC OF A NEW YEAR

For a birder addicted to checklists, the sense of discovery and newness is so raw on the first day of January that it never fails to surprise us that others don't feel it, too. Everything has an aura of magic about it. It's as if our eyes after a long blindness were suddenly opened, and each bird, no matter how common, is transformed into a rare and unusual specimen. We call these birds "zooties," and once a year every bird is a zootie. It's akin to Andy Warhol's "fifteen minutes of fame" except it lasts about fifteen seconds.

Before first light on the dawn of a new year I set out a pad and pen on the dining room table, and beside it my binoculars. So deeply ingrained in me is the urge to find one hundred bird species in the month of January that I can barely resist it. This is a throwback to my Colorado days, and though I have never been successful at it, the old familiar twitch still plagues me. And it all begins with that first bird.

At first light I looked out the window and saw a chickadee and a downy woodpecker. Ninety-eight to go.

A perfect failure rate, however, tends to dampen my enthusiasm to the challenge. Do I really want to spend the next four weekends driving across the state in pursuit of zooties, or would I rather stay home and read a book? Within an hour I had fourteen species. I felt the tug but resisted.

The geese pulled me out. They came from the west,

hugging the hillside in a ragged formation, heading for the sewage ponds or open fields near the Big Blue River. I told my wife I was stepping out for a short while, to both flesh out my bird list and to hunt for a cackling goose. This is a new species for Kansas—not that they haven't been here for thousands of years, for they have, but rather that the esteemed scientists at the American Ornithological Union recently "split" the Canada goose race into two separate species. The details are far too complex to enumerate here so here's the easy explanation: the cackling goose is the smallest of the races, with one subspecies barely taller than a mallard.

There was a little diversion on the way when I noticed a small falcon in the center of town. Hoping for a merlin, I whipped around the block for a better look. By the time I returned it was gone.

A friend of mine once told me the key to success is to get the hard-to-find birds first. I agree. It also adds excitement to the challenge, the thrill of seeing something unusual.

I found the geese at the ponds, a gray mass darkening the waters. Keeping my profile lower than the embankment, I moved closer. I was still hunkered down when I heard them take flight. They rose in a cloud and dispersed in two directions, and I tracked them, scanning their ranks for a smaller member with a grayer throat and stubbier bill. It was like looking for a needle in a haystack only these haystacks were moving. They winged away and faded against the indistinct horizon and were gone, leaving me standing there like a jilted suitor.

There was no time to pout because an immense flock of small birds zipped by, weaving in wide loops around the ponds, their tinny cries like distant wind chimes. They might have been Lapland longspurs, a real zootie, or the more common horned larks. Their speed and mass made it impossible to determine their race, and soon they, too, flew away.

Several years ago my wife and I drove to Waconda Lake to look for two rare gulls that had been reported. After an entire day of picking through the thousands of gulls sitting on the ice, we finally nailed the two zooties. It was supposed to be a trip that would push my count over the hundred mark. Instead, the two gulls were all I netted. The distance outweighed the gains.

The next two days were spent working on my upcoming Christmas Bird Count. My wife and I drove the backroads to the north and south of Waterville, marking down properties that looked birdy. My definition for "birdy" simply means an area with varied habitat and, to add a touch of rusticity, an abandoned house or barn that might harbor an owl. Later I check the plat maps to ascertain who owns the property and start making phone calls asking for permission to enter. This is not only a delightful way to see the country but it also gets me into the field for more birds.

Just north of the intersection of Sunflower and 4th Road we located a large raptor, about a third of a mile off the road. Through the binoculars I could tell it was a large gray falcon, easily the size of a red-tailed hawk. Only the gyrfalcon is that large. Owing to the rarity of the gyr, however, there was no way I was going to claim it unless I got a better look. Since I'd stupidly left my spotting scope at home, I braced my binos on the hood and studied it. When it flew, it imitated all the other zooties and disappeared over the horizon.

Through my years of trying for that magic number in January I've learned a few things my friend never told me. It really helps if zooties cooperate; hurling invectives or field guides at departing birds does not further your goal; strong drink assuages the sting of failure; plus, there's always next year.

This January, I'm going to catch up on my reading. I'm not chasing birds all over creation. I'm not.

As I write this, there's a pine siskin at my feeder. Not that I care, mind you, but it's bird number thirty-two.

# IN BIRDING, NO SURE BET

After reconciling myself to forgetting about the insane challenge of trying to find one hundred bird species in Kansas in January, I dug through the pile of books I received as Christmas gifts and selected *Gilead*, by Marilynne Robinson. The weather cooperated with my newfound liberation by coating everything with a layer of ice and then spitting snow on top of that and cracking the thermometer so all the mercury emptied out. Only a fool or an idiot would want to go outside. I put on a pot of coffee, donned slippers, and settled comfortably into a recliner. January was mine to relish.

Such complacency came cheap. I could afford to gamble my decades-long dream when so much of the game was left. The cards I had been dealt were five weekends and an upcoming Christmas Bird Count, and from where I sat, looking out the window (keeping an eye out for nuthatches and creepers), I could afford to hold back. I could hedge my bets.

Everything hinged on the count. If I found a lot of birds then I might entertain the irrational thought of attempting what had always defeated me. If things didn't pan out, I would blissfully return to reading my book. I would stare out the window and look for movement and not once let my restlessness gain a foothold. I would tell everybody that I didn't care. I would say, "There's always next year." And I would know in the deep fastness of my heart that I lied. For what becomes of us when we no longer have anything to look forward to, no dreams, no challenges, no obstacles to overcome?

Saturday morning came with a thin sliver of moon rising in the east. My tracks broke the virgin snow blanketing the road leading into Prospect Hill Cemetery, cutting twin swathes to the gazebo. The only sounds were the rustle of wings in a nearby pine and the brittle crunch of snow underfoot. Stars glittered like ice crystals, cold and distant. My gloved finger found the play button on the cassette recorder and the whinnying cry of a screech owl echoed in the darkness. There was an answer, and another.

The process of finding new birds was as sluggish as the water trickling under the ice of Coon Creek. It was also painful. There was a moment at the beginning of the count when Warren Buss, Jeanette Pralle, and I walked a snowy backroad when our faces were so frozen we could no longer pish, that the sound issuing from our lips was more hiss or sibilant croak. A red elongated sun lifted above the distant cottonwoods. I had warned the others to first travel the roads they knew would get sloppy in the afternoon's thaw. But it never thawed.

By midmorning a gray fogbank appeared in the south. Within thirty minutes it had swallowed the sun and colors and the horizon itself, and with it came a breeze that congealed our blood. The afternoon was as cold as the morning or more so, and the roads slicker than ever. Twice Warren told me to stop, and both times I replied I was, or wished to, and yet the truck continued on unfazed by the brakes.

But even at day's end, when I tallied up the count and realized I'd passed the halfway mark, I wasn't ready to commit. The day had been fun and exciting and special but the thought of pushing myself to always seek out more birds sounded like too much work. And yet, thinking of the ones that got away had the unfortunate result of making me wish to remain in the field, and that edginess found an ideal outlet in my wife's request to go shopping in Manhattan the following day. I could have begged off, but I thought it wouldn't hurt to stop by a few spots, like the exit channel at Tuttle Reservoir, or the river below the old mill at Rocky Ford. I mean, you never know.

In the short amount of time my wife allowed me, I knocked them dead. Prairie falcon by the old stone house, herring gull flying overhead, waterfowl in the rapids below the mill, golden-crowned kinglet and rusty blackbird in the trees by the river, and so much more that I found myself caught up in a birding frenzy. I was on a roll, and the hundred mark suddenly seemed easy.

But there was a sobering moment when we drove the slick roads circling the K-State feedlot on the north end of Manhattan. Not one cowbird could be found in the thousands of other blackbirds swarming the site, though we drove slowly and scoped everything out, our eyes watering from the stench, all thoughts of lunch souring. The place had always been a sure bet, guaranteed to have dozens of the parasitic bird, and yet we drew a blank. And I thought how odd it is that we accept the zooties as something earned or rewarded but the ones we miss haunt us.

With a dozen feet of bad road to go before joining the main highway, Lori pointed to a small clump of weeds. It was full of white-crowned sparrows, a bird whose presence at the feedlot was practically unheralded. I couldn't help but laugh out loud, and in the laughter I heard the sound of a contentment that goes beyond words, beyond emotions, beyond artificial goals. To live fully we must have dreams.

It was bird number sixty-six.

# THE LAW OF DIMINISHING RETURNS

## North of Waterville

I t must have been a place, an evening, such as this that inspired Robert Frost to write his poem, *Desert Places*.

> *"Snow falling and night falling fast, oh, fast*
> *in a field I looked into going past,*
> *and the ground almost covered smooth in snow,*
> *but a few weeds and stubble showing last."*

And little else visible, the distant trees vanished in a white fog, the air white, the land white, and in that colorless expanse only my truck and myself and the telephone poles marching away into oblivion. The cold a living thing, nipping at my ears, stabbing my eyes.

No gyrfalcon here, no merlin nor any other bird. The wind knifes through my clothes and still I refuse to retreat to the warmth of the truck. There is something here that draws me, some mystery bird, some gray ghost from the far Arctic, and yet it remains cloaked. I pace the road, restless, haunted, unable to leave. As once I did when the world was younger.

Strange how far a song can take you. Loreena McKennitt's *Snow* is a background to the silence about me, a tune accompanying the thickening air, and it brings me back to when we were leaving the Chiricahua Mountains of southern Arizona. It had been one of those trips that brand our souls, and departing filled with me with an unnamable yearning. Leaving wounded me somehow. On the road heading north I pulled to the shoulder and got out and stood staring at that range across the broad valley. I was rooted to the spot, with the song's closing lyrics playing in my mind. "The world seems shrouded, far away, its noises sleep, and I as secret as yon buried stream plod dumbly on and dream." And I dreamed, and the dream was of staying.

There is something at play here on this winter eve, even as then, some deeper thing than the mere ticking off of a new bird species. But in the deepening gloom, with the cold hardening, it remains nameless and unseen, just beyond the limit of sight. As if the fog shrouds it, too.

When at last I leave it is like a mystical umbilical cord connecting me to this place is being sawed in half, and inwardly I throw back my head and howl like a wild beast. At times we are barely removed from our animalic natures.

## Public land southeast of Blue Rapids

Parker's law of diminishing returns: when searching for a specific number of birds in a limited amount of time, for every new species found the next will exponentially be more difficult to locate.

Everywhere I go my binoculars are at my side. Through them I see the world, the red-breasted nuthatch scampering up the rough bark of a bur oak, the cloud of Lapland longspurs hugging the snowy ground in a tight knot, the swarm of brown-headed cowbirds mantling a forsythia like a dark shroud. Every new bird less frequent.

One gray day I find myself on a dead-end road. This might

have been surprising but my state of mind has been solely on birds, and yet I have not prepared for the frigid conditions. I drive as far as I dare and then switch to foot. Passing locusts dripping with thorns and icicles, I slide down a snowy incline into a small clearing beside the frozen river, where several acres of milo have intertwined with wild licorice and velvetweed to form an impenetrable thicket. The road here more memory than fact.

Each step is shadowed and preceded and accompanied by birds. The field rustles with their wings as if a sudden wind raked the dried seed stalks. Pishing brings sparrows roiling up, drab miniature jack-in-the-boxes that pop up for a quick look and then dive for cover. Several I identify as white-throated, bringing my total to seventy-two. So this road then is not so dead-ended but led to where I needed to be.

My teeth are chattering but the thought comes to me that even if the returns from here on diminish, if each new bird or new desire or hope or dream in the remaining years of my life be harder to fulfill, there will be no diminution in the searching, that rather than taking away or lessening I am in fact enriching and being enriched. And maybe even that as all roads eventually come to their ends, so do our quests, but the ending, no matter their success or failure, is not what gives them meaning. It's in these little stops along the way, and the places they lead us to.

Or maybe I'm so cold that rational thought is impossible and I am merely gilding a foolish undertaking.

## Stockdale area, north of Manhattan

A serendipitous holiday brings me southward where I study gulls on the river below Tuttle Creek Lake. They undulate with waves rolling from the discharge tubes, balanced on ice floes irregular and edged like shattered glass. Watching them makes me giddy, but I pick out two Thayer's gulls, wanderers from the farthest spit of land on the northern hemisphere. Two more species follow but the rest of the day is a fruitless meander across two counties.

It comes down to this: standing beside a rusted barbed wire fence, listening to the tap-tap-tap of a small woodpecker that flew into a wild tangle of thorny trees and brush. Is it the ladder-backed woodpecker, a Southwestern bird seen here yesterday, or just another downy? Until it moves I cannot know, and I will not move until I do.

This is where the road has taken me. I may miss the bird, but I will not be diminished.

# DISPATCHES FROM A MANIC-DEPRESSIVE BIRDER

**It's not Oklahoma but you can see it from here**

I've always felt that no town should be judged by its appearance in winter. With the absence of concealing foliage or colorful flowers every flaw is exposed to view. It's not the town's fault that January is so bleak and dreary.

I'm now willing to make an exception. Geuda Springs, Kansas, population 212, thirty-something miles south of Wichita, is a squalid, ill-kempt, wretched dump. Its dirt streets stagger crookedly, each yard competing for the most trash and barking dogs. The cheeriest structure is the bar, a pair of railroad cars joined together and painted brick-red. The single church has been converted to a residence. Even God has fled.

It's possible I'm an unreliable witness. All day my mood has risen with each new bird—Cooper's hawk in northern Riley County caught silhouetted against a red slash of dawn, common loon swimming in the outflow channel at Tuttle Lake, rough-legged hawk north of Burns—but lunch lies uncomfortably in our guts, and an afternoon dry spell only emphasizes our intestinal misery. We've come south in my quest for one hundred bird species in Kansas in January, and I now fear that the vile meal has broken our luck. My mood plummets.

I'm angry at myself for violating a cardinal rule to never eat at a Mexican restaurant owned by white people. The "Authentic Mexican Food" sign in Winfield should have scared me off, but we were hungry and feeling adventurous. If my warning bells chimed when I saw "sancho" on the menu, they pealed with abandon when the waitress professed ignorance of *chile verde*. Every explorer's dreams die hard.

Geuda Springs looked better from a distance, which is why we're here. The snowy owl south of Oxford isn't to be found no matter how many roads we traverse, our binoculars tracing every remnant snowdrift or billowing plastic sack singing on barbed wire fence. After spying the church in the distance, Lori asked if we could drive through town. It's a mistake.

"I'd be a dedicated alcoholic if I had to live here," I tell her. The place has all the charisma of a penal colony. Lori pulls out the map and charts a course for the next bird.

I remind myself that not every species on my list will be found, that birding is as much luck as skill. It doesn't help.

## Belle Plaine and beyond: not so belle anymore

The trees in the cemetery are splintered and broken, as are all the trees in central and southern Kansas. Belle Plaine, French for "pretty plain," is a lovely town, but the red crossbills I wanted are not in evidence. Like the trees, they may have fallen prey to the ice storm.

Unable to locate the sewage ponds in Mulvane, the next town northward, we stop at the museum. This is partly to ask directions and partly to let Lori have some fun; she's more interested in history than birds, so this is how we find common ground during road trips. At my query, the curator frowns. "We don't have sewage ponds here," she says. I certainly hope you do, I want to say, but I remain civil.

She phones the sheriff, asks a few questions, and then gives me directions to the water treatment plant on the west side of town. The road is littered with broken branches and limbs, and the Taurus bumps over them, scraping bottom. The pond is mostly frozen and barren of waterfowl. I have now missed an additional five species of birds I had hoped for. My mood is sinking like the Titanic.

## Once called Oldsquaw Pond, now victim of political correctness

Call it the Ritchie sand pit, or pits, as there are several. They lie northwest of Wichita in an area relegated to grubby industries such as gravel mining and rubbish burial. In a birder's lexicon it is the "Oldsquaw Pond," named for a particular species of rare waterfowl that often shows up here. One was seen last Friday, in fact. We're here looking for it, as well as two species of gulls and assorted waterfowl.

"Oldsquaw" was determined to be a sexist name several years ago by a stuffy panel of cowardly academics. At their recommendation, the name of the bird was changed to "long-tailed duck." While the appellation is certainly accurate, at least for the male of the species, most birders find it difficult to warm to the new name. Nowhere in my records is there any mention of a "Long-tailed Duck Pond." I hope it stays that way. In our efforts to appease everyone, we are losing the music of our language.

I have never in my life been this cold. The wind is in my teeth, Arctic in nature, brutal in force. Keeping the scope steady is impossible, especially with frozen hands, but I'm feeling lucky. I've already found great-tailed grackle on I-35, and there's a huge glaucous gull in view, bobbing on the whitecaps. More gulls are streaming in, winging across the face of the full moon, which brightens as the sun touches the horizon.

My luck is improving: ruddy duck, American coot, bufflehead and lesser scaup quickly follow. My count now stands at eighty-six, and there's still tomorrow.

## The fat lady clears her throat and steps to the podium

My euphoria succumbs to a gluttonous feast at the Golden Corral Restaurant. Dawn finds me exhausted after a night of fitful sleep. It's ten degrees outside with a wind chill somewhere far south of zero. The thought of standing outside for several hours makes me queasy.

The ponds are now iced over. Unable to find ducks, I look for donuts, hot coffee, and the road home. I miss my exit and complain bitterly about the lack of adequate signage. Lori says, "You can't do this anymore if you're going to be that way."

I am so close, and yet so far.

# THE BIRDER WHO CAME IN FROM THE COLD

## The devil, you say

A friend said, how many are you up to, and I said, ninety, and he said, are you making any money on it, and I said, no, I'm losing my shirt. We both laughed. You need to learn how to get paid for it, he said.

Curiously, he never asked if I was having fun.

The morning after I returned from a 350-mile loop through west-central Kansas, and right after making plans to find another bird, I looked up "obsession" in the Oxford English Dictionary. This was sheer perversity on my part, but I was curious about its origin.

The oldest use of the word dates to 1513, when it referred to the "act of besieging." By 1605 the word had taken on a darker tone, defined as "The hostile action of the devil or an evil spirit besetting anyone." Modern usage drops the supernatural aspect with "any influence, notion, or fixed idea which persistently vexes or assails, especially as to discompose the mind."

Personally, I favor the middle definition. Spending all my time and money trying to find one hundred birds in Kansas in January? It's not my fault: the devil made me do it.

## "It ain't pretty"

I walk in the door with twenty minutes to spare, kiss my

wife, rub my rabbit, slam down a beer, claw into better clothes. It's the annual Blue Rapids Chamber of Commerce dinner and I'm almost late. The duffel bag, scope, and tripod are dumped in the middle of the floor. The car remains littered with the detritus of a long road trip: the thermos lost under one of the seats, maps folded haphazardly, remnants of a half-eaten lunch crushed in a paper bag. I'm ready in five minutes. Now if only my mind would catch up to my body.

It's hard switching from one state of mind to another. One moment I'm racing from one reported sighting to another and the next I'm listening to a speech on economics. I'm not here and not there either, but inhabit a ghostly middle ground.

As the speaker drones on, I catch myself drifting backward. I can't shake the frustration I felt after driving up to the gate at the Jeffries Energy Center north of St. Marys and asking the guard permission to scope out the lake. Sure, he said, all you have to do is sign in. But the guard inside wasn't so cooperative. He shook his head and told me he couldn't allow birdwatchers in. Hunters yes, birders no. You mean I can kill ducks but I can't look at them, I said. His eyes smiled but his face did not. That's it, he said.

But most troubling was something that came to me as I was speeding off after barely glancing at the trumpeter swan at Lake Shawnee in Topeka. I recalled reading a letter where the author decried listing on the grounds that it not only reduces the wonder of birds to a checkmark but also turns the birder into a robotic, insensate drone. At the time I deemed her daffy, but I now realize she's partly right. Any pleasure I'd felt upon finding a new bird was rapidly subsumed by the need for another. I was a junkie needing a fix.

Pete Janzen, a friend in Wichita, had warned me against this. "I know what listing can do to a guy," he said, "and it ain't pretty."

Most troubling, though, was when he called it my "Quixotic dream." Again the OED: "Inspired by lofty or chivalrous but false and unrealizable ideals." I didn't like the sound of that last phrase, not one bit.

## Coming in from the cold

My dreams began filling with birds, but these were not the species I'd been looking for. These were grotesque, deformed birds, with twisted legs and splintered beaks, with black holes for eyes and cries like the grinding of broken glass. No longer the hunter, I was the hunted.

The miles tend to blur together until all that's left is the sameness of the road. Place names where birds were found were abridged to shadowy pinpricks on an unreadable map, associated with a particular avian species but detached from any tangible recollection other than that of winter's fierce grip. More real than the long-tailed duck at Clinton Lake was the unrelenting north wind, and the gray sky, the gray land, the gray water. The swamp sparrows pished up from the frozen cattail marsh below Milford Dam were intrinsically bound to the aural memory of footsteps crunching through ice-encased reeds. Each new bird—Bewick's wren north of Tuttle Creek Lake, merlin at Fancy Creek State Park, black-billed magpie west of Kirwin—possessed its own unique imprint of ruthless winter.

It was a duck that broke my resolve. My arrival at Wilson Lake near Russell coincided with a freezing drizzle that turned the road slick and treacherous. The horizon disappeared, visibility reduced to less than a half-mile at times. And for all my searching I missed three critically-needed birds and nailed but one, a northern pintail in an open lead of water framed by ice. I thought I would freeze to death scoping out the lake.

On the return leg, bitterly chastising myself for not taking to heart the economics lesson, I cursed the endless miles and the pittance of a reward. The sun went down long before it set.

The end came far to the west, after another four-hundred-mile trip garnered a single bird, bringing me to ninety-three. With two days remaining in the month, I told my wife I was through. She didn't argue.

Night had fallen by the time we pulled into the driveway. Wearily, I opened the door and turned on a light. "Sheba, we're home," I called. Our Angora rabbit leaped from her cage in a joyous bunny dance. I knew exactly how she felt.

# THE ROAD SO FAR

# LOST BIRD, LOST SOUL, DECISIONS MADE AT AN INTERSECTION

What constitutes the genome of our personas? If a pill could erase that part of me which frequently left me incapacitated, would that be good or bad? Would I still be me without bouts of depression or would a stranger wear my skin like a cloak and peer through my eyes? This is something I wrestled with late in 1994 when I started taking Prozac. Snow fell heavily that year, and deep, and an ancient murrelet tried making a night landing on a wet highway near the Denver airport. It set down hard.

Some years lie lightly on us; others threaten to bury us. Chekhov's comment that "Any idiot can face a crisis, it's the day-to-day living that wears you out" has rarely been truer for me than that year. Our youngest son had been removed from our home due to a horrific event that still reverberates a decade later, and we were being dragged through the system, shredded piecemeal, losing parts of ourselves with each counseling session, each new psychologist, each setting sun. A five-year fight to save over four hundred acres of land had come to a head with an election, and though voters had approved a sales tax hike to support the purchase of open space, even in victory I felt defeated, for I knew the land I'd fought for and cherished was effectively removed from my grasp, its future now the responsibility of others. My mood swings had turned giddy, though rarely upbeat. I tried medication, but what I found was both startling and disturbing. "Several times I've felt in a funny mood, as if my body was trying to become depressed but the medication wouldn't allow it," I wrote in my diary. "It's a distinctly confusing state of mind, one I'm unable to decipher. There also seems to be a general listlessness, and things that interested me are sliding away."

The murrelet had it far worse than me, though when dawn came on November 14 we both were wounded grievously. The bird was found on the highway and given to a friend, Duane Nelson, who immediately called and asked if I wanted to be there when he released it. I did, for seeing such an unusual bird, a pelagic species of the North Pacific that rarely comes ashore except when nesting, was almost unheard of in the Rockies.

I found his car at Cherry Creek Reservoir and followed two sets of tracks through the snow to the shore, where he and a friend stood over a small cardboard box. Inside it was the piebald bird, smaller than I'd pictured. It appeared thoroughly bedraggled, forlorn. I cradled it in my hands, trying to warm it. I didn't think it had a chance of surviving.

But there was life there yet, and it swam out past the narrow scrim of ice ringing the shore and made for open water. Breathlessly we watched it struggle, ten feet, fifteen, thirty, but its movements were like a clock winding down, each movement a heartbeat slower than the last. It had no buoyancy, and when it stopped to rest it slipped beneath the water. Surfacing with difficulty, it headed back to shore. We collected it on the ice and placed it back in the box. Its feathers were brittle and sharp.

I offered to transport it to Birds of Prey, a raptor rehabilitator near our house, to see if they could help it. Placing the box in my car, I kicked the heater up full blast and ran the gauntlet for home.

The center was staffed only part-time, so I phoned prior to driving out. As we were speaking the bird convulsed, twisted its head back unnaturally, and slumped over. Everything beyond that was moot.

That night, feeling restless and empty, I went for a walk. Fog was closing in, the dusk lowering until all that remained were the eerie glow of the fog and the gibbous moon hanging above. All sounds snuffed out, and only my tracks in the snow to point the way home. With visibility reduced to less than twenty feet, I closed my eyes and spun in a circle, erasing all cardinal points save the moon.

I thought of how easy it would be to get lost, and perhaps how pleasant, too, wandering until hunger or weariness felled me, each step a heartbeat slower, shedding sorrows and heartaches like castoff clothes until all that remained was a husk that drifted featherlike to the snow. There must be some solace in the act, some grace, I thought. And yet, there was no way to lose myself in a field surrounded by settlements. Disoriented, yes; lost, no.

I set off toward the moon, snow crunching underfoot, passing through brittle cattails and orchard grass until tall cottonwoods stood stark against the sky and street lights filtered through the fog. The sound of passing cars trespassed on the silence. I had come to an intersection; home was three hundred feet to my right.

Being lost killed the murrelet, and lost now would surely kill me. Being found would mean giving up the field, giving up my child, and most assuredly giving up a medication that was more Faustian pact than deliverance. I stood there in the ghostly luminance until cold settled in my bones.

Our memories are imperfect at best. Events we have lived through, places we have been, often slip beneath the surface and disappear until something comes along and renews them. New reports of ancient murrelets in Colorado, Illinois, and Iowa hurled me back a decade, when I stood at a cold intersection and had to decide my way. That I have made it more or less intact is testament to the support of my wife and family. I wish the murrelets well. I wish all travelers, lost and alone, a safe passage and a home at the end of their flight.

# THE LONG NIGHT, WRESTLING WITH ANGELS

When Jacob approached the tribal lands of his brother Esau, who hated him, he sent messengers asking that he be received graciously. On their return, the messengers said that Esau, accompanied by four hundred men, was moving to meet them. So Jacob divided his people into two groups, thinking that if one was slaughtered the other could escape. He sent gifts to Esau hoping to find favor. The night before they were to meet he sent his family across the Jabbok River, and remained behind alone. He was in great distress, and needed time to think.

I drove into Grants, New Mexico, reeling from a recent divorce, wallowing in self-pity, afraid of the new world that was mine. The men I was to serve with were a motley bunch of losers, each with his own nightmare of guilt or failure, but we all wanted the same thing—a better life, a future with hope, a guarantee of security. It surprised us all that we had washed up in such a godforsaken place, guarding the Kerr-McGee mines thirty miles north of town. The miners had gone on strike and threatened violence; we were there to stop them.

I was raw enough to have no inkling of what to do if trouble came. Inspector Haines's admonition to "drop three or four of them and the rest will get the idea" seemed somewhat impractical if not illegal, but it was merely symptomatic of larger issues that plagued me. Somehow I had to find my way back to myself, but I had no idea how to do so. My partners were no help. One young man, whom I hated because he was a reflection of myself, took care of the matter by blowing his head off. Others numbed themselves with alcohol or grew surly, nursing their bitterness like the last ounce of cheap whiskey. I asked questions that had no answers.

Nights were long and boring, punctuated by the screams of toads coming from the shallow playas and occasional bouts of terror, as when a guard at another mine radioed that he'd seen men creeping up on my position. We'd been warned to watch the dynamite bunkers, so I danced from shadow to shadow with slippery hands and a finger caressing the shotgun's safety. Nothing came of it.

The Feights took care of the barracks where we stayed. He would kid me for all the letters I wrote but made sure my mail was delivered first. His wife, being the only woman allowed in the barracks, was something of a novelty, but her calm reasoning and easy manner helped us relax.

One night, headquarters radioed that a gang of strikers outside the mill were getting rowdy. They were armed and drunk, and, shortly, the dispatcher said they were coming our way. I was near the head of the canyon with a partner, Leo Gabaldon. We counted sixteen sets of headlights sweeping our way.

"What do we do?" I asked.

"Tell 'em to go away," Leo said.

"Right," I said.

He moved the truck to block the road, with my side facing the oncoming vehicles. As they stopped men spilled out, roaring yells and taunts. They looked like enraged ants, swarming to close the distance between us, picking up stones and waving rifles. I drew my pistol and set it in my lap. One man picked up a football-sized stone and hurled it two-handed, and as it spun through the air in slow motion as if it were in no hurry to reach its destination I calculated its arc and decided it would come through my window.

I thought that since the rock was going to kill me perhaps I ought to shoot the man responsible. Just as I raised my pistol and sighted on his chest Leo gunned the engine and popped the clutch. We rocketed off the road as the stone slammed into the bed of the pickup. It sounded like an explosion. The truck dropped off a steep hill, blew across a lower road and screeched to a halt in front of a rain-filled playa.

With us out of the picture, the strikers drove to the mine and proceeded to destroy it. There were gunshots and explosions and dust and screams, and after a while half the vehicles came out and headed back toward the mill. The others left by backroads. We moved in to investigate.

When the lawyers wanted us to testify only I volunteered, the others saying that the miners would kill them. And me. On the drive to court in Gallup I was seated between two state troopers, and armed men rode before and behind us. As often happens at the last minute, the lawyers settled their differences with handshakes. I was let go.

Mrs. Feight told me that scar tissue forms when you fall down and skin your knee, that the scar is thicker than the original skin. Next time you fall down you're that much tougher, she said. I took the lesson to heart.

That night above the Jabbok River Jacob wrestled a man. Or an angel, or God, depending on the interpretation. They wrestled all night, and when dawn came his opponent wanted to break off. Though he dislocated Jacob's thigh, Jacob would not let go until the man blessed him.

In my state of mind I could have taken the easy way out

like the one guy did, but between the danger and Mrs. Feight's wisdom, and the long nights with only my own tormented company, I learned that life is never given but must be claimed. It must be clawed at and gripped with a ferocity we seldom believe we possess, and it must not be released until we demand, and receive, what we want.

I claimed that blessing. And when I left Grants a week later, my steps, though still wobbly, were getting steadier. I wasn't going great guns yet, but I was going.

# A REQUIEM FOR GRANDFATHERS AND
# MEADOWLARKS

On the day my grandfather started dying I was out at Irving looking for meadowlarks. Strange how interconnected they might be, looking for a lost bird in a dead town while death comes for a man I thought might outlive us all. Ninety-seven years old, an ex-West Texas deputy sheriff, Benjamin Smith, "BoBo" to us grandkids, suffered a stroke and collapsed. A CAT scan indicated blood on the brain and most of what he ate or drank ended up in his lungs. Coherent speech was gone.

The death vigil had begun.

But I didn't know this at the time. I was at Irving on a mission of sorts, parked early in the morning in the shade by the stone monument. The roadside ditches were filled with water from the two inches of rain that fell several days ago, and chorus frogs were singing loudly from the flooded fields. The catalpa trees were in full bloom, huge ivory petals contrasting with the lime-green leaves. Purple phlox added color to the underbrush. Overhead, two long streaks of cirrus clouds fell toward the tree line as if the sky were weeping. It was nine o'clock and already the heat was building, humidity like a wet blanket.

What prompted my visit was a letter from Martha Nance, a subscriber who lives in Prairie Village, Kansas. An Irving native, she asked if meadowlarks still sang in the town site.

It was a good question and one I didn't have a ready answer for, so I felt duty bound to reply. The open fields surrounding the woods where the town once stood should have them, but usually when I visited I slipped into the trees in search of secretive birds, making my way down the overgrown side streets of the ghost town. I was raised with the song of the meadowlark ringing in my ears, and though I always felt it to be the quintessential Western bird, we tend to lose interest in common things. I wanted to find her a meadowlark and let her know that the world, or least that part of it, carries on.

As a personal quest goes, however, I immediately lost sight of my objective and disappeared into the woods. Silence greeted me. Cobwebs gleamed in sunlight slanting through the trees. My boots and socks were soaked within a hundred feet. Ticks inched their way up my pants, so I tucked them into my socks, unsheathed my Leatherman, and picked the insects off with pliers, simultaneously crushing them. I'm not sure the Leatherman was intended for such a purpose but it's a crucial piece of hiking equipment.

The only sound was an occasional yowling of peacocks from the Winslow property. As I delved deeper into the woods I started seeing movement—butterflies fluttering above stands of iris and phlox, cabbage whites and tiger swallowtails and a single little wood-satyr that had me following it like a Pied Piper through stands of cedars barely surviving in the deep shadows. It was so quiet I could hear my heart beat.

I pushed on further, breaking out into the open near the river. At the forest edge I started hearing birdsong: cardinal, pewee, red-eyed vireo, indigo bunting. By now the sun was reflecting off the pale gravel road and bearing down like a furnace. The light hurt my eyes after the darkness of the woods.

On the way back to town I made several stops to listen, but no meadowlarks were heard. Dickcissels kept up a steady banter under an azure sky hung with vultures, and I saw a red-tailed hawk carrying a two-foot-long snake to its nest in a cottonwood.

An e-mail awaited me at home, saying that my grandfather was in the hospital. I called my parents to find out what happened as a gloom settled over me. But above all I kept thinking of Irving, that town sinking into the woods, fading away with only memories remaining plus a few isolated concrete walkways buckling up through the lush grass, and of how a girl growing up there had loved hearing the song of the meadowlark. Somehow the bird had become an intrinsic part of what was happening with my grandfather. Maybe if I could find a meadowlark I could somehow save my grandfather's life.

He passed away two days later. I was too busy doing other things to have it sink in, but after a hectic weekend we arrived home to collapse on the couch and try to unwind. I thought of how people, like towns, come and then go but their memories, at least for a while, remain. Eventually they become little more than names marking the span of their lives, footnotes on the historical record. For now we hold these memories close to our hearts, those of us who knew the people and the towns, but we ourselves finally die off and slumber beneath the Kansas soil, and the stories fade away.

On Sunday evening my friend, Dan Thalmann, and I returned to Irving to continue the search. We wandered the dirt roads and two-tracks for a mile in each direction, usually in the truck, sometimes on foot. Mosquitoes were voracious, their buzzing a constant whine in our ears. Dickcissels were plentiful, singing their clarion songs from power lines and fence posts. Red-winged blackbirds trilled from the marshy areas near the river. We heard a yellowthroat, a nighthawk swooping over the trees, a pewee, but no meadowlark.

The town is gone, my grandfather's gone, and, apparently, the meadowlarks are gone, too. I desperately wanted a meadowlark for Martha Nance to let her know that life is transient but the natural world abides, that some things of our past remain. But memories are all that we are left now, memories that, so long as we draw breath, never fade nor tarnish. It's all we have, but somehow, in some way, it must be enough.

# ONE FINAL TRIP TO THE LONE STAR STATE

It was with a heavy heart that I turned the truck southward and followed the invisible paths of migrating birds. I was heading to Texas to do a bit of gardening, to plant the ashes of my grandparents, but it wasn't that which hung like a dark cloud over me. It was the thought of being apart from my wife that weighed like a stone on my heart. My grandparents were beyond feeling, had passed beyond the mortal boundaries of this world and were witness to whatever lies beyond, so whatever I did with them or for them was mere ritual.

I know little of death but I have experienced loneliness in my time. When I said my wedding vows I meant them, and thought it would be the end of a bitter and sad period of my life. There are times in every relationship when one must be apart from the other, whether by career or happenstance, and those times have been difficult for me. That might make me a weak man, and I, for one, have never been able to reconcile that part of me to the image I hold of myself. Besotted with love, let that be my credo. But whether weak or frightened of a hollowness that once almost overwhelmed me, I am what I am, and this trip southward was a shadow on my soul.

Or perhaps it was more than I dared to admit. This was finality. It was closure, and on many fronts. I had never before seen that part of Texas—Eastland, a small town west of Ft. Worth, where my mother was born and my grandparents lived prior to moving to an even smaller town on the desolate plains of West Texas. Having declared their fill for the 650-mile journey, this was also to be the last trip my parents would take there. It was, literally, now or never. And there was, of course, the matter of mortal remains to consign to the dusty Texas soil. For that, my mind skipped over the details and bored into the minutiae of trip-planning: where I would camp, what birds I might see, how long I would be gone.

It was dark when I left our house, a darkness even dawn could not dissipate.

\*\*\*

My grandmother, Lois Armstrong Smith, was one of those women who are not complete unless they are doing something for somebody else. She was selfless and giving and had the most charming smile. That smile rarely left her face during the years I knew her, though at the end of her life I was not able to be with her. Others were, though, and she sensed them at odd times. She claimed to have felt a hand upon her shoulder, to hear strange and wonderful music, to be within a company that both comforted and mystified her. Her physician placated her by saying it was a normal occurrence for someone in her position. He may be forgiven for letting science rule his thinking, but I think it's a shame he wasn't able to see that the thin membrane separating us from that other world sometimes grows tenuous.

My grandfather could not have been more different. Brown (B.B.) Smith was a good man though selfish to a fault. A hardscrabble farmer turned deputy sheriff, his favorite hobby was regaling audiences with tales of his exploits. He ridiculed his wife for talking about the spirits who visited her, but after she departed he had his own dealings with them, and it scared him witless. My mother told him it was his wife come back to haunt him. He tried making light of it but it must have been a humbling event. He was used to dealing with black and white matters, not supernatural ones.

The first road trip I ever took was right out of high school. I headed to Imperial, Texas, to stay a week with them. They fought and argued and bickered and loved each other immensely. When I drove out to a quarry to hunt rabbits, my grandfather warned me to stay on the road or I'd get stuck. Being young and dumb, I disregarded his advice and pulled onto the shoulder once I found a likely spot. My car instantly sank to its axles in a weird kind of silt and gravel that seemed bottomless. It was a walk of many miles back to town. I still recall the burning sense of shame I felt for not having listened to him. He did his best to make me feel small; my grandmother tried to set me at ease.

They were the best humanity can offer, and the worst. They were, in other words, merely human. I loved them both.

*** 

There were cousins I'd not seen in over two decades, my parents, an aunt or two—I'm useless with relatives. I can navigate flawlessly with a map but a family tree leaves me baffled. We met at Eastland Cemetery under a hot Texas sun that scorched the skin and left us drenched in sweat.

I carried the urn containing the ashes of my grandfather to the gravesite and passed it to my cousin, who set it on the ground. It seemed more a family reunion than a solemn occasion, and I wonder if I missed something. I snapped photographs, hugged family members, but only paused for one quick moment to study the urns and reflect on their cargo.

This is all that's left of a life, I thought. It seems there should be more.

\*\*\*

On the road it's all hustle and bustle, with little time for contemplation. Tomorrow my mother will show me where she was raised, the farmhouse collapsed and rotting into the dirt. We'll drive to Breckenridge, thirty miles away, and see the place my grandparents lived in retirement.

And then I'll nose the truck northward and head for home, to my wife, my rabbit, my friends. I will take away things not easily understood, things that will take the rest of my life to sift through. But I think it'll come to me eventually, what it all means. At some point a hand will lightly rest upon my shoulder, and a voice will guide me to that next step. And I will not be afraid, for others have gone on before and are waiting for me.

# VISIONS OF BEAUTY IN THE NIGHT SKY

This much is indisputable: when Comet NEAT neared the sun, a jagged bolt of plasma rose to meet it. The image, captured by the SOHO spacecraft and available on the Web, is a real eye-popper.

Almost everything else about the comet, from its trajectory, size, origin, and celestial import to NASA's handling of data has been the subject of countless tirades. But on a warm spring evening with lightning playing on the contours of the horizon, I saw the comet through an opening in the clouds. That, too, is indisputable.

As is the case with so many things in my life, it was a book that piqued my interest in astronomy. The impact was on par with an asteroid dropping on my head and explains why I bristle whenever anyone attempts to ban books. I won't deny that there are a slew of truly bad books on the market but they're just like Brussels sprouts—if you don't like 'em, don't eat 'em. A single volume by Isaac Asimov, *Quasars, Pulsars and Black Holes,* metaphorically grabbed me by the lapels and tossed me into deep space. I've never been the same since.

In conjunction with this life-altering event, my father decided to build a telescope. I also started hanging around Mr. Brown, a friend of the family's and a member of our Baptist congregation. Mr. Brown was a knowledgeable astronomer and offered to help me. That I learned little more than the constellation Orion, the Pleiades, and the stars Sirius and

Betelgeuse shouldn't reflect so much on him as on his teenaged pupil. Boys of that age are eager to discover things other than supernovas and double stars, and I quickly understood a telescope to be a fine instrument for checking out the lighted bedroom windows of the pretty girls in the neighborhood. I probably should be ashamed of this but I'm not.

The telescope was made from a kit and required forty hours alone for polishing the glass mirror. It was a beauty, a long white tube with contrasting black eyepieces. So powerful was it that a glimpse of the moon made me feel like an Apollo astronaut hovering over the lunar surface. And it was adaptable to my environment. Rather than limiting its use to nocturnal hours, I found that when placed inconspicuously within a snowball shrub, the telescope gave unparalleled views of the girls in the swimming pool a block away.

Our memories latch onto the oddest things. Concurrent with my budding astronomical interests were a house-sitting service I performed for the Browns and riots that exploded in downtown Albuquerque. I can't remember what infuriated the lower classes to acts of civil disobedience but when the ensuring hubbub threatened to expand to our neighborhood, my skywatching was curtailed in favor of retreating behind locked doors and reading H.P. Lovecraft novels. The impending apocalypse of our neighborhood by hordes of the unwashed, mingled with the terror induced by Lovecraft's writings, set me on edge. I finagled the 16-gauge pump shotgun from my father and set it beside Mr. Brown's favorite chair, saying it was necessary to defend his hearth and home. The rioters were eventually subdued and life returned to normal. I'm sure I went back to stargazing but strangely can recall little more about it.

When Comet Hale-Bopp passed by in the '90s I was

awestruck at seeing it pendent in the northern sky. My grandmother passed away around the same time, as did the Heaven's Gate religious sect, who committed mass suicide in an effort to transport themselves to the comet. Though we missed her very much we couldn't help but joke that she, too, hopped on Hale-Bopp. However, it's doubtful she would have countenanced the cultists and would probably have booted them off in short order to drift among the discards of space rock and ageless ice. We Baptists were never very forgiving of the beliefs of others.

Other than that, my dealings with the night sky have been filled more with wonder than knowledge and usually involved owls, goatsuckers, moths, or carpenter ants, all firmly attached to this terrestrial top spinning around the sun. Until the advent of NEAT.

Historically, comets attract lunatics and wackos with distressing frequency, and even in this age of enlightenment the rational man is sorely outnumbered by those who see significance in every celestial event. NEAT, named for its discovery by the Near-Earth Asteroid Tracking system, was a rare treat for the conspirators among us. Not only did the sun reach out and brand it with a blast of solar lightning but a ghostly eye formed above the comet, which some took to be the Eye of Horus as depicted on our dollar bills and which signifies a beneficent Providence watching over us. This really got the New Agers frothing at the mouth. No longer a mere bit of space rock, this was a message from some celestial being. That shortly thereafter the computers of numerous amateur astronomers were hacked only deepened the mystery.

Thankfully, things were a bit calmer in Blue Rapids. My wife and I located the comet and only suffered one mosquito bite. It didn't have the classic comet shape but appeared like a pale fuzzy smear against a backdrop of stars. No June bugs or wood roaches flew into our open mouths, though we had several near misses. Horus didn't announce himself nor did the world stop turning. Our computer wasn't hacked.

But for a few divine moments we left this planet and soared on the winds of space, and it was like seeing something never before witnessed by human eyes, an artifact from the dawn of creation, a portent or harbinger, or a slip of skin glimpsed through a slightly parted curtain, inexplicable, illicit, feverishly captivating.

# TORNADOES OF THE MIND

For years they haunted my dreams. There were always two of them, coursing like bloodhounds, ranging over treeless fields, tracing out a darkly glowing lemniscate, two looping coils conjoined in the center, the symbol for eternity. And always they were to the west, advancing from a distant range of mountains veiled beneath dark lowering skies. Intermittently lit by flickers of lightning, their long tails twisted and writhed, dipping down like serpents' tongues from a midnight sky, as if licking the air to detect my presence. This was a personal thing: they hunted me, and I fled.

Nightmares rarely leave room for escape, nor is reality much better. Where in my dreams the tornadoes and I eternally reenact the scene, in the real world there is a basement, and into that basement my wife and I descended at the urging of the weather radio announcer. The moment was surreal, almost imaginary, fraught not with danger but a complicated stew of emotions. Blame it on the sky, which held none of the menace of that in my dreams. Blame it on an unwarranted faith in modern technology. Or blame it on the scars, which never heal.

It's hard not to take tornadoes personal because my first experience with them left deep furrows in the sinews and flesh of my psyche. The tornadoes that ravaged the Denver area on June 3, 1981, shouldn't have been a surprise, yet they were. Meteorologists had always claimed the city's proximity to the mountains endowed it with immunity, but that was before the shortgrass prairie was buried under miles of cement and asphalt. As the city grew larger, so, too, the storms that evolved in the canyons west of town morphed into something much more powerful. When they spilled out that afternoon there was hell to pay.

You must understand this was not the Great Plains, not Tornado Alley. This was the mountainous West, and when that first tornado raked across Second and Sheridan, bringing down an apartment building and shredding the roofs of several houses, we harbored a terror that nature herself had come undone. Our very foundation was torn asunder.

I heard it on the radio and then, as I was downtown loading my work truck, I watched a pale funnel cloud pass between two skyscrapers. The civil defense sirens wailed like lost souls. Retreating to the safety of the service building, I called my wife, who was home with our two young boys. I warned her of the tornadoes and told her to take cover. Neither of us knew that the largest tornado in Denver history was bearing down on our neighborhood.

The first details were chaotic. By that time I was on the south side of town, but when the news reported the tornado's path, straight up Eppinger Boulevard, I turned my truck for home. A deep dread filled me. I wondered if I had a home, or a family, to return to.

For almost two hours I clawed my way through dense traffic, taking shortcuts and side streets. I was a madman behind the wheel. All haste crashed to an abrupt halt when I entered my neighborhood after passing through a police barricade.

Downed trees and rubble blocked roads dyed green with shredded vegetation. Scraps of metal wove through power lines like tinfoil. Houses were empty-eyed, windows blown apart, roofs missing. Dazed people stood talking in groups or weeping alone. Everyone looked numb. The trail of the tornado was easy to see; it had scythed everything in its path. I raged to hurry but couldn't.

Our home was undamaged, my family safe. The tornado had missed us by six houses, leaving a stratum of shattered glass and splinters in our yard that took months to clean up. But the nightmares began that night and have never gone away. Dulled and faded, yes, but like the lemniscate they spiral away and back with depressing regularity, and each time they draw closer.

The strong cell that approached Blue Rapids last week had none of the dramatic visual elements of my nightmares. The sky was bruised and roiling but not black; the wind stripped leaves off trees and roared like a freight train but not unlike other days when the skies were clear. All I could discern of the approaching storm was what the weather radio and Doppler radar told me. I've been through worse, but this time I had the weight of information pressing down on me. The National Weather Service assured me it was worse than it looked.

Tornadoes touched down in Belleville and near Linn. I tracked the storm to the county line, where the radio bleated again, this time announcing that rotation was detected six miles south of Waterville. Take cover immediately, the radio said.

I'd never had the occasion to consider what sort of things one would want to save in the event of a disaster, but now it confronted me like a toothache. We are notoriously a materialistic society, and I'm as guilty as the next. Had I time to sort out which things I hold dearest and which I things I could jettison without a care, I would have made a fine list that in no way would have been practical. Family photos seem to be the first thing people grab, or jewelry or cash. My stash amounted to two books (ones I'm currently reading), my laptop computer, our Angora rabbit, a cup of coffee and a pistol.

But even as we headed down the stairs, I felt both nervous and silly. As if hiding wasn't bad enough, my wife's expression was one of cynicism. "Why the gun?" she asked. I wanted to say to defend against looters but that sounded implausible, so I just said, "I feel better with it." Maybe I could shoot the tornado and save Blue Rapids.

The sky darkened. Hail pocked the windows. Lori read a magazine while I fretted and rubbed the rabbit. It was over within a few minutes. Afterward, I stood outside watching a long tendril probe out of the retreating clouds, snaking through the air as if wanting to caress the earth. A little bit further, it seemed to say, just a bit more and I will unleash the Hounds of Hell. I will find you.

It was a storm that could have been dangerous and fizzled out, for which I am grateful. If only the storms in my mind were so benign.

# THE GREATEST GIFT

It's the first really hot day of summer and I'm mowing the yard. The sun beats down like molten lava, superheating air thick as molasses. Sweat pours from me, dripping into my eyes, soaking my shirt. I stink so bad that vultures track my moves. Something's wrong with my right foot, each step sending a jolt of pain lancing up my leg. But I scarcely feel any of that. I'm here but I'm not. I've gone back in time.

I first saw her at a Christmas party at Temple Baptist Church in Albuquerque. She had come with another guy and I had come alone and that's the way the evening ended, too.

She saw me when I walked in, but how could she have not? I was dressed somewhat atypical for a Baptist meeting: jeans with both knees out, old plaid shirt, raggedy brown corduroy jacket, scuffed combat boots. She couldn't have seen the bottle of whisky in my left jacket pocket nor the Colt .38 snubnose in the right. She couldn't have seen the depth of sorrow I carried. She couldn't have seen the dark intent I held that promised this to be the last such foray into a church group before resigning myself to a violent and unrepentant life in a small town a hundred miles away. She couldn't have.

Yet her eyes found mine from across the room and drew me to her. At that moment I neither knew nor cared where her date was, only that it was best he stayed away for a while. I asked her out. She accepted.

Later, in the dark hours of early morning, I lay in bed

staring at the ceiling, struggling to recall what her body looked like, what she wore, how her hair was made up, and nothing came to me but the form of her eyes. They seemed almond-shaped, the pupils gunmetal gray, or slightly amber, or clear like a hot summer sky bleached of all hue; I couldn't remember. There was only the shape, and the depth, and the realization that I could drown in them and never solicit rescue. When she gazed at me it wasn't as if she was merely watching me, no, she was *seeing* me, looking deep into me and reading my hopes and fears and dreams and most private, secret places as if written in the pages of a diary visible only to her. And I liked that, a lot.

I sensed that hers was a natural loveliness that knew neither guile nor haughtiness. She wasn't like the other girls I tried to impress, the real beauties of the church who were model-perfect, and who instinctively knew it in their refined bones, in their lithe graces, in their throngs of adoring toadies, in their elevated, almost holy stations guaranteeing them a place in the pantheon of success. She was as real and genuine as the dawn.

Sleep being elusive, I finally rose to write a few sentences in my diary. "Met Lori Herrmann," I scribbled under the date, December 23, 1973. That was all that came out. Back then I had this weird notion that a diary should consist only of deeds; later I realized that thoughts and emotions tell a better story, with much more effectiveness.

Evening the next day, I'm standing on her front porch ringing the doorbell. I'm dressed smartly in clean jeans and shoes, a good shirt. I've shucked the whiskey and the pistol, slicked back my hair. I'm a new man turning a new leaf. When she opens the door and I see those eyes again it's like the sun rising on a darkling plain, banishing all shadows. I am dazzled, ensorcelled, enslaved.

Several months later I'm leading her down a murky trail under a sky spangled with stars, brilliant in the rarified air at ten thousand feet in elevation. A bright glow emanates from the west, just over the wind-stunted pines. We hike one mile from the tramway until the trail breaks from the trees and fades onto a rocky promontory. A stone shelter silhouettes against a thousand thousand lights, a sea of glittering jewels, a galaxy fallen to earth—the lights of Albuquerque, a mile below. She sits on a hard stone bench as I sink to one knee. Marry me, I say. She accepts.

The wedding comes off without a hitch other than we move the date up and neglect to inform the organist. After a quick reception we're northbound toward Taos, and the next day we wend our way over the mountains and descend into Las Vegas to look for a place to live. We're madly in love and homeless and it doesn't matter.

It all seems so sudden, but that's the way life is. It never turns out quite like you expect, and yet it does, and in doing so you realize that true happiness could have been realized only through the events as they played out, the meeting, the falling in love, the children, the heartaches, the joys, the darkness and the light, the redemption. Nothing else would have worked.

Sweat burns when it gets in your eyes. I put the mower away and suck in a deep breath of air redolent of fresh-cut grass. I'm thinking of thirty years of being married to this woman, thirty years this week. Andrew Hudgins, in his prose poem *After the Lost War*, wrote, "This is the greatest gift: to know that someone sees you as you are and loves you anyway."

I limp across the sun-blasted yard, heading for the house. There I will find a cold drink, a respite from the heat, and my greatest, greatest gift. My vision is blurred. It's not just the sweat.

# BLUE MOUNTAINS FAR AWAY

For a moment after I climbed from the darkness of the kiva all I could see was white light. The early morning sun, slanting above the distant line of juniper-covered hills, reflected off the pale sandy gravel atop the ceremonial pit, blinding me. As I waited for my vision to clear, first the outlines of the ladder jutting above the roof of the kiva, then the ruins of the old pueblo and beyond them a rising wave of green ridges coloring to the blue and purple of distant peaks, a phrase kept running through my mind: *blue mountains far away*. Pecos Baldy was an azure knob to the north, graced with a small patch of eternal snow.

The phrase, eloquent and remarkably concise, comes from the title of a book by Gregory McNamee. In his introduction, McNamee writes, "In the heart of the Greater Southwest, you cannot find a landscape that is not bordered, somewhere, by a blue fringe of mountains." Such a landscape, he says, constitutes the foundation of his existence, the only place he could feel whole. Those sentiments were my own in another life and another place; I would have wholeheartedly agreed with him when he adds, "Once you come to expect blue mountains on your horizon, you cannot be happy in the flatlands or in canyons without hawks."

I was raised in the American Southwest, my horizons bordered by the Sandias, the Manzanos, the Jemez, the Pecos. For half my life I lived in Colorado, where my blue mountains included the Never Summer Range, the Indian Peaks, the Williams Fork, the Laramie. Each range was different, each precious, each central to my character. But McNamee is wrong. Though my horizons all had blue mountains, I found contentment in the flatlands of Kansas.

Our personal geographies are mapped during our formative years. Within our bloodstream pulses the memories of our home places. We may become lost and go astray, but it is enough to rekindle those memories, to relocate our position on our internal map, once we stand within the boundaries of that home place. Our heart knows even if our mind doesn't.

My father was born with the Pecos River in sight. As a young man, he'd sneak up to the river early in the morning as frost lay on the land like a thin layer of snow, his breath fogging the air, the shotgun heavy in his hands. When he could hear ducks conversing he'd go to ground, belly crawling until he was within a few feet of the bank, and then he'd leap to his feet, swinging the shotgun to lead the birds as they exploded from the water, spray hanging in dawn's light like a handful of diamonds thrown carelessly into the air. The shot booming across the West Texas scrublands.

He did not know then that mountains loomed on his horizon, that he would someday stand in that selfsame river six hundred miles away leading a rainbow trout with a white-winged dry fly, the arc of his rod glinting in the morning sun. Or that in years to come he would stand in the Pecos River with his middle son and baptize him in the ways of trout and clear water and mountains. Those blue mountains called him home.

Like him, I was born in a land of creosote and mesquite beneath an overpowering sky. And though my earliest memories were of mountains, buried within my consciousness was the memory of wide open spaces. This has led, I believe, to a duality I am often at odds with.

Though I was raised in Albuquerque, it never felt like home. This was not something that was put into words, nor, indeed, could it have been. At the time I did not posses the language to explain my unease. That would come later, after I hopscotched north another five hundred miles, this time to the shadow of the Rocky Mountains. The concept of home eluded me there, too, but to the east, where the sun lifted above the horizon, to those mountainless flatlands, I was called as if by a siren song.

And yet I would have argued to the death that I was incapable of leaving the West. I needed mountains as surely as I needed oxygen or heartbeat. Indeed, they were intrinsically linked. But the geography of my homeland, the heart of my personal map, was in another place, one I didn't discover until years later. When I did, it was a homecoming like no other. My heart recognized the place even if I did not.

Standing there as the sun warmed the twelve-thousand-year-old settlement, it came to me that a person can have more than one home. These disparate places are hardwired into our souls, they flow in our veins, they beat with our heart. They provide the continuity that links our past to our future.

The Pecos River, just over a distant ridge, binds my father's history to mine. It is an indissoluble thread in the fabric of our lives, weaving the flatlands of West Texas and Kansas with the mountains of New Mexico and Colorado and, by the nature of its origin and its demise, creating within me two homelands.

It wrenched my heart to leave. To know a place one must know its elements, the poet Gary Snyder says. I named them as we departed: the birds, the wildflowers, the trees, the butterflies. The river, tumbling from the mountains, whose headwaters are formed by the melting snows of Pecos Baldy.

My geographies are woven into a pure and perfect map. I have lived with blue mountains on my horizon, I have walked in canyons filled with the cries of hawks, and yet I have found home elsewhere. The distance is not so far. No matter where I live, no matter where I call home, there will always be blue mountains on my horizon.

# QUERENCIA

I was suspended somewhere between full-blown depression and melancholy yesterday, or, as, Tom McGuane put it in one of his novels, "sad for no reason." It's as good a description as any though it leaves out the part about the black hole that threatens to suck me in and never let me go. Writers and artists are often introverts and thus spend all too much time looking inward when the real world is outside our own thoughts and feelings, something we sometimes need a jolt to bring home to roost. I can't say I've ever learned how to shake off the gloom or even adequately understand it, but if ever there was a medicine for melancholy, sitting on a front porch of a house in rural Kansas must rate high on the list. Equally well, for me at least, would be to get in my car and drive to Alcove Spring and stand in the narrow valley with the creek burbling below and shadows lengthening as the sun dips beneath the tree line and let the world unfold before me.

It's hard to remain in a depressed state when confronted with a pig family in the middle of nowhere, oinking and grunting on the road into the canyon. By the time we get to the parking lot at Alcove Spring I'm already feeling human again, looking forward to a short hike and a whole lot of soaking up the natural world like a sponge.

Crickets, katydids, and cicadas are enjoined in a three-part harmony only a few decibels below ear-shattering. A bird whose call I do not recognize belts out a long melodious trill and then falls silent. The air is humid, warm, aromatic of mold and growth and altogether fresh, the kind you can't buy in the city no matter how fat your wallet. With each step I feel the weight of my darkness slipping from my soul.

There's a Spanish word that's almost impossible to translate. William F. Buckley, in *Racing through Paradise*, says, "It is used in Spanish to designate that mysterious little area in the bullring that catches the fancy of the fighting bull when he charges in. He imagines it his sanctuary: when parked there, he supposes he cannot be hurt...So is it, borrowing the term, that one can speak of one's *querencia* to mean that little, unspecified area in life's arena where one feels safe, serene."

From ancient times until the present, there are places on earth that seem to possess the power to heal. Some are sacred by virtue of historical context, such as Mecca, the Temple Mount, or Bethlehem. Others remain more mysterious and less well known, tempered by a vague mythical quality impossible to explain: the Black Hills of South Dakota come to mind. And there sites that are endowed with a sense of quietude and calm that transcend the outward manifestation of forest, stream, limestone outcrop, expansive grassy meadow, or tangles of dogwood, poison ivy, and wild plum. For me Alcove Spring is such a place. I go there to commune with the ineffable.

To speak of *querencia* is to infer conflict. The bull would not need a safe haven were not for the little man waving a red cape and flashing the sharp sword. We would not need sacred places were it not for the longing. That these places lie on the maps of our hearts is testament to our need for solace.

I do not consider the house and land we own to be mere wood, plaster, and weedy lawn. It is my refuge. Within its borders I breathe a deep sigh of relief and consider myself an intricate part. It alone can't chase the shadows away, but I am grounded in the cycle of seasons, summer's growth, winter's sleep.

It is late evening by the time we pull into our driveway, but I'm still restless and want to stay outdoors. I sit on the porch and soak up the view. Crimson beebalm and golden lilies are blooming in the flower bed. White daisies nod in the breeze. A young cottontail bounds into the open, pauses when it sees me, then slowly snips off a purple-blossomed stem of alfalfa and sucks it down like a strand of spaghetti.

I have my wife, who's inside working on the computer. I have a cold beer, sweat drops rolling down its sides to form a shallow puddle. And I have the latest James Lee Burke mystery, *Jolie Blon's Bounce*, which will whisk me, for a time, to the steamy bayous of southern Louisiana.

But for a moment I pause, one finger holding my place in the first chapter, and listen. I'm going out of my skin, redirecting myself toward something that does not know or care about me. Across the field a thrasher sings, his tune changing every few stanzas. In the distance comes the soft cooing of a Eurasian collared-dove, a species freshly wandered up from Florida. The song is strange, out of place on the Kansas prairie. I can't help but smile.

I will slip below the waters of melancholia again, sidestep that black hole if I'm lucky, but for now I'm finding my way back out of the gloom, feeling my way like a blind man, one step at a time.

Here is beauty enough for one day, wonder enough for a lifetime. I want to live fully in this moment, this moment that is now.

*Querencia.*

# ALL THIS AND MORE

It was a typical day anymore, a little stressed, thinking of money shortages and irritated people and the tenuous economy and the cold winter setting in with a promised boost of natural gas prices, and of our sons and their wives and broken relationships and a granddaughter being raised fatherless, and all the rest of it. I was lying in bed, Lori softly breathing beside me, the night still and silent. My eyes open, unfocused. Covers pulled up to block the chill of the room. All that.

All that weighing on me, pressing down like a weight.

The night was like velvet, the room silent as a tomb. No passing traffic, no distant sirens, no rumble of jets overhead. I felt myself rising above the sleeping earth, the river curling around the town, the little lights twinkling in the cold night, the highway a link to the great big world beyond the fields we know, the small pinpricks of light of farmhouses, the broad constellations of distant towns, and higher still I went, until the land opened like a three-dimensional map, and I could see our rural house surrounded by so much darkness, so much openness, so much promise. A faint smile tightened my lips. Moonlight shimmered on the hills and reflected off the quicksilver ponds nestled in their hollows.

Restlessness tugged at me. Though I wanted nothing more than to stare down at what we have found, this blessed and uncertain life we've fallen into, I felt pulled in several directions. At first annoying, and then insistent, I succumbed to its will and turned away, looking far to the southwest, the curve of the world delineating deeper space and the faint stars beyond. I began moving with the speed of a comet, the earth blurring and rushing past.

The Flint Hills smoothed and rolled flat, woods and creeks thinned, until I crossed into the red dirt wastelands of Oklahoma and the Texas panhandle. The high plains of New Mexico were barren in the night, the Sangre de Christo Mountains rising in the west like the spine of a dragon. I passed tiny Las Vegas glimmering against the low foothills, skirted Santa Fe, and stopped above La Bajada Hill. In the distance the Sandias huddled over Albuquerque as if nurturing it, and I felt my parents there, and my estranged brother, and I thought that this was home, too, but not home, something in my past that while summoning me could not hold me. Nor could I approach any nearer; something blocked my way.

Again I was pulled, this time northward. Raton Pass rose before me, an outthrust of the Rockies, and then I was over it and onto the shortgrass prairies of southern Colorado. The mountains fell away to the west and then curved back, the Spanish Peaks momentarily catching my eye, and then Cheyenne Mountain rose like a bulwark above Colorado Springs and I whispered to the rushing air, "Track this, NORAD," and I was gone before they could register me on their instruments, a ghostly and surreal body moving at the speed of light. And there was Denver, spreading out like a wide-flung galaxy, so peaceful and lovely from my altitude, a glittering ocean washing up and over the foothills and beyond, and snow whitening the ragged peaks, alpine lakes shining like hammered steel in the starlight, forests dark and silent. I felt myself being pulled so many ways that I jerked like a marionette, dancing across the sky. Disjointed, my mind an explosion of memories. I threw back my head and howled in anguish, a primal scream thundering in my ears. And yet the night remained mute.

I was in Denver Carpet, the 15th Street Viaduct arcing over the Platte River, the east windows shattered, glass strewn on the concrete floor, the flimsy box I was standing on collapsing beneath me, my hand slicing down a broken pane leaving a wet smear, pools of crimson as I walked back to the truck, enough blood to alert the entire Denver Police Department when the alarm later failed. The phone call in the early morning, *Did you cut yourself?*

Why that memory? Decades past, the viaduct gone, the building gone. All of us gone.

Our firstborn son to the north in his new subdivision. I hovered above his house, seeing the destruction of the natural world on so massive a scale, the hurly-burliness of growth for growth's sake, a cancer on the earth. Him with his immature and spendthrift wife, with a child his and not his, like a shadow no sunlight can fade.

And what of our youngest son? I looked out over the endless miles of lights and wondered where he was, lost, wordless for over a year now. Disappeared.

But the strongest pull of all was that of the mountains. I turned to face them and was gone, suddenly standing at the base of Long's Peak, the thousand-foot sheer drop of the Diamond before me, the frozen waters of Chasm Lake creaking in the night. Below me was Peacock Pool, emerald green, fed by snowmelt, its surface dimpled with rising trout the summer day I was there, now congealing under a layer of ice. The night air must have been frigid, but I couldn't feel it. I was spirit, not embodiment. No physical thing.

And then the tug came again, faint and sweet like when our rabbit nudges me with his nose to get attention. I turned, high above the plains, the Rockies at my back, and looked out across the miles to the east. No paling of dawn. Out there, sundered from these crags, these icy waters, these forests of spruce and fir, was home. I left, swift as thought, and again found myself high above our house.

A damaged peace washed over me. Below me was my wife, and our rabbit nestled beneath the kitchen table, and it all seemed so ideal, yet a shadow hung on me like a cloak. I thought of the question an old friend asked my wife recently: are you still glad you moved? Glad, yes, and deeply thankful. And as I pondered the concept of thankfulness I found myself rising, spinning, and I stretched my arms out in an embrace to all that I could see, caught there between heaven and earth, swimming in a sea of stars and melancholy.

I have all this and more, I thought. Can it not be enough?

And then I dropped like a falling star, and in the darkness I touched my wife on the shoulder. I thought that sometimes the act of giving thanks is swallowed by an abiding and relentless sorrow, and yet we must carry on in our imperfect way, struggling to find our way home, to measure what we have as well as what we have lost. There are holes in our hearts that burn like fire this thanksgiving season, but it's the price we pay for love. All we can do is give thanks for what we can and mourn what is lost and never lose sight of the treasures we possess. This is our greatest strength and our greatest weakness, but our hearts know this, even in darkness.

# THE QUESTION OF GHOSTS

My job was simple: snap a few last-minute photographs, burn them to a CD, and take them to the community center, where they would be integrated into a movie about present-day Blue Rapids. A fellow photographer and I perused a list of places that needed to be included, chose our selections, and then hurried off, time being a compelling factor.

This was guerilla documentation, hit and run, drive-by shooting using cameras instead of Tec-9s. Within minutes I had bagged the storage units on the east end of town, the old Hannah poultry plant, the depot, the Presbyterian Church, the veterans monument on the town square, the elevator, the bank, a few businesses and, at the end, Greenwood Cemetery south of town. The trick was to get as much in the lens as possible and still include a marker or sign that described the location. For the cemetery I parked near the entrance where rows of pines overshadowed the sign and the road entered and forked to flow around evenly-spaced rows of headstones. As the shutter snapped I thought of dead people and dying towns and wondered if the correlation was illegitimate or if my mind had sensed something, some vibe or undercurrent that made our actions questionable.

Projects, like towns, evolve. What began as an idea to compile a database of old photographs of Blue Rapids, sort of a pictorial history of the place, branched off to include a current image of what the town looked like at the beginning of the twenty-first century. Partly this was an outcome of being inundated with ancient black-and-white photos that required enormous amounts of time to sort, scan, copy, and replicate, and partly it was the difficulty of finding credible documentation of how the town appeared a hundred, fifty, or even twenty years ago.

So while our task was so much simpler than that which would follow—one day's record versus that of 135 years—we still found it impossible to fully escape the past. It was as if every photograph we took was sandwiched between others, afterimages or shadows superimposed upon the virtual emulsion. Those buildings, parks, or cemeteries carefully framed within our viewfinders hinted at not only what was there but what was no longer there, not so much in the actuality but in the analysis. We weren't seeing double exposures, we were seeing ghosts.

*** 

This of course was worse for the old-timers than for us relative newcomers, but even so the images bled together whenever appropriate to the historical context or the viewers' perspective. Say we took a photo of the community center, built a decade ago—what people saw wasn't just the current steel-and-stone façade but echoes of the Albion Hotel, the street mucky, a horse-drawn sled mounted with runners out front, used to ferry visitors from the depot like a primitive taxi. Rather than the faded station sign on the railroad tracks we saw trains chuffing by with German prisoners of war sticking their hands out to catch the fresh fruit residents tossed their way, or locomotives spewing coal-black plumes that hung in the air like smoke roiling off prairie wildfires. Time's sequential march jackknifed back on itself.

I needed a photo of the engraving above the fireplace mantle in the old Women's League building, and knew I had several somewhere on file. While hastily searching through hundreds of photos on my computer I came across one of a whitewashed frame house with Lori's brothers and sisters standing on the front porch. It hadn't been taken that long ago—maybe two decades, give or take—but it surprised me in its timeliness, for we had recently completed the gutting of that house of all its possessions, a laborious and emotionally wrenching experience that left us all drained, and none more so than Lori's grandmother, Ilda Herrmann, who had lived there for thirty-some years before failing health forced her into the nursing home. Seeing it once again full of children was akin to seeing Lazarus stepping dazed from his tomb.

The power of such images is irresistible, but their power resides not in the image alone but in what they represent. They're a form of time travel or a Pandora's Box, which upon opening blurs the boundaries of time and reveals the insubstantiality of the ages. When faced with disaster people often attempt to secure their photographs first, their reasoning being that the photos are priceless, irreplaceable, that their loss would amount to nothing less than the erasure of the past, a forfeiture of one's personal history. And yet they are such simple things, mere slips of paper embossed with visions of times of yore. Our past. Our ghosts.

We made one final trip to Ilda's to retrieve the lawn mower. The house had already been sold and the new owners were remodeling it, stripping wallpaper and tearing out walls. But before unlocking the shed I stepped out by the front curb and looked at the house, trying to find traces of what it once was, of the people who lived there, of their guests and visitors whose voices and laughter might still whisper through the empty rooms and narrow stairways. Nothing came to me. All I saw was the house itself, its loose rain gutters, the crumbling porch, the cracked shingles.

Jacques Derrida, a French philosopher, once said, "Psychoanalysis has taught us that the dead—a dead parent, for example—can be more alive for us, more powerful, more scary, than the living. It is the question of ghosts."

It applies to rural towns and old houses, too. But where were the ghosts now that I looked for them? Perhaps their visitation hinges on factors beyond our reckoning, or the methodical emptying of the place was still too raw in my memory to trigger anything other than a bleak sadness. I was surprised at their absence though, just as I had been surprised at their appearance in the project's images. One never knows about ghosts.

# LEARNING TO LET GO

We are ringed with horizons both external and internal. Just as I once stared across the Chihuahuan Desert and wondered what lay beyond the next rise, I felt rooted to a place I called home, and yet home would be elsewhere in the future. Or so I sensed. Yet that horizon was a limit I knew I must someday test.

The dilemma, of course, was in knowing when to leave.

Such thoughts did not spring full-blown but were dredged up earlier in the day during a journal-writing workshop in Manhattan. It was an initial shaky step toward something different, partly at my wife's insistence, partly for curiosity's sake. I'd recently left a job that fulfilled me in a way none other before had, and I felt the future stretching before me like a broad darkling plain.

Our instructor asked us to write a short essay on food, weaving our five senses into the fabric of our words. I wrote of green chile stew. Preparation brought all five senses into play: the rainbow of ingredients, the aroma of the simmering chicken broth, the knife tap-dancing through the pungent chiles. But I surprised myself by seeing the dish as both home and an act of rebellion. Mexican stew is not your basic Midwestern staple, and whenever I cook it I feel slightly seditious. Home, though, was not something I expected.

No longer in the classroom, I suddenly stood beneath a rarified turquoise sky of a New Mexico autumn, the Rio

Grande Valley golden with cottonwoods lining the bosques, the acrid smell of piñon smoke stinging my lungs.

What followed drew me deeper.

We split into duets to speak for two minutes about our childhood. My partner was a tiny elderly lady who grew up dirt poor on a hardscrabble Flint Hills farm, with too few friends and an unquenchable lust to write. My tale was of a childhood so uneventful that life simply didn't register, that it had no more relevance than the air I breathed. I was content and young, having no past to draw upon or to measure against an uncertain future. But there was more, of course.

I told her I enjoyed wandering the desert north of our house, and again I made a mental leap back in time and space. I basked in that aureate light and gazed across the valley to the ruler-flat horizon of the West Mesa, serrated with eroded volcanoes, and beyond it the peak of Dootl'izhiidzill, the Sacred Mountain of the South. More horizons flooded in, my life as expressed by a wider field of vision.

When the instructor asked if we'd discovered anything about ourselves, the room fell silent. I was somewhere in New Mexico, a much younger person, when I was pulled back to the present. She stared at me, as if divining something in my expression.

I waved a hand in dismissal, but she bore in.

"What did you find?" she asked.

"Horizons," I said.

There were so many, and in the telling others rushed in, like the view of the flat-topped buttes staggered along the river north of Bernalillo and the juniper-freckled hills rising to the blue mountains behind Zia Pueblo. Most vivid was a low rise with clumps of honey-colored grass across from the junior high school I attended, an empty field waiting to be developed. I imagine it's filled with houses now, and has been for decades. But then it was a horizon, and it was mine. I would stare at it and wonder what was on the other side, and imagine myself striding off one day to find out.

Later on we moved to a new subdivision a mile away, and I was able to climb that rise and disappear into the scrubland toward our new home.

A horizon, I came to understand, was only another word for mystery, and crossing it was an act of breaking free, of severing the bonds that confine us to one place. And those horizons never ended; there were always others waiting to lure me.

Those memories were simply a trigger for something deeper, something I was reaching for even as they crystallized. I left the class in a daze, and found myself sitting paralyzed on our patio, watching small flocks of snow geese flying over and one lone Swainson's hawk swimming in that fathomless blue ocean.

And then I saw them, glittering as they caught the sun's reflection: filaments of gossamer riding the breeze.

Young spiders of several species migrate by a method called ballooning. On a warm day with a light breeze, they climb to the highest point around, usually a tree or post, and, facing into the breeze, they release long strands of silk. When the strands are lengthy enough to provide lift, the spiders cast off.

They never know where they will land. They may go a few hundred yards or into the next state. Gossamer has been found at forty thousand feet, carried by the jet stream across entire continents.

Such is the faith of the small things of this earth. Refusing to let their horizons be limited, spiderlings fearlessly launch into the unknown.

It's all a matter of timing. Conditions must be right, but in the end the decision rests with the will of the spiderling. To leave there must be desire.

Sometimes our needs shift, our horizons crowd in. Knowing when to accept change is never easy. Maybe, like the spiderlings, it's a belief that just outside our purview is something better.

What's over that horizon? I'll never know until I see for myself. Taking my cue from a tiny insect, I let out my lifeline, and, with one eye firmly fixed on home, I let go.

# BENEDICTION IN A BREEZE

Any ideas of mankind being the most advanced life form are routinely dashed whenever one reads the newspaper, watches CNN, or picks up a news magazine. Walking down the street of an evening in a rural town is a delightful antitoxin to the latest news, but lately I'd been spending my evenings tending to our elderly rabbit and trying to catch up on my reading, a hopeless task but a pleasant one, so I was missing out on neighborly interaction. My old Baptist minister was fond of browbeating his congregation, usually through animated body gestures that often included removing his suit jacket and flinging it across the stage, plus turning red in the face, that God gave man dominion over the earth and so anything we did was therefore sacrosanct. In the same breath he railed against the sinfulness of humanity and offered salvation for those who made the long walk to the front altar. Such duality led me into a state of confusion that not only lingered but has grown ever more strident.

If people were the reasoning beings they think themselves to be they would eject their televisions from their homes each election year and use them for wingshooting practice. Likewise radios unless one listens to classical music, but then care would be needed to silence it when All Things Considered aired. That one-hour radio show on NPR is the best we have for getting detailed, relatively unbiased news, and yet it often equates to fueling our helpless rages. I've always been something of a newshound but I can barely take it any longer.

A deep funk was settling in when I retrieved the mail. Normally seeing a dozen nighthawks strafe the town park would be enough to make my heart pound with excitement, but these particular birds were migrating south, accompanied by a cloud of swallows of various species, and I had been slack-jawed witness to them not an hour before. Dark clouds building to the west added a touch of melodrama. Knowing that one of the classic symptoms of lemming-like behavior is when we refuse to stop engaging in what clearly is self-destructive, I should have tossed the news magazines into the trash before opening them. I didn't.

Each week both Time and Newsweek offer one page of notable quotes uttered during the prior week. It's the first place I turn to if for no other reason than to get a laugh, sometimes bitter indeed, as in two weeks ago when President George W. Bush replied to Senator John Kerry's proposal to rescind tax cuts for the wealthy by saying, "The really rich people figure out how to dodge taxes anyway." No further explanation was necessary, and anyway the cynic in me hears the song of one who knows the tune. This quote from a sitting president should be enough to determine the outcome of the next election but probably won't.

My funk changed from gloom to utter doom when I read two entries in Newsweek. The first was by a convicted robber named Robert Carroll Coney, 76, who, along with his common-law wife, was released from a Texas jail where they had served forty years. "We're going home," he said, this after a judge found that Coney's confession to a 1962 robbery had been prompted by having his fingers crushed between cell bars. That Mr. Coney is black comes as no surprise.

The next quote hit hard. "How does it corrupt the tradition of the Last Supper?" asked Elizabeth Pelly-Waldman after her daughter Haley took her first communion using rice wafers. As church doctrine requires that communion wafers be made of wheat, the diocese of Trenton, New Jersey, promptly invalidated the communion. I can only deduce that the Catholic hierarchy spends too much time drafting dogma and not enough time reading the scriptures, where even a cursory glance should humble them. This sort of behavior is my biggest gripe with modern religion. Today's Christian leaders would do well to study the parts of the New Testament where Jesus condemned the Pharisees.

So distraught was I that I raided the refrigerator. The meal I concocted was for use only in emergencies and consisted of saltine crackers, peanut butter, dill pickles, and Tabasco. A more satisfying repast would have been chocolate donuts and beer, but even by my admittedly lax standards it was too early in the afternoon to imbibe, and anyway the freezer was devoid of donuts, cold storage being the place any sane person keeps them.

A full belly helped but didn't completely compensate for the anger I felt. As I stared morosely out the window, I remembered that the plains tribes believed that hearing the sound of rustling cottonwood leaves was the best medicine for melancholy. A lone cottonwood rises from the woods bordering the railroad tracks not a third-mile distant. Needing strong medicine, I clapped on my hat, grabbed the binoculars, and hightailed out the door.

I took the opportunity to study the small butterflies darting around my neighbor's flower beds. One was a fiery skipper, new to me, but before I could congratulate myself a large pale spider scuttled out and snatched it. This was Tennyson's "nature, red in tooth and claw" but somehow it's less unsettling when done by the more primitive species.

Moving on, I crossed a grassy field chest-high in sunflowers and ragweed, dipped into a shallow depression matted flat by deer, and climbed through heavy timber to the open railroad tracks. A breeze whispered through hackberries, stirred the locusts and mulberries, but stronger was the resonant clatter of the cottonwood. It sounded like clear water running over gravel, or a waterfall, or rain falling. It sounded like a benediction. I closed my eyes and sank to my knees. The tracks burned through my jeans and I did not care.

# A MEADOWLARK FOR MARTHA

Any obligation we feel toward others is strictly voluntary. It is an elective we choose. But this I took on willingly, knowing full well that eventually, by dint of persistence, I would find a meadowlark for Martha.

Martha Nance, formerly of Irving, Kansas, and now living in Prairie Village, Kansas, had written me a letter asking about several species of birds she'd seen in her yard, notably a spotted towhee. She also posed a question, and the question took on a life of its own, transforming itself into a personal quest.

"Is the Irving town site still full of meadowlarks like the ones I used to listen to when walking to school through the churchyard?" Martha asked. I didn't know, never having paid a whole lot of attention, so I drove out there to find out.

Irving lies a few miles southeast of Blue Rapids, but there's nothing left of the town except for a stone monument in a small grassy clearing and remnants of sidewalks incongruously strewn through heavy second-growth forest. The old site is bordered on three sides with agricultural fields and the Big Blue River on the fourth. Meadowlarks were not to be found.

At the same time, my grandfather suffered one of those strokes that signify the end of a long and eventful life. Between searching for meadowlarks and his death watch, the two events became inextricably bound together. That I am no longer able to drive to Irving without thinking of my grandfather or of meadowlarks is significant to the depth of emotions that were stirred by the events of last spring.

After my initial failure to find a meadowlark for Martha, I searched off and on many times, even soliciting help from my friend Dan Thalmann, but the town, though filled with songs of any number of other birds, never echoed with the fluted trill of the meadowlark. Irving's streets are overgrown and congested with trees but it is ringed with open fields—prime habitat for meadowlarks. I was certain of it.

Another year goes by. Winter's hold lessens and slips. Spring teases, then arrives full-blown. We go from jacket weather to sunscreen in a span of a week. The demarcation between winter and spring is not something so trite as a day marked on the calendar but a verifiable, provable fact. Our phoebe arrived right on time (one day later than last year, but remarkably close, as if he, too, followed a calendar), and promptly added his *fee-bee* to the chorus of cardinals, titmice, and chickadees. The skies were filled with geese heading north.

A harrier came off the hill to the south, circled lazily until it found a thermal, and rose in a tight spiral on a column of heated globules of air. When it was merely a speck against the high cirrus, it soared northward on outstretched wings until it disappeared in the haze.

Killdeer flew by with their shrill *kill-dee's,* followed in quick succession by a kestrel. The season's first grackles winged past.

It wasn't only the migration of birds that marked the season's change. Tulips thrust up in colors so vibrant that it was as if my eyes had forgotten the hues and were seeing them for the first time. Scarlet buds furred the maples. The faded yellow grass of the field was supplanted by shades of emerald. The air grew damp and sticky.

But it was the song of the western meadowlark that gave me pause, stirred something within me reminiscent of guilt or a nagging sense of incompletion. The song never fails to stir me, only this time it instilled what can only be described as a longing. But for what?

And then it came to me, slowly, a snatch of a phrase, a sentence, a letter I had received almost a year ago. I took down the framed letter that hangs on the wall above my writing desk and read it again. Would there be meadowlarks in Irving?

Keeping one eye on the sky for migrating hawks and the other on the road, I made my way out of town, stopping first at the sewage ponds. A few ducks swam in the waters ruffled by the wind, mostly goldeneyes and ring-necked ducks, but three scaup swam into view from the grassy bank. Two males, one female, the males subtly different. I studied them as they approached, noting the head shapes: one rounded, one peaked, one with a glossy sheen, the other purplish. What I had found was the first greater scaup to be recorded in Marshall County, something of a prize. A swirling mass of Bonaparte's gulls descended, small, distinctly-plumaged gulls that put shame to the notion that all gulls look alike.

The road to Irving was filled with meadowlarks, clouds of them scattering to perch on fence posts or graze in fields of winter wheat. But when I parked at the monument and cut the engine an almost preternatural silence descended. Slowly, building to a crescendo, birds began harmonizing, and I picked them out, one by one, all woodland species. No meadowlarks.

I drifted down to the broad plain below the town site, near where the bridge once spanned the river. Tree sparrows shifted furtively in the thickets. A sharp-shinned hawk flew by searching for lunch. I quartered the roads, my windows down, listening hard. Nothing.

I pulled over with a view toward the old barn that stands sentinel in the close-cropped fields west of town. By my reckoning I was near where the old schoolhouse was, which would put me about where Martha had once heard them singing. The wind sighed through the trees, kicked up dust in the street. For a good half hour I watched for migrating hawks, hearing only the staccato whistles of bluebirds. It seemed my quest had reached another dead end.

And then the song came on the wind, a verse, a stanza, a chorus. The song was crisp and sharp, ineffably lovely. I felt a burden that I had not known I possessed slip away. Meadowlarks surrounded me, all of them singing.

I found Martha her meadowlarks, yes, but it was certainly much more than that. Perhaps, in some way I could never explain, I also laid my grandfather to rest.

## SKY CURRENTS, DRY FLIES, AND THE
## CAST AS QUEST

When I slipped from the camper that morning I whispered to Lori that I loved her. My actual expression was along the lines of "If I don't come back" or some such thing, words that seemed melodramatic but somehow important enough to stress should anything happen to me, though I couldn't say why. Something about not having my river-legs yet. When by late afternoon I hadn't returned, she grew worried enough that the entire family set out to find me.

There is a river whose headwaters lie far out to sea. It is fed by tributaries of extremes—heat from equatorial climes, cold from ice caps—and as these tributaries converge they form currents that sweep the earth, riffling over and under pressure systems. The air we breathe is Mongolian, Peruvian, African. The dust painting the twilight scarlet is sub-Saharan, Australian outback, stardust left behind from the Big Bang. This river flows above us and around us and through us, sometimes an eddy, turning back on itself like the worm Ouroboros, and sometimes a foaming torrent that strips limbs and bark from trees and kicks sand in our eyes. Never entirely still, this river flows eternally.

My father and I walked down to the river and split up. Fly-fishing is at heart a solitary endeavor. As he disappeared downstream through the willows, I gingerly stepped into the water and tested the footing. The stones were greasy with a patina of moss. After pausing for a few moments to read the river, I peeled off a dozen feet of line and flicked the rod back and forth to belly it out. Bouncing a white-winged dry fly along a riffle boiling around a boulder to swirl along the edge of a slack-watered pool, I thought how fly-fishing was all about expectation and hope, of becoming one with the river as much as trout or stonefly or nymph, of connecting—or hoping to—with something outside our own borders. When the fly disappeared in a tiny dimple barely noticeable in the current, I set the hook.

Much later my father came by to watch me. I didn't see him there on the bank, a solitary figure dressed in an old flannel shirt and chest waders. At the time I was mesmerized by the motions of double-hauling, a complicated maneuver that speeds up the line to form tighter loops that punch through wind and distance. I was really laying it out, more for the sheer exuberance of casting than in the pursuit of trout, feeding out as much line as I could control. For the moment, and for many moments thereafter, it was enough just to be a part of the river.

Did I fall in and drown? Such was my wife's fear when I didn't return, and so they set out to find me. I met them halfway to camp, hale and whole and yet not. Perhaps in some way I *had* drowned, for being out of the current made me feel disembodied and vaporous.

It was the last time I cast for trout, my life taking a different turn, channeled by terrain only partly of my own making.

Now I stand in another river. The season's first frost has come, irretrievably changing the complexity of the land and hastening the gentle fall of leaves. The unbroken northern sky is open to my view, my feet planted in brittle stands of brome and alfalfa, my right hand curled comfortably around rubber-clad binoculars. The current is from the north.

There is no reading this river, no riffles, no pools, no pocket water to dap with a dry fly, nor clouds to provide definition or a place for the eye to alight. Bluer than the bluest water, it is a smooth, textureless partition revealing nothing. Whatever is hidden must be sought. Within it, behind it, under it, are hawks.

I raise the binoculars and scan the horizon, left to right in an arc, and then lift the glasses one field of view and repeat. And repeat, until I am staring almost straight up. It's like casting, really, the act of expectation and hope, the desire to connect. Fly-fishing, like hawkwatching, is only partly about technique, the rest enforced by luck alone. Today I'm feeling lucky.

Nothing in my past prepares me for what I see. An American kestrel engages a peregrine falcon in a duel, the pair darting so fast that it's hard to tell the two apart other than by size and coloration. The peregrine finally breaks free and disappears. Swainson's hawks pass through in small kettles, and one, consisting of eight hawks and one pelican, soars in concentric circles that take it across the pale gibbous moon hanging low in the west. Violet-green swallows—impossibly rare in this part of the state—pass overhead, and as I stand in mute shock thinking that nothing could be finer, the river brings more.

Above me, in stark contrast to both the sky and each other, are two hawks. One is a Krider's hawk, an albinistic red-tailed hawk, the other a Harlan's hawk, its exact opposite with coal-black plumage. The white hawk stoops on the black. Just before collision the black hawk flares and whirls upside down, and they lock talons and plunge in a freefall, white and black, black and white, a spinning piebald form gyrating out of control until G-forces tear them apart.

Suddenly it's snowing gulls, black-headed Franklin's by the hundreds, swooping down to kiss the earth before rocketing skyward, weaving intricate patterns whose meaning is known only to them. Embraced in a web of motion, I can only stand in the current and keep my feet. My fingers caress the binoculars as I raise them. And I cast, and cast, and cast, into that fathomless, gift-giving river.

# NEVER FORGET: A CAIRN FOR MISTER BUN

*A cairn is a pile of stones, usually pyramidal in shape. Sometimes found high above timberline, where they are used to mark a path through frost-heaved scree, or along rocky Arctic promontories where they announce, "I was here," they also denote a monument, usually of someone of renown. Thomas Pennant, in "Voyage to the Hebrides," published in 1772, wrote, "As long as the memory of the deceased endured, not a passenger went by without adding a stone to the heap...To this moment there is a proverbial expression among the highlanders, allusive to the old practice; a suppliant will tell his patron, I will add a stone to your cairn; meaning, when you are no more, I will do all possible honor to your memory."*

Sara Everton, protagonist of Harriet Doerr's novel, *Stones for Ibarra*, finds an ever-increasing pile of stones stacked outside the hacienda's front gate on the anniversary of her husband's death. When she asks a hired hand what it means, he says, "When people pass by and remember, they bring stones."

I was told that if I write this there will be people who think I've gone off the deep end. "It's just a rabbit," they'll say. Some will understand, though. If it helps, substitute dog, cat, horse, or hamster. But let me be up front about this column—this wasn't written for you. This is for me, and a certain little snow-white Angora rabbit with sometimes-pink eyes and sometimes-blue eyes, with a temper that could be easily assuaged by his favorite treats, who loved super-premium-gourmet rabbit food and Post Raisin Bran, who loved nothing more than to lay beside me and get rubbed for hours and hours, and who was by any and all means spoiled rotten. As were we.

Mister Bun came into my life ears first. Lori had just returned from a meeting and carefully set a cardboard box on the kitchen floor. Before I could ask what was in the box, a pair of white tufted ears and two curious, frightened pink eyes slowly rose out. When our eyes locked, he slowly sank out of sight.

Lori had stopped at an Angora breeder's home north of Manhattan with the intent of buying a young rabbit and wound up rescuing a middle-aged bunny with bowel problems. This was excellent from Mister Bun's standpoint because he had been slated for destruction. It was also a big step up from a small cage behind the house. Here he had the run of the place, his cage situated in the back room just behind the computer. He was possibly the only rabbit in Kansas to have his own remote-controlled air conditioner, though in honesty we shared it.

Once he got over the intimidation of new digs, he was quick to capitalize on his newfound freedom. Regular rabbit pellets? Forget it—he wanted gourmet stuff. Sleeping in a cage with the door closed? A resounding thump from his back paw let us know his disgust, so I wired the door open. He loved being with us, and would spend each evening lying beside me on the living room floor. The new furniture we bought was left to Lori alone; I had a pillow.

Sometimes he slept under the kitchen table, sometimes against a bookcase, sometimes in the back room, almost hidden under the desk, with only his ears poking out. He had his favorite places and kept to them with a rhythm only he knew. He was lonely for another rabbit—a girl rabbit—but accepted me as his soul mate. He disliked being brushed and tossed the comb around whenever he saw it.

For almost four years he was my constant companion. He was my muse, my friend, my familiar.

Three weeks ago he stopped eating. He had been losing weight and acted as if his front right paw was crippled. We were seeing the slow decline of a rabbit who's led a full life, the vet said. But the decline wasn't that slow. Several days later he started eating again, voraciously, and we fed him a steady diet of apples, bananas, wild alfalfa, and the little green and yellow treats found in his gourmet food. Things he loved and should have eaten in moderation. For two weeks he rallied, even gaining weight.

Then his other front leg went out. He remained outside of his cage, and I hand-fed and watered him. A day later his back legs stopped functioning, and he could no longer eat from his dish. I would spill some in front of him, selecting only the treats. Every free hour was spent by his side, stroking him to a blissful daze.

On Wednesday morning I rubbed him for two hours, and then, when the first wan sunlight gilded the hackberry tree in the back yard, I wrapped him in a towel, took him outside and set him on the grass. Though almost paralyzed, he began eating. "You're a wild bunny now, Mister Bun," I said. His eyes were blue when I shot him.

That afternoon I began stacking rough stones above his grave. I chose flat ones of native limestone, found along the river where the bones of the hill lie exposed. They were carefully chinked together to form one layer, then two, then three. On top I set the last of the gallardia blossoms and an apple.

Yeah, he was just a rabbit, a little snow-white long-hair Angora rabbit with sometimes-pink eyes and sometimes-blue eyes, who would sometimes run after me for one last rub before bedtime, who would thump his back leg loudly when sensing danger or peeved about something, who would steal my pillow when I left for a moment and not leave it until I rubbed him some more, who had a sweet and loving disposition unless we tried sneaking in generic Raisin Bran, who spoiled the two of us rotten. He was just a rabbit—just a rabbit!—and his name was Mister Bun.

Bring stones.

# HUNTING FOR THERMALS

There were three hawks circling above the low hills fronting the Big Blue River north of town. At first I thought they were engaged in a mating flight, two males vying for the attention of a single female, but there were no dangled legs, no grasped talons and tumbling freefalls, only an ever-widening gyre, as if they were searching for something. The morning was warming but still brisk enough that a sweatshirt was needed when standing in the stiff south wind. They're hunting for thermals, I realized. Looking for lift.

I was far below them, almost invisible in a small meadow at the base of the railroad grade. Seehan Creek tumbled clear and cold from the culvert, spilling into a broad pool before dropping down a rocky channel like the notes of a canyon wren. My left hand and wrist, submerged beneath that silky flow, were growing numb. My right hand held a knife.

A phoebe hawked at the mouth of the culvert, flitting back and forth to snatch insects from the air, its tail wagging as it lay in wait, keeping time to the pulse of the earth, a steady, rhythmic dip and upward snap. Butterflies danced by—goatweed leafwing, spring azure, eastern comma—splashes of burnt orange, ethereal blue, purple-fringed nightshade beneath speckled amber. Rains had flushed the winter hues from the land, leaving it emerald green.

It's a long way from wherever I was to here, kneeling on the banks of a clear-running stream, but if I tried to retrace my steps all I saw was darkness, and rage, fierce and sharp like lightning stabbing the night, accompanied by a bedlam of voices, accusing, betraying, belittling. The voices were my own, and inescapable.

I had been in a bleak mood when I left the house earlier, but it plummeted to a new low when I ran over a black snake. It was crossing the river road in the shadow of the hill, mindful of its own business, and along I came, blind in my despair, and our convergence left it writhing in the dust, its spine crushed beneath tons of steel.

Guilt hammered me. My self-esteem further eroded when it was nearly impossible to locate a pair of singing black-and-white warblers even though they were within forty feet, my hearing so reduced that aural details were incomprehensible. It made me feel even less human.

On the trail to the spring I stepped across an orange-collared ringneck snake, motionless in the damp soil. Chorus frogs croaked raucously, and field sparrows, newly arrived, trilled their dropping-ball melodies. Almost by rote, I methodically wrote down each bird species seen, though *why* was a question that nagged me. Why when I might not be around to derive any benefit from the records.

From the spring I cut across the saddle and down into Seehan Creek, which was flowing briskly, its music filling the vale. Climbing the muddy hillside, I broke into the open of Stella's Meadow and crossed over keeping one eye on the sky for migrants and the other on the ground for butterflies. I walked past the outhouse, keeled over as if tired from all its years of standing erect, and entered the trees again, crossed the stream at a narrow channel, and cut through a field of wild roses and blackberries to where the stream bubbles over a rocky shelf and cascades past a mossy, columbine-draped boulder looming over an emerald pool. There I sat down to write.

I listed the reasons I felt I was angry. It was a long list, and a surprising one. The usual culprits were there, but once written a pattern emerged. Things that had spiraled my emotions downward like a whirligig all had to do with what I perceived as injustices—intolerances, cruelties, discriminations, inequities—things that had been directed toward my family and friends and, to some extent, myself. Things beyond my control, not caused by any fault of my own. Or perhaps I was deluding myself; when in depression's clutch, it's hard to think straight.

"Despair is the worst betrayal, the coldest seduction," Marge Piercy said. Seduction it is. Depression doesn't inflict, it entices. It beckons a hooked finger and beguiles us to succumb. And when under the chemical overload our brains sometimes produce, our neurotransmitters misfiring, our wiring crossed as when a switchboard operator patches a call through to the wrong connection—for such is why these things occur, according to scientists—there's a warm, almost euphoric sensation to submitting. Almost a release.

But not for long. The mind begins to feed on itself, sucking all life from the soul like a vampire, and left in its place is guilt, anger, shame, feelings of worthlessness, and a bone-deep exhaustion. Reason and clarity are usurped by paranoia. When under what clinicians categorize as major depression, thoughts of escape focus on one solution—the final one. Women attempt this more than succeed; men do.

I watched a chorus frog move from the water's edge. It leaped higher than I thought possible, clinging to the rough surface of the shelf, pulling itself up to crawl onto a narrow ledge and advance to within an inch of the waterfall, where it flattened itself against the limestone and became invisible to everything in the universe except for me.

I felt a great peace descend. And I knew then what I would do. I would walk to the culvert, dip my wrists in the cold clear water until they were numb, and then take the new Columbia River knife and slit them to the bone, and let my lifeblood paint the stream crimson and my life bleed away in that loveliest of places. End it there. Be done with it. Sleep.

How long I sat there I do not know. Nor can I say why I didn't follow through. After a while I folded the blade and clipped it to my pocket, and stood up, letting water drip from my arm. The hawks had moved on, leaving the sky bare. Perhaps they had found their thermals. I was still looking for mine.

# LEARNING TO WALK AGAIN

The arroyo behind my grandmother's house in Albuquerque was usually dry except for after a thunderstorm, but one cold winter several deep pools remained. Iced over, they formed irregular white patterns on a sere brown wasteland, fringed on one side with hillocks of industrial materials, jumbled piles of shattered concrete, trimmed tree limbs and uprooted shrubs, and the omnipresent mounds of illegally dumped garbage. For a young boy, this was an enchanted playground, especially when there was always a chance of finding a tattered copy of *Playboy* magazine. Being the good Baptist kids we were, we would grab them and sequester ourselves within that trashy redoubt, keeping one eye out for visitors. And, being the good Baptist kids we were, we were always cognizant of God, who was surely frowning down upon us. We didn't stop, but it sure robbed us of some of the thrill.

Bodies of water, however ephemeral, were uncommon in the areas we frequented, so it was only natural that my brother and I were drawn to the pools. Our interest didn't lie only in water but also in its aftermath. After one severe deluge we found a vast glistening mudflat that proved to be more liquid than solid; any object hurled into it disappeared with an obscene resonance, leaving a gaping hole that slowly filled with brown ooze. We couldn't walk in the muck, though. The ice was another matter.

As with the mud, we bombarded the largest pond with

chunks of cement. They hit with a loud crack, spraying shards of ice like broken glass and skittering across like a car out of control. Once we determined the surface was thick enough to withstand our missiles, we ventured onto its scarred veneer. Our steps were tentative, as light as we could make them, hesitant, fearful. Somewhere near the center, with me in the lead, a section of ice tilted up, dumped me into the frigid water, and snapped shut over me.

The cold must have been a shock, but I can't remember it. There was only the ethereal blue light filtering through the ice and me below, choking on water, scrambling madly to break through that hard membrane, my panicked motions conjuring pale irregular bubbles that danced around me like a swarm of angry bees, all of them catching the pallid light and refracting it, enhancing the sense that all reality, all motion, was to be found only in this liquid embrace, hidden away beneath an innocential film of ice, and the world outside, with its rushing cars and jets arcing across the skies and the myriads of people scurrying through their daily activities, all merely an illusion. And then I broke through and my brother's hands clawed me to safety, and the cold struck like a hammer.

To be deposited so ungainly, so swiftly, surely was God's fierce retribution, I felt. God is not mocked, whatsoever ye sow so shall ye reap, all that. And it would be easy to say that in the weeks to come I vowed off dirty magazines however freely acquired, my thoughts as pure as adolescently possible, but I was haunted by that blue light and the glittering white door that closed behind me with such stark finality, and I was taken to staring at it in my crippled mind's eye. I returned again and again to that place. If it would only open I could see to the other side.

I acted normal. Did my homework, played with friends,

went to church on Sundays. But something was different. It was as though I had voyaged to a foreign country, only to return with an accent or a new mode of dress, though certainly nothing in my outward demeanor gave any inkling of the change. Perhaps for the first time in my young life I had glimpsed things eternal, far beyond the homilies heard each Sunday. Whatever lay behind that door was nothing to be feared. I sensed that, and still do.

But that was an involuntary approach to the edge, youthful indiscretion nearly turned fatal. A week ago it was willful, if such can be said for my state of mind. Not ice this time but a thin canvas of skin and veins and heartblood and a razor-edged blade to open that door. Followed by a withdrawal of sorts and a long dazed walk back to the truck.

If not for my diary I could not say what happened next. My mind seems to have lost track of itself; chores just finished, places recently visited, conversations I've had, leave no imprint. The present is all, with occasional snatches of the distant past, as when I once slipped into gelid waters to emerge altered. Disorientation comes easily, and once, when cleaning a glass door, the transparency of the window befuddled me and I almost fell through. It was like falling from a great height, the air liquid, invisible. Misfiring synapses are so exhilarating.

One morning, after my wife left for work, I sat on the porch listening to birdsong. Where do I go now, I wondered. How do I make it in this new environment. *Slowly*, came the answer. Take baby steps, just like when you went onto the ice. Feel your way home.

That afternoon I dug the lawnmower from the shed and fired it up. The grass was deep in places, especially along the north fence where brome creeps into the yard. A long strip of shorn grass followed the wake of the mower. I could look back and see where I had been, and where I needed to go. It was all so elemental, so simple. I lined the mower up with the first row and paced off another hundred steps, and then another, and another, creating a map even a man blinded by blue light could follow. Each step was stronger, more confident. The icy doorway could wait.

# FOR EVERY SEASON, A MONTH

# JANUARY—THROUGH THE GATE

From the saddle of Pawnee Pass it's easy to see where you've come from. If you pause to catch your breath and look back, maybe drop your pack with a groan and allow your rubbery legs to stabilize, your eyes can retrace the trail as it zigzags down the rocky incline, a tall cairn anchoring each bend, and far below the trail straightening out to cross a treeless meadow before teetering on the cliff edge above Lake Isabelle and then falling out of sight, swallowed in the dark pines. And below that Long Lake, sunbeams winking off wind-tossed breakers, and stepping downward yet more Brainard Lake, where the trailhead marks a clean demarcation between civilization and wilderness. But the pass is not a destination, it's a gateway.

Face west and the trail goes on. It forks before descending into a broad valley watered by Cascade, Buchanan, and Hell creeks, sending runners to the adjoining peaks, Shoshoni on your left, Pawnee on your right. Beyond, mountains roll away in staggered ranges, snowy, precipitous, coldly and terribly beautiful.

The ancient Italians knew something of gates. Their purpose was for going out and coming in and as such represented beginnings and ends. So important were they that a god was placed over them—Janus, dual-faced, one visage looking forward, the other back, suspended forever in the past or the future, never inhabiting the present. And so, after Rome conquered Italy and welcomed its gods into an already crowded pantheon, Ianuarius was added to the calendar, marking a clean break between the old and the new. January. The gate.

The paths of our lives are harder to trace than any dusty trail leading through frost-heaved stones in the alpine tundra. There is no looking back as from a 12,541-foot pass such as Pawnee, no visible track meandering uphill or down, no Continental Divide to provide such an elevated and lofty outlook. We have only the pinnacle of the year, a manmade contrivance with no bearing on nature's circadian rhythms, a single day from whose height we can pause and take stock in our peregrinations, to examine our steps to determine if our boots are on the right path or if corrections are in order. To measure our resolve. We are not Janus, though we can see into our past and a little ways ahead, if only vaguely; not godlike, with no certain cognizance of the future; but human and capable of pausing, and in that pausing to peer inward not at tundra or tarn but into the soul. A capacity surely brushed with divinity.

So we pause, while outside winter comes down hard and the waters turn to stone and the land to iron and the air to ice crystals that lacerate the skin, and shadows of woods lie dark and deep. The sun low in the south, casting a wan light that does not warm but more sharply defines the nakedness of things, and then not for long, though for longer each day. We pause and check our backtrail and in doing so unconsciously honor Janus.

"The unexamined life is not worth living," Socrates said. The problem of course is in finding time for an examination. The gateway guarded by Janus is the ideal time, and many of us choose it to assess our progress. We vow to shed pounds, to make amends with an estranged relative, to read the classics, to write that poem that's been nagging at us, to buy a new wardrobe, to find a new girlfriend or boyfriend or husband or wife, to do any of the limitless things people conjure up to make themselves into another thing, another being, all brought about by an internal disquiet that whispers we can be better, that there is time yet to transform into what we want to be. That the trail goes on. This is the gift of January.

I've never been one to dwell long on New Year's resolutions and my track record is spotty at best. I've resolved to lose weight, to exercise more, to sock away more money in the bank—to do any number of things actually—and few were successful. Mostly what I did at the completion of one year and on the brink of another was to sit alone at my writing desk and review the year in my diary. As if to glean something from it, to gauge my mileage. As we would at Pawnee Pass: four and a half miles from the trailhead, another mile or so to the crest of either peak, and unlimited miles if we take the center trail. On and on and on, like life.

A few years back I resolved to live more, to see more, to love more, plus I posed a challenge to find one hundred bird species in Kansas during the month of January. I failed on the latter, mainly due to flagging interest in the amount of ground needing to be covered to accomplish the task. I like to think I was more successful with the former.

Nowadays my thoughts are more in the present, notwithstanding that a diarist is, like Janus, constantly looking backward. I've reached that age where I understand life is finite, that it can be taken away in the next breath, and the realization is less disturbing than it is enriching. That we cannot see far down our trail is our good fortune, for the journey itself is the important thing. We can examine our lives and look back over our past and try to peer into the future but it's the step by step by step that gets us nearer to our destination, the placing of one foot before the other and the locomotion thereof.

We stand in the gateway, cast one last look behind, shoulder our packs and pass through. The old behind us, the new ahead, and us unapprised of what tidings it brings. The trail goes on.

# A BRIDGE ACROSS THE SEASONS OF OUR LIVES

*February is merely as long as is needed to pass the time until March. —*Dr. J. R. Stockton

Created in the 8th century B.C. to fill a void in the Roman calendar, February was merely an afterthought. It signaled both the end of the year and a time of purification. So little esteemed is it that we drop its first "r" and hasten through the enunciation of its name. It occupies that misbegotten stretch of time between the wintry days of January and spring's vanguard in March. It's the shortest month, the number of its days erratic. It's the month my son Ben tried killing me.

I always forget that.

Somehow, though, it doesn't forget me. It's as if the scar tissue was timed to rip open on a certain day of the year. That day is today, the third.

I was finishing up at work, mentally working on my next column, one about February. In it I would mention the first signs of spring, how birds start tuning up, how if you get down on all fours and peer under the yellow tufts of grass you'll find fresh green shoots, and how the sun's rays hold a new warmth. And then my knees buckled and I sobbed and did not know why. When I got home I asked Lori when Ben had done his thing—we dance around the phrasing as if in fear of it—and she said, without hesitation, "Today."

Some years my reaction is less dramatic. As Lori says, we just get crushed without knowing why.

Years of therapy and counseling followed the incident, with a steady strangulation of emotions. He finally disappeared one day but we heard that he was working at a tattoo parlor. He met a girl and had a daughter and then left them. His life was in shambles.

Last February we heard he lost his job. Strange how we find ourselves back in the role of grieving parent, though the amount of grief we are to experience is yet to be revealed. As Lori said, "That job was everything to him." I don't understand the machinations of the tattoo trade nor do I want to, but it's what he had and he had so very little. I wondered about his mental state, how many hits he could take before he packed it in, whether, indeed, it's in him to cancel his own ticket. Or if, by hanging out with the crowd he finds comfy, his days are numbered by the very nature of their association with risk.

For a few days this oppressed me, but when we watched a movie, *In the Bedroom*, it became an open sore. The main thrust of the movie was how the violent death of a son impacted the parents. It was riveting and sad and terrible and had a nebulous ending with two people trying to rebuild their shattered lives. I wondered how Ben's death might affect us. I wondered about Ben, too, where he was, what he was going through. Will we know if something happens to him? How long would it take for us to find out, if ever? Those thoughts haunted me.

We were in bed, the soft hum of the humidifier lulling us to sleep, when it seemed something bumped the bed. Some body. I jumped, Lori jumped, and for a moment I imagined a man standing there looking down on us. I rolled over, my heart hammering my ribs, and saw only the bookcases and the open doorway. Neither of us said a word. I considered inspecting the house, if for no other reason than to burn off a feeling of dread that enveloped me, but the bed was soft and warm so I stayed there, sleepless. I wondered if Ben was dead, if the bump was his apparition come to see us one last time, if we had both felt the moment of his passing from life to death.

I felt the mattress sag as though someone sat down beside me. My leg shifted from the weight, and my hair, I am certain, stood on end. Iciness coursed through my veins. I was facing away and refused to look behind me as if by ignoring the presence it would go away. My skin crawled trying to escape the weight.

And then it lifted and I heard the furnace start and the soft sound of Lori's breathing. He's gone, I thought. He's dead.

Morning came. Walking by our bedroom, out of the corner of my eye I glimpsed someone standing in the room. I skidded to a stop and stared, but the presence was gone. Though a terrible fear gripped me, I stepped into the empty room and looked around. Ben, I said. Ben.

We had no way of contacting him, no way of knowing the truth of my suspicions. That entire February was a torment of expectation. Every phone call scared us. I can't do this, I thought. I can't go on. And somehow we do.

Time, at least on this earthly plane, does not heal all wounds. But I believe that someday we will find a resting place where all our troubles will be washed away. I possess no theology or philosophy to certify such a belief, but see it in an old photograph sitting on my desk. My wife, much younger, is looking over her shoulder, a small smile on her lips, her eyes luminous as the sunlight falling on her hair. In her expression I see what we were before the shadow. I see so much promise, so much joy. Too much to forget, or leave behind, or have taken away.

Several months ago Ben phoned. We were out, but he left a short message on the answering machine. He didn't talk long but said he was okay. We never erased the message but kept it to remember his voice.

The days of February are short but they bridge winter to spring. February tells us there is hope, that darkness is not forever, that better days are ahead. Our final purification awaits. Close your eyes and see.

# LEAPING INTO MARCH

Eight years ago we flew to the Texas Gulf Coast for a week-long birding adventure, the first of what we hoped to be many more leap year celebrations.

Four years ago we went a little more extreme. We sold our house, quit our jobs, and moved to Kansas. It was more midlife crisis than leap year adventure, at least that's the story I like to tell. Lori prefers the intercalary aspect: we "leaped" right out of our city lives. And that works for me, too.

Time and financial considerations this year prevented us from taking a leap to Mexico, which would have been my first choice. Instead, on the spur of the moment, Lori decided we needed to head to a bed and breakfast in Glasgow. We could explore a new part of the state, visit some small towns, and, she promised, I'd have a quiet room to write in. I couldn't refuse.

It wasn't the best day to travel. The sky was the color of hammered steel. Wind buffeted the car. Along the way the land rolled to the horizons, opening up west of Clay Center with a few hills visible in the distance—real hills, with wooded slopes and windswept crests providing the explorer distant vistas of the Solomon River valley. But here on the cusp of springtime the land lay fallow, leached of color save for shades of gray and tan, with an occasional green swath where winter wheat thrust through the damp soil. Towns were deserted and lifeless.

Rustic Remembrances B&B lies about five miles northeast from Glasgow. Since we arrived earlier than the scheduled check-in time, we drove into town to have a look around.

There are few towns that would look their best on a raw day like this. Glasgow was no exception. It looked exhausted, as if it had just run a marathon and hadn't had time to catch its breath. But even it looked positively vibrant compared to Simpson, the next settlement to the west.

A massive limestone school once dominated the place, but now it was half demolished, its stones being hauled off to Missouri. Across the street was a steakhouse where we ate supper. It looked like the only thing that kept the town on the map. According to a newspaper article hanging on the wall, weekend business triples the town's population of 110. The owner, Tony Prochaska, cooks the steaks on an old propane grill prominently placed outside the kitchen door.

The B&B was well worth it. For a spinning enthusiast like my wife, the place was a dream. Llamas roamed the grounds, as well as Jacob and Katahdin sheep, prized for their wool, and chickens, miniature donkeys, bronzed turkeys, and a host of other animals. Our cozy room was decorated with antiques and had a small table where I could write. I could easily have stayed a week.

Morning came with a roar of rain and wind.

After a huge breakfast and several hours of stimulating conversation with our hosts, Larry and Madonna Sorell, we began our slippery journey back to pavement. We hadn't gone a mile when part of the driver's side windshield wiper blew off. I pulled over and tried reassembling it, but half of a tab that held the end piece together had sheared off. All I could do is bend the metal arm up slightly so it wouldn't scrape against the glass.

But I had really wanted to take a photo of the town of Simpson, its dismantling stone by stone. Still, having ninety miles of rain-swept road ahead gave me pause.

My imagination runs riot when something goes wrong on a trip. A tire goes flat, the engine overheats, and suddenly I picture the car slowly disintegrating, the hood peeling away as if jettisoned, a wheel falling off, the car spinning out of control as a fully-loaded tanker hauling liquid nitroglycerin slams on its brakes and jackknifes and catches your car in mid-swerve and explodes in a huge ball of fire that vaporizes the rain and melts the roadway into sludge and roasts everyone to cinders and, well, you get the idea.

At the intersection I turned left instead of right and headed for home.

Rain pounded down, pooling in the road. The car hydroplaned. I cut my speed and used the wipers intermittently to prolong their life. Driving was slow and monotonous. The swish of the wipers, the hum of water beneath the tires, and the rain pelting the windshield creating a low-level tension. I was worried about the wiper. My hands gripped the wheel in a white-knuckled grip as I fought to steady the car against hammering gusts.

Visibility narrowed and colors washed away to muted pastels, but even in the midst of the maelstrom I began to take note of the terrain. For miles we drove through treeless, hilly country, with low scudding clouds pressing down on crenellated ridges. We passed wooded ravines surging with rills of blackwater, old barns collapsing under the weight of time, and rusty skeletons of crumpled windmills. The land was empty, as if the wind had scoured it clean of humanity. So wild and destitute and primitive was it under the storm's battering that in spite of the concentration needed to maintain my course I was captivated by its beauty.

It was a feral land on an untamed day, and my heart, in

this bissextile year, surged in response, leaped like a trout on a hook, leaped with boundless joy into the whirlwind that is March.

# THE GIFTS OF APRIL

One of the peculiar traits associated with diarists is that they're constantly looking over their shoulders, dwelling in the past more than the present. Or at least they do when writing. While some might consider this a monumental waste of time, there are rewards to be accrued, too many to be named, for sure, though I will focus on one, and a paradox to boot—a diary, properly maintained, acts as a crystal ball to peer into the future. Not bad for a few scraps of paper.

It can be disorienting to glance back through time with the purpose of looking forward, but such is what I've just done. Rooting through my past entries to last April, I jotted down everything that we can expect in the coming month, beginning with that most appropriate of days, All Fool's Day. But this is no stretch of the imagination, no practical joke, no lie. Everything I tell you will come to pass. You just have to watch for it.

It goes without saying that April showers bring May flowers, but March ends with plentiful rains and the season's first thunderstorm. Soon the skies will fill with the acrid smell of prairie fires as farmers burn their fields, and the sun will no longer set so much as welter in a haze of smoke. What isn't burned will turn green almost overnight; already we're well on our way toward painting the Kansas countryside into a localized version of the Emerald Isle. Grass and weeds—

especially weeds, at least in my yard—push through the damp soil and spring riotously into the sun's energy.

It looks nice, winter's drab veneer swapped for vibrant colors, but it comes at a price. Sometime during the first week of the month I'll be forced to dig out my lawnmower. This year I intend on giving it a little maintenance—change the oil, sharpen the blade, that sort of thing—and then I'll be pacing off our yard, whiling away the hours with the roar of the engine in my ears. It takes me four hours to mow my yard and another across the street, mainly because like a fool I bought a twenty-one-inch push mower. Everyone admonished me to get a riding mower but I refused. I was going to mow only a small section of our lawn and let the rest revert to tallgrass prairie. I forgot about ticks and chiggers until they asserted themselves. Still, it's about the only form of exercise I get anymore, so I shouldn't complain.

I also like to point out that people on big, powerful riding mowers are less connected to the earth and undoubtedly overlook the small things that make life worth living. They remind me of SUV drivers whose self-esteem is based on the amount of steel encasing them. My neighbor on his massive blue Dixon would never have seen the tiny Henry's elfin butterfly had it been in his yard instead of mine. Those whirling chain-driven blades would have fricasseed the poor thing and never would he have been aware of it. Me, I saw the butterfly, cut the motor, and studied it through my ever-present pair of binoculars. It was what we birders call a lifer, though the term "lifebird" doesn't carry over to the *Lepidoptera* family as well as might be hoped for. "Lifebutterfly" doesn't have much rhythm to it, nor does "lifebutter" and especially not "lifefly." More study needs to be done on this subject.

As our tilted planet wobbles and aligns itself more in line

with the sun's direct rays, life in all its myriad forms becomes more apparent. Two days ago my wife slapped me on the forehead. "Mosquito," she said. It seemed early but I can only take her at her word. I can't recall saying anything stupid at the time. We'll see more of that in the weeks to come. (Mosquitoes, not me talking stupid.) With all the rain we've had it might be a bad season for West Nile Virus. Let's be careful out there.

Pelicans and swallows will arrive any day. House Wrens will busy themselves around our yards, looking for a place to raise their young. Hawks are moving, migrating from as far away as southern Argentina, passing over in a direct northward flight that leaves no room for tarrying. As important as birds and raptors are to me, I find myself growing more interested in butterflies. It's part of becoming attuned to the rhythms of the natural world, and of finding my place within them. This, too, is part of the calendal cycle.

For these are the gifts April brings: mourning cloak, tiger swallowtail, common sootywing, clouded sulphur. There is magic in these names, and saying them aloud affirms the great cycle of life, of birth and death and renewal. It's a realization that the great things of this earth are found in the small things. The world with all its many splendors, its Yellowstones and Grand Canyons and Niagara Falls, are nothing compared to the subtle sheen on the wings of a red admiral.

Repeat after me: great spangled fritillary. Eastern tailed blue. American lady. Falcate orangetip. Banded hairstreak. Olympia marble. What more could we ask for or expect in this life or the next?

In the calendarial cycles of the universe, April is the life-giver. Throw open your windows, rush out your doors! April is here, and its gifts are free.

# MAY—THE BUILDING BLOCK OF SUMMER

If summer were a puzzle to piece together, or a LEGO toy to be assembled block by block, May would be the month when the final piece is set into place. I'm trying not to be too loose here on calendrical details but ever since I was an inmate of the public school system I've felt that true summer was that season stretching from the last class bell at the end of May to the opening (and dreaded) peal signaling the beginning of yet another school year in September. Such was the nature of my innocence that I believed there were only two seasons, those of school and summer. Nowadays the school year operates on its own illogic and dismisses by mid-spring, but thankfully I served my time when the calendar made sense. School and May were simultaneous in releasing their hold on me, and every minute and every day of that month was another piece or block I enjoined to form a composite of what awaited me.

I am long since graduated from the tyranny of school, freed now to enjoy the blossoming of summer unhampered by classes and boring teachers. In real world terms this means I'm so busy I can scarcely find time to breathe. One of our bitterest ironies is that we never realize how good we have it until it's gone. This shameful omission on our part is nearly impossible to rectify though I've found that infusions of hot green chile takes some of the sting out of it, or at least replaces it with something more pungent. Weeping in your beer also helps but should be done sparingly.

If we've learned anything from this it's that we should live each moment to the fullest, or better yet, as the poet Gwendolyn Brooks suggested, "Exhaust the moment." Easier said than done, of course. Implicit in this is the folly of anticipation, and yet the writer's hands are tied. If I am to attempt to outline the changes we may expect in the natural world, my steps by necessity take me from the moment the redbuds bequeath their gaudy colors to the sultry firefly gloamings of early summer, all in the space of a few paragraphs. My nature resists. Spring, like barbecue, should be taken slowly.

As I write these words rain drums on the roof and sluices through the downspout, momentarily drowning out the thin slurry whistles of Harris's sparrows. If it's true that April showers bring May flowers then we're in for a real treat in the coming weeks. For all the concomitant misdeeds the month can bring—thunderstorms, straight-line winds, tornadoes, hail—wildflowers are the finishing touches to the most picturesque segment of the year.

In fact, it's not just these northern Flint Hills that bloom but the avian world as well. Our most flamboyant species, the orioles, tanagers, buntings, and warblers, will arrive any day. Birders can barely contain themselves for excitement. Each day brings a new wanderer back, until by the end of the month they should all be on their breeding grounds, their territories staked out by song and persistence and perhaps some fighting, the nights ghostly with the eerie calls of nightjars. Everywhere we go, even if it's only outside to take out the trash, we arm ourselves with optics.

Though splashed with scarlets and golds and azures and roses, the predominant color of a Kansas spring is a shameless, luxuriant green. It defies decorum, like a brazen trollop plopped down on the front pew of a Baptist church.

After winter's dullness, our eyes can scarce take it in. Seeing the prairie rolling away with its ponds shimmering in the light and the glint of moving water in the wooded bottoms never fails to connect on some primal level.

My wife's uncle always says this is God's country, but if so He sure goes on a bender now and then. This year I broke down and bought a weather radio. The model I purchased has the new SAFE technology that allows programming for specific counties and natural disasters, which supposedly cuts down on the amount of whooping and hollering it does. The question in this age of terror awareness is how many disasters should we be apprised of. Every nasty event one could dream up with the exception of an incoming asteroid is included, though even that's probably covered under the "civil emergency" category.

Determined to not sacrifice too much sleep over useless interruptions, I studied the manual to decide which warnings to remove. Out went alerts for tropical storms, hurricanes, coastal floods, volcanic eruptions (I am not making this up), avalanches, tsunamis, dust storms, high winds, earthquakes, fires, child abductions, 911 telephone outages, material hazards, and nuclear reactor meltdowns. The alert to "evacuate immediately" gave me pause, but in the end I removed it. I prefer the "shelter in place" warning anyway, finding the idea of hunkering down usually the best course of action if for no other reason than the proximity to the refrigerator and my books.

Plenty of other warnings were left programmed to remind me that May can be a contentious month. Indeed, it's depressing to consider the number of calamities available to us. May can lift us up with its sublime beauty or stomp us flat without a care. Let's learn this lesson: Life is transient and fleeting. Throw out your calendar. Exhaust the moment.

# A MONTH NAMED FOR A BUG

June is the month of love, when wedding bells toll through the countryside and beautiful brides dressed in white are escorted down the aisles by their fathers and given in marriage to their handsome grooms. According to my research, this tradition has been in place since the fifteenth century and had less to do with the timing of love than the timing of the annual bath, which took place in May. Though most people today are a bit more fastidious in their grooming, the tradition remains in force. More weddings are performed in June than any other month. And more June weddings are going to be screwed up in the eastern third of the U.S. this year than any since seventeen years ago.

You gotta love it. After all the debates and tirades over allowing gays to wed, and after the government's decision fell to the divine interpretation of marriage being between one heterosexual man and one heterosexual woman, it took an act of God, or nature, to really throw a wrench into the wedding plans of thousands of couples. Gays, at least for this cycle, aren't affected much, but those heteros who are tying the knots next month are getting tied in knots over the emergence of what few saw coming: bugs.

Not just any bug, but really big bugs, with loud whirring wings and evil red eyes and voices loud enough to be heard for a mile. Lots of them, too—hundreds of billions, the experts predict. Enough to abolish outdoor weddings and drive them indoors, to drown out the preacher's intonations. And, remarkably, Kansas is unaffected this time, and will be for another eleven years.

The emergence of Brood X (as in the numeral ten), or periodical cicada, has played prevalently in national news in the past few weeks, but for us Kansans this should come as no surprise. We all know the month was named for a bug, regardless of what we learned in school. Though our teachers drilled into our heads that the sixth month of the Gregorian calendar was named for the Roman goddess Juno, wife of Jupiter, we secretly knew that it was named for *Cotinis nitida*, the green June bug.

This is no coincidence. Around the time of the solstice, typically within a day or two of June 21, flights of the handsome beetle fill the skies, and, sometimes, our homes. So prevalent are they that they have been woven into the fabric of Americana, coined in regional idioms, toasted with mixed drinks, named for dances, special events, even airplanes. June bugs are *big*, not just in size but in our imagination.

If only if stopped there. May goes out with a bang with the Memorial Day weekend, the traditional start of the summer camping season. As June waxes, so does the insect population. Make no mistake, it's a buggy month, filled with ticks and chiggers and fireflies and mosquitoes and butterflies and monster beetles and, well, you get the idea. A few are lovely to look at, others are fascinating to study, and some are potentially fatal; most are merely a nuisance. Any idea that humans are at the top of the food chain is quickly dispelled by an early morning walk.

Indeed, I am already mottled with insect bites. Several have been scratched until bloody, making me wonder, not for the first time, if the designation of "Bleeding Kansas" was made not for warring factions preceding the Civil War but because of all the bug bites the early pioneers suffered from.

Here in Kansas our brides aren't about to let a few bugs alter their wedding plans. Not for nothing is our state motto "ad astra per aspera," to the stars through difficulties. June weddings and June bugs can coexist in perfect harmony.

Children often get restless during weddings, so why not give them something fun to do? Capture a bunch of June bugs and tie strings their legs and let kids fly them like kites. June bugs are also renowned for their taste, and when powdered and mixed with hot milk forms a delicious malted beverage. Toasted June bugs have a sweet flavor and are full of important nutrients. Several bowls of them placed strategically around the table will make for a memorable wedding banquet.

And let's not forget a special drink for toasting the bride and groom: the June bug! Mix one ounce Midori watermelon liqueur, three-fourths-ounce rum, three-fourths-ounce banana liqueur, one ounce sweet and sour, and one ounce pineapple juice, blend and pour over ice. Quaff a few of those puppies and you'll be feeling your oats quick as a chicken on a June bug.

Ah, June. The peak tornado season has passed, to be supplanted by the ascendancy of bugs. Wildflowers paint the prairie in soft pastels, the days are hot and languid and made for sitting on a porch and sipping June bugs. Spring gives way to summer. Take a deep breath—can you smell it? It's the smell of love in the fresh Kansas air. That, and maybe a bug or two that flew up your nose.

# SHOTS IN THE NIGHT AND SHOT NERVES—WHY DO WE NEED NOISE TO CELEBRATE?

The first bullet struck the spotlight above the main gate, the sound of the gunshot concurrent with the explosion of glass, metal, and filament. The second bullet sliced lower, singing off the chain-link fence in a deadly stereophonic chord that buzzed in both ears like an angry hornet. A third shot was my partner returning fire with a 12-gauge riot shotgun. It was my introduction to the world of angry people with large-caliber weapons, and so close, so perilously close, to the Fourth of July.

That wasn't the worse of it, strangely enough, though it posed a far more lethal version of what was to follow. It was my idiot brother who made that July so terrible, who flayed my nerves until they screamed in torment, who kept me bathed in sweat as nightmares stalked my dreams. My idiot brother and his idiotic firecrackers, and my parents who betrayed me in my hour of need.

It's one thing to be at a location where you know a certain segment of society is out to harm you, or at least broadcast that your presence isn't welcome, and quite another to be caught unawares at one's place of refuge. In this instance my refuge was my parents' house, 120 miles from where I worked as a guard at a New Mexico Public Service Company generator plant. After being shot at, threatened, publicly accosted, my tacos deliberately spiced hotter than Satan himself could manage, and followed by menacing thugs, I desperately needed a place to unwind. It wasn't to be.

Wadded into a conglomeration of violence and longing, that summer was a pivotal point in my life. Everything changed after that, some in surprising ways. By the end of my stay in Las Vegas I had developed a penchant for inflammatory cuisine, an abiding love for the quietude nature affords, a dislike of loud noises, and a near-pathological loathing for our nation's celebration of independence.

If that July was dangerous at my job, at home the menace was more insidious, and more recurrent, for my younger brother had finagled a copious supply of firecrackers, previously forbidden by strict edict of my parents. For some reason they turned a blind eye to his actions, ignoring my imprecations, threats, and pleas, leaving me defenseless against a foe I could not defeat by firepower.

I was jumpy. He knew it, and he exploited it by tossing firecrackers whenever my back was turned. It didn't matter if I was in the yard or sitting in the living room, where our couch abutted the rear wall and a large picture window. Whenever I opened a book or stood outside gazing at the turquoise sky, a loud explosion would send me face forward into the ground. He would cackle like an old witch and scamper off before I could get my hands on him. The thought of shooting him was sweet indeed, if not terribly impractical.

Before then I never had an aversion to fireworks; afterward was another matter. Between the bullets ringing off the diesel tanks and my brother's antics and the local celebrations in backyards and streets, I came to dread the inevitable riot of noise that accompanied the holiday. It's amusing how veterinarians routinely warn that fireworks induce stress in pets but nothing is ever said of people.

It's probably wrong for me to blame the Fourth of July for what essentially was a few people wielding firearms and explosives, but there's no getting past the fact that the holiday provides an excuse for loutish people to indulge in noisome activities that at other times would constitute an egregious disturbance of the peace. Not only that, but it's an assault on our hearing. It's gratuitous noise in an already noisy age. Were we to sit in our cars and lean on the horn at regular intervals we'd be arrested and hauled off.

I suspect there are others like me, veterans, law enforcement officers, or ordinary folk caught in a crossfire not of their own making. More than a few have moved beyond the memories, have allowed them to fade like old photographs. Left behind is the imprint but the emotive immediacy has slipped away. Others, though, still flinch when vehicles backfire, when a nearby hunter cuts loose—or when firecrackers and fireworks turn a quiet neighborhood into a freefire zone. It's not so much the sound as its suddenness; we're taken unawares and feel terribly exposed.

Each year I tell myself to relax, that it's just for a few weeks. I've even attended the local celebration at the fairgrounds, thinking that by willingly participating I am somehow in control, that its effect will be lessened. After all, it wouldn't do to have my patriotism impugned. But I'm always unimpressed, finding the din too much for me to handle.

This year was, if anything, worse, between the window-rattling demolitions on the fairgrounds and the neighbors who really tied one on. I feel like a beaten dog. But a cool breeze wafts through the open window and the song of the meadowlark comes as a pure and perfect balm for my jangled nerves. They're reminders of what Henry David Thoreau expressed when he said, "In wildness is the preservation of the world." Or at least the preservation of people who crave silence.

Next year I'm taking the advice of the vet—I'm finding me a secluded place in the country and I'm holing up. And I'm also looking forward to the day when people revolt against the abuses of the holiday and demand an abolition of personal fireworks. Let there be community celebrations to honor the creation of our nation, but for those fools who need loud noises to feel good, let them put a bucket over their head and bang it with a hammer. It'll add a personal touch to their festivities, and the rest of us won't have to listen to it.

# SUMMER NOT ENDLESS, AUGUST BETRAYS

They are not ruled by calendars but by angle of sun, length of day, warmth of air that one breathes, one aviates, and they were both on alert. The ground squirrel, perched jauntily on its hind legs, stared through the rusted strands of barbed wire, past the brome grass bowed with its seeded crown to a sky glowering with dark clouds. The dragonfly, emerald eyes luminous in the gloaming, watched upstream as it hovered above a tiny riffle on Seehan Creek emerald with moss, reflective in the emerald light filtering through the emerald canopy. And me, crouched on slick stones beside the creek, hearing the whisper of rain as it pattered against that tall canopy, a spectator like them, a seeker, though what I was looking for remained a mystery even to me. I had come in search of August, as if it could be discerned like a constellation in the starry sky or a blade of grass, or a bird, or flower.

Not all who wander are lost, Tolkien said. And yet August has its share of wanderers, some astray, some moving to cycles and rhythms we can barely conceive.

Restlessness pervades the senses. August ultimately betrays, beginning with its summertime languidness, its dog days, its scorched pallid skies and sense of freedom, but it closes like a trap with migration in full swing, shorebirds leaving the Arctic for the tropics, monarchs moving en masse toward the

Sierra Madres, southbound hawks hitching rides on thermals, reduced daylight, children sidling bitterly toward school, back to the daily grind, light's out, party's over. From the first week to the last the pace picks up like a dropped ball that bounces high and then lower and lower yet, quickening as the distance lessens between impact and perihelion. When it comes to rest, autumn is practically knocking on our doors, leaving us breathless with wonder at where our summer disappeared.

Could any of this be seen in the wild lands bordering the Blue Earth River, known now as the Big Blue? On an afternoon darksome with advancing clouds from a cold front sweeping down from the Arctic, heeding the suggestion that I get out more often, I went looking.

I was tricked from the start. The cantillations of birds greeted me, a springtime symphony of parulas, titmice, chickadees, and sparrows more reminiscent of May. Wildflowers bloomed in meadows and along roadsides, in borrow ditches, and on rocky shelves. Tree frogs trilled in the deeper shadows of the woods, and the distant cadence of chorus frogs came from the river. Wet, humid heat shrouded me, and the whine of mosquitoes was loud in my ears. This was spring and summer rolled into one.

And yet—were the tips of the sumacs losing their emerald hue for a rose blush? Their seed clusters were ripening to a vivid red. Midsummer flowers were fading, colorful petals transforming into fuzzy seed heads. Prairie grasses were paling, showing the first shades of auburn and gold. Leaves carpeted the grass. If I looked closely I could get a hint of autumn.

Without a clock or calendar it might have been impossible to tell which month I was in. Such is August's nature. Before rending our hearts it teases us, playing with our sensibilities, our reasoning, twisting everything around so that we scarcely comprehend the time of year or our place in the land. August is the trickster, the coyote of the calendar.

Once the sixth month and now the eighth, owing allegiance to no fixed number of days (first conceived with thirty, then twenty-nine, then thirty-one days), named *sextilis* in Latin but renamed for an emperor, everything about the month is deceptive. Even the dog days are gone, Orion's hounds leashed: the ancients believed that when the sun and Sirius, alpha star of Canis Majoris, rose together in late July and early August they combined their heat to create the searing days known as the dog days of summer. Thanks to our planet's wobbly rotation, even this is no more, a thousand years fled. Sirius the Dog Star now rises with the sun near the end of August and dominates the heavens only in winter, when it joins the hunter Orion to wage war on the bull.

A tree was talking to me. I stepped up to a tall sycamore and placed my ear to the rough bark; the voices were within. Indecipherable, yet almost-human, the sound was like nothing I'd ever heard. I moved on, treading on twigs and leaves stripped from the trees during a previous windstorm. The meadows were layered with colorful fragments of sycamore bark, curled at the edges like wood shavings.

Robber flies challenged my intrusion, darting from the trail only when almost stepped upon, circling back to block the trail once more. Green darners and meadowhawks patrolled the skies above the clearings, while along the waterways skimmers and emeralds hunted the shadows. Wood satyrs wove drunkenly through thickets. I passed from drizzle to understory and descended into the creek bed. The air grew heavy and still, filled with vague whispers.

There was no hint of August here. Whatever I thought I had seen of it was suddenly questionable. But evening would fall early, I knew, and continue to fall earlier each night, a constant whittling away of daylight so subtle that we are led to believe the summer is without end. Hot weather would return but its span was now limited. The sun would track across the heavens, rising and setting in a different place each day. The songs of frogs and birds would be silenced. The red-tailed hawk sitting on the fencepost would be gone. Leaves would fall. Change was upon us and yet all but invisible.

August is here. Do not be deceived. Trust nothing.

## SEPTEMBER DREAMS, REAL OR IMAGINED, AND THE OPEN ROAD

For now the heat has abated, dark clouds riding low, the morning cooler and humming with cricketsong. I'm sitting here listening to Lyle Lovett's "This Old Porch" and thinking of West Texas, mostly of the Davis Mountains and a roadside rest area just across the border from New Mexico, one with a huge emblem of Texas jutting up into the Texas sky, and of how I felt when I parked beside it, a quickening pulse for my homecoming to a place I'd once renounced. The open road lay before us. All we needed was contained in the camper and Lyle Lovett was blasting Texas songs and we pulled out and headed south and sliced through El Paso on the interstate and past and then dropped into what seemed to be the middle of nowhere, sharp hills rising from creosote flats, and I thought of how it must look in the springtime when bluebonnets blanketed the ground. I've rarely felt so free. Why Lovett's song triggered these memories I can't say; indeed, I barely understand the lyrics. But implicit is loss, longing, homecoming, anger, and pride, and I guess that just about sums up life in general, so the song is fitting by any measure you choose.

My dreams of late have been wild, ranging across the twisted landscape of the imagination. Oddly, most have involved me wearing my old work uniform, or, in one instance, armed with my Kahr 9 mm pistol. I'm always being stalked, hunted, or menaced. Often I've had my pistol drawn and ready;

once, a suddenly-opened door had me yanking out my service revolver, and in that midnight opening I sensed a forbidding presence no bullet could harm.

Last night my wife and I were following a shadowy man through narrow alleyways and streets to a dark endless corridor lined with boxes and trash and doorways leading off into gloomy interiors, the light fading until darkness fell like dusk, and a feeling of menace blossomed into two shapes materializing behind us. I pushed Lori behind me and aligned the night sights on the closest figure, three green glowing dots level with his chest, my finger tense on the trigger, ready to fire, ready to kill and kill the other one too and then kill whoever stood in our way as we backed out, but nothing happened, of course. Dreams tend to collapse in the middle, leaving us forever wondering what might come after, how our dreamlives would conclude. One moment I have an arm shielding my wife, pistol in hand, adrenaline surging like a red tidal wave, and the next I'm awake in the darkness of the upstairs bedroom, the green glow from the clock radio telling me how late it is, or early, and I hear Lori lightly breathing, the air conditioner rumbling, the ceiling fan whispering. I listen for anything out of the ordinary. My finger still feels the trigger, so vividly that I consider opening the nightstand drawer and pulling out the pistol just to feel the cool stainless steel. And I don't.

September always puts me in that mood. It's not just because it's my birthday, an event I've come to dread more than anticipate, but the loss inherent within the next four weeks. Nighthawks are winging south, and whenever I see them on that trajectory I cry out for them to stop, to not leave. As they disappear into the distance I feel part of myself bleeding away. That they are joined by ever-increasing numbers of hawks, passerines, dragonflies, and butterflies is enough to bludgeon my emotions to insensibility.

Our feet are rooted to the earth as surely as trees or shrubs. I'm speaking metaphorically of course as getting in the truck and driving off on a six-month excursion through the Southwest is perfectly plausible if not impractical for any number of reasons, financial ones being the first to spring to mind. This is just one of the great injustices we labor under, labor being the warden overseeing our particular prison.

Even the sun heads south, sailing past the celestial equator on the twenty-second in an inexorable slide that eventually places it so low to the horizon that only a weak, ineffectual heat can be felt. But for one moment day and night are equals, and then darkness is the rule rather than the exception. It's all downhill from there.

That constant movement makes me restless. I may be looking north to catch hawks in the distance but my heart is tugged southward. If everything else is leaving, why can't I?

All life is transient though we often try to convince ourselves it's not. September reinforces the point, bashing us across the face with a proverbial two-by-four as if we were nothing more than an intransigent mule. Even the most stubborn of us finally get the point when we see the leaves flare to gold and scarlet and drift away in a cold north wind. Grasses yellow; apples hang heavy in the trees and drop to the ground; the start of school puts a damper on any feelings of escape we might harbor. Summer's swan song can be heard in the metronomic pulse of field crickets. Orion's bow will be drawn. Sirius will glow like fire in the evening sky.

Writer Heather McHugh said, "It's not nice dreams I'm yearning for; it's true dreams." Right now I'd settle for nonviolent dreams, or dreams where I find the steering wheel in my hand rather than a pistol. I assure myself there's no need to be lachrymose. September has its own true dreams, primary being the wonder of migration, the slowing pace, a turning in rather than looking out. Best of all, they can be experienced without interruption. They won't drop us in the middle of the plot. We can go on, blind as we are, eager for what's around the bend, or over the hill, at the end of a dark corridor, or, better yet, just across the border.

# GOODBYE TO ALL THAT—THE YIN AND YANG OF OCTOBER

On the last day of summer I found a new bird for Marshall County. This timed perfectly with William Bliss Carmen's observation that "something in October sets the gypsy blood astir," even though a stickler will point out that technically the bird was not found in October but in the preceding month. All too true but irrelevant, I say. The tenth month is one of subtraction, so surely we can add something to embellish the tale. That the bird was discovered under exhilarating circumstances almost too embarrassing to mention is also fitting to October's schizophrenia. It's doubtful I'll ever return to the Black Vermillion Marsh without recalling the time I found a marsh wren after engaging in a wild and spontaneous dance.

Sometimes I'm lucky enough to be able to chase birds at the slightest provocation. An e-mail on the Kansas Ornithological Society's listserv informed me that three long-billed curlews had been seen flying over the marsh earlier in the day. "Flying over" is birder code for "We got to see it but your chances are less than zero." I had just finished an article and had a few hours free, so I threw the scope and binos in the truck and went after them.

It takes about twenty minutes to get there from my house, and once there there's not a lot to see. A first-time visitor expecting something along the lines of Cheyenne Bottoms or

Quivira National Wildlife Refuge will be sorely disappointed. More inundated weed field than wetland, it exists at the discretion of the Kansas Department of Wildlife and Parks, which floods it each fall to create habitat for migrant game birds like waterfowl. "Creating habitat" equates, of course, to chumming in birds so hunters can have effective fields of fire, something that would put you and me away for a goodly spell were we caught doing it. A rocky dirt road splits off 14th Terrace and heads east toward the Black Vermillion River but it's closed to unauthorized vehicles, which are mine and yours. A small dike on the north side of the road separates the viewer from the marsh proper. To see over the dike you must force your way through head-high ragweed and goldenrod and other pollen-intensive plants, many of them linked together almost invisibly by spider webs.

I had done just that several times before working my way over the dike yet again. As I scanned the marsh, mostly brittle grass with shallow runnels meandering toward the center, I tried pishing something up. I clicked, I clacked, I clucked, I hissed. A dickcissel popped up, followed by a Savannah sparrow. I was congratulating myself for finding the season's first migrant sparrow when I glimpsed the largest jumping spider I'd ever seen. It was climbing my shirt and passed from my sight even as I felt its hairy legs scribble up my neck.

If one image can adequately describe October, it is this: periods of calm followed by intense activity.

I launched into a feverish bout of self-flagellation. In the end I don't know whether I killed the spider from a direct hit or from fright, or if it did a swan dive off my larynx and escaped into the deep weeds. At any rate, there was no battered corpse to prove that my dervish dance had been anything other than ecstasy over autumn's impending arrival. While trying to still my pounding heart and catch my breath, I glanced around to see if there were any witnesses. There were no humans but a wren, and a transient wren at that. Not ten feet away, it studied me with a quiet intensity that every living creature exhibits toward children or lunatics. I must have given it quite a stir.

Naturally, the curlews were not found.

"What of October, that ambiguous month, the month of tension, the unendurable month?" Doris Lessing asked. Indeed, it can be as hard to live with as a spider climbing your neck. Decades ago there was a series of TV ads showing a white-gowned Mother Nature being offered a sample of Chiffon margarine, which she mistakenly identified as butter. When the narrator crowed that she had been tricked, a lightning bolt blasted the set. "It's not nice to fool Mother Nature," she spat, and perhaps that's how October feels about being named the eighth month and then booted down the line.

It's the most schizophrenic month of the year. It's the school yard bully with a heart of gold. It takes away and it gives back. As we progress from start to finish the days shorten, gardens slumber, temperatures drop, trees denude, birds and butterflies depart, and familiar summer constellations slip over the horizon. And yet, for the loss of leaves, there is more color. For the loss of daylight, there are bluer skies. For the loss of birds, there is the occasional surprise, like the wren.

I'm trying hard to be optimistic here because October is my favorite month, my nature dominated by the idea of loss while inherently rebelling against it. Perhaps I'm as schizophrenic as the month but at this stage of my life there's probably no changing it. I lament the passing of birds even while delighting in finding new ones, and of seeing familiar hawks soaring past in a seemingly endless procession. I dread the idea that our pet rabbit will almost certainly not see November. Life and loss are intrinsically bound, and nowhere more evident than in October.

What of October? We learn to deal with ambiguity, we say our goodbyes, and, knowing there are few other choices, we endure.

# NOVEMBER IN A WINDBLOWN SEED

In the ashen moonlight slanting through tall barren trees William Morris, the British poet, saw November. The light transformed midnight into "dreamy noon, silent and full of wonders," he wrote, and

> *The changeless seal of change it seemed to be,*
> *Fair death of things that, living once, were fair;*
> *Bright sign of loneliness too great for me,*
> *Strange image of the dread eternity,*
> *In whose void patience how can these have part,*
> *These outstretched feverish hands, this restless heart?*

I, too, have seen November, not in moonlight filtering through the half-naked trees flanking our gravel road, nor in the variegated shadows cast by the death and rebirth of the full moon in the waning days of October—hunter's moon, blood moon—nor in the deep prairie grasses burnishing the hillside into shades of russet and umber and ochre, but in frost glittering on cold stone, in an icy wind coursing over the land, slipping through the desperate clutch of boughs to bend low the goldenrod and asters in fields grown empty of birdsong and cricketsong. The loneliness Morris wrote of clings to me like wood smoke. In the growing darkness of winter's approach I find an oppression that has no name or shape but seems somehow to focus on a pile of rocks behind the house, situated between a pair of low elms and an Osage orange, sprinkled with withered bunches of wild alfalfa and the season's final blooms.

When poets speak of November their words are mostly filled with loss, dread, loneliness, or sorrow. Alexander Pushkin wrote, "A tedious season they await/ who hear November at the gate," while Thomas Hood, with barbed whimsy, called it the month of noes, as in "no warmth, no cheerfulness, no healthful ease/ no comfortable feel in any member—no shade, no shine, no butterflies, no bees/no fruits, no flowers, no birds, no bees." To Charles Lloyd it was "dismal," to Helen Hunt Jackson "treacherous." Charles Baudelaire saw in it the onslaught of winter, when he would be "exiled, like the sun, to a polar prison."

In the mornings, when spindly shadows flee the pursuing sunlight or gray dawn is met with gray woods and gray heart, I walk to my rabbit's cairn and stand over it and struggle for words to say. The wind harvests the bright leaves of the hackberries and maples only to abandon them, and slowly the grass lies beneath a blanket that sings autumn's own peculiar chorus under the rustle of footfalls. I set more stones in place until the first shafts of sunlight strike the cairn like the tolling of a bell. In evenings, the sun long down, last light bleeding away into the hollows and darker recesses of the woods, I again stand above the stones, and say farewell.

As all is farewell now. In November, "a little this side of the snow and that side of the haze," as Emily Dickinson put it, we become acquainted with the end of things. Yet even as the last leaves drift to earth, as the colors, once so gaudy and vivid, now die away, something lingers just below the surface, some nagging thought or memory, of a November promise. And it eludes me, even as I trudge back to the house, whose lights glow with a warmth unknown in summer, a coziness of refuge, of sanctuary, like a solitary candle burning in a vast and terrible plain.

Can there be regeneration in the gathering gloom? Does November hold something that we can look upon in the benighted dusk and proclaim, as Morris did in an earlier stanza, "Is it not fair, and of most wondrous worth?"

I thought not. And yet, as one morning I sat beside the cairn, the asters nodding in the breeze, their purple blooms now exploded into fuzzy seed heads, a sudden gust sent them yawing and swaying, and I watched the seeds whirl away, as insubstantial as hope, each a tiny perfect microcosm containing the rudiments of germination and propagation, with embryo, placenta, and egg, the matter of life itself. Here was the promise of spring in the fading of autumn. November, I had thought in my grief, was like the cold and bitter wind stripping away the tinsel of summer until all that remained was the desiccated husk of December. I was wrong.

On a sunny Saturday afternoon with no hint of November in the air my wife made a phone call. We drove south, the Flint Hills opening before us, the roadway spotted with tawny litter scattering in our wake, and after an hour's drive we turned east toward the mad jumble of land enfolding Tuttle Creek Lake. There, a lone house stood at the crest of a hill and behind it a cluster of outbuildings. Inside were cages, and in them were Angora rabbits.

One, a small black-faced female with silver ears and mottled flanks, placed her front paws on the bars and studied me. And I cannot say why this was so, only that it was: that in a room filled with rabbits, some tortoise, some black, some snow white, some tan, there was only the one, and we watched each other until I crossed the room and unlatched the gate and pulled her out, and she huddled close to me, heart to beating heart, and then she stood in my hands, our noses almost touching, her dark lustrous eyes staring deeply into mine.

In that instant I saw the "wondrous worth" Morris wrote of, and the coming November void held no fear for these feverish hands, this restless heart.

# SOLSTICE, OR THE PROMISE OF DECEMBER

If December had a voice it would be in the gentle whisper of snow falling through naked trees, or the wind sighing above a narrow tree-fringed valley, each tarnished leaf and spindly twig motionless as if giving lie to the ceaseless current of air moaning aloft. As if in another time or place, or far removed from this brittle landscape with its tenebrous woods and rocky bourns half-buried under leaf wrack, where the echoes of footfalls break off sharply as if truncated or silenced by something unseen in the air, or dampened beneath the gnarled limbs of towering bur oaks, or smothered in the darkness congealing between the gathering boles. This still, small voice that spoke long before there were ears to hear, or time, or a calendar. Or a December.

Do the crows flying overhead comprehend this? They weave the air with invisible strands, the warp and weft a pattern of their own reckoning, untraceable to others. If I could, I would call them down to me on this shadowed forest floor and ask them what they know of the end of things. If they sense its approach in the lessening of light, in the endless bitter nights lumined by the silvery gilt of moonlight, or cavernous beneath patined clouds suffocating all light however pallid, each night longer, and darker, until sunlight seems a faraway dream. Will they think the night ascendant? That their blackness will merge with night's blackness and so disappear? Or do they realize that all ends are but beginnings?

For most of our collective history we have wondered this, huddled around our hearth fires, looking for signs in the heavens or portends on earth. The knowing is one thing, the intense darkness another. We have forgotten all too readily. The earth is a circle and all therein even as the sun is a circle and the seasons are circular and return with exquisite precision, yet in the cold midwinter we fear the mounting gloom. Have feared. Not now.

We sought solace in the burning of bonfires, in donning sprigs of mistletoe, in warding our windows with prickly-leaved holly, in gathering rowan trees to hang inverted in our dwellings. We built intricate monuments to chart the course of the sun, whether Stonehenge or Newgrange or Maeshowe; we raised monoliths across the breadth of Europe and Egypt, constructed Aztecan temples and Chacoan pueblos, and in medieval Roman churches the sun slanting through a small hole in the roof tracked the meridian line which, surrounded by symbols of the zodiac, demarcated noon and the extremes of the solstices. Have, not now.

This desire to know the end and the beginning was as much a physical longing as a spiritual one. We called it Lenaea, Alban Arthuan, Inti Raymi, Shab-e Yaldaa, Mi na Nollaig, Dies Natalis Invicti Solis, Brumalia, Jol. We called it the winter solstice. We made celebrations to drive the darkness away, adulterating them into festivals of excess such as Saturnalia, ancient even before the Romans and the Persians, where children became rulers of the household and masters slaves, and, in the words of Seneca the Younger, "we...take a better supper and throw off the toga." Have, not now.

We deduced from the placement of the North Star that our planet is tilted, that the sun's light is not equal, that it shifts and lengthens and withdraws. We added a new holiness to the season and called it Christ's Mass. We saw the world from space and so proved our computations. Darkness became metaphor for death and resurrection and no longer catered to our uncertainties. Christ's Mass eclipsed solstice, and in return was usurped by the jangling of cash registers and the redcoated bellringers warding the entrances of supermarkets and malls. And greed. And excess. Saturnalia redux.

It is easier to hear December in this valley where I stand as motionless as the spindly twigs and tarnished leaves, with blackbirds weaving the low sky and calling out in their dog-voices, the insubstantial whisper of wind like the sound of distant tides. Competing voices are silenced. December murmurs and beckons.

And if it could be followed like the tracks of voles through a snowy meadow, December would lead us from first snow to the stronghold of winter's reign. It would show us the end of things. It would sink us in unforgiving cold and infinite night. It would drag the sun earthward as if to embrace it. And at the last moment, when despair is imminent, it would turn a corner and release us.

This is the message of December, that in the darkness there is hope. That the end is a beginning. We know this, have known it for thousands of years. Have almost drowned it out. Have almost forgotten it. Almost, but not.

We must listen again. We must hear the still small voice of December. We must listen to solstice, to its promise.

The crows depart. Darkness swallows the trees, rises in the creeks like floodwater. I make my way toward the truck, a half-mile away. Night falls hard and fast. Cold intensifies. Snow falls.

It will not last.

# RIVERSONG

# WHERE WATERS MEET

For a large portion of my life I was always more interested in headwaters than confluences, beginnings rather than ends. Maybe it had something to do with geography, for headwaters, at least where I came from, are born in remote, mountainous areas; confluences are everywhere. But that was the Mountain West, and this is the Great Plains, and nothing is the same anymore, except for confluences.

They surround us, overlooked by all but those who seek them out. Possessing a quiet dignity, they lack the grandeur of cascading waterfalls or the exuberance of whitewater. More whisper than shout, they are nature's version of mathematics. Add enough confluences and you get the Mississippi. Subtract enough and you get Elm Creek, a glassy, meandering rivulet snaking for only a few miles as the crow flies and a few miles more as the runnel runs. Elm Creek passes below the bridge on Highway 9 east of Blue Rapids, writhes through willows and overarching cottonwoods, snakes silently beneath Broken Bottle Bridge, and straightens—as much as any body of moving water straightens—in the final stretch before merging with the Blue Earth River. Confluence.

I was thinking of confluences after my recent out-of-body experience, after seeing from high in the night sky a river of sorts that tumbled from its headwaters in West Texas, flowing uphill, parallel to the Rio Grande, before riffling through Albuquerque and passing on northward. It was just a stream actually, a minor tributary to something larger and yet to be revealed, but in that old New Mexican town my stream converged with another, one whose headwaters were in the mountains of Nevada. That, too, was a confluence. River as metaphor for life. Seeing the convergence of our lives gave me an urge to see the real thing, the meeting of waters, and so on a crisp autumn morning I slipped into heavy waterproof boots, slung my binoculars around my neck, and set off down Elm Creek.

From the bridge, the creek has only a few hundred yards remaining of its singular existence. Nestled between high banks, the dell is intimate and close, carpeted with fallen leaves, its upper terraces bristling with cottonwoods bending over the water as if straining to hear its song. A bitter wind sighed through the boughs. The water was still, untouched by wind or current.

I worked my way down, my boots sinking in mud and soft silt. Cutting through the plowed field would have been easier but I wanted to be as near to the stream as possible. The confluence would be our shared experience.

A shrill scream of an enraged hawk shattered the silence. I searched the trees but came up empty, and yet the cry relentlessly accused me. *Where are you?* I suddenly remembered times in the past when a similar cry was heard near here, disembodied, wraithlike. Ghosthawk. Its voice soon trailed off and I continued on with only the dialog of crows.

Near where Elm Creek weds the Blue Earth River the stream widened and deepened, more backwater than flow. The banks fell away and the broad river whispered past. I walked out onto a wide sandbar, behind which the creek lay imprisoned. Disappointment nagged me, but then I noticed a small trickle of water wending its way around the shoreline, almost hidden behind an accretion of waterlogged twigs. It looped toward the river as if heading upstream and emptied into the shallows along the shoreline. It wasn't much to look at it, but standing at the exact spot where Elm Creek relinquishes its self and becomes another entity was like peering into the innermost workings of nature. This is the still, small voice that whispers of larger things.

Of course, this is also due in part to timing. A creek in winter is a shadow of its potential. Returning in springtime would reveal another side to this freshet, with a current laughing between its banks, surging to its incarnation as a major tributary of a watershed encompassing some seven thousand square miles before emptying, eventually, into the Gulf of Mexico.

And yet, a wintercreek is a reflection of the season. The rush of spring and the bounty of summer give way to somnolence as the land turns dormant. No more birdsong, nor laughter, nor shouting, gone the song of tractors in the harvest, this is what remains—the quiet heartbeat of the planet.

I straddled the confluence and became, for a timeless moment, part of the river, part of the earth.

# SHOOTER AT COON CREEK

There is a small hill to the southwest of Waterville where the ages lie exposed like the bleached bones of a skeleton, and man's brief chapter is told in stages. The hill is cropped at the top, flattened by the tons of ice that once slid down from the north, the land falling away in brush- and tree-choked draws that converge in the lower elevations to form a watercourse that traces a finger of erosion to the junction of the Little Blue River. Three shallow depressions shadow the base of the hill, former burrows of pioneers who lived like badgers. Across the narrow valley stands a modern house and barn, and beyond that, at the apex of a rounded knoll, stands a whitewashed outhouse built by WPA workers in the middle of the last century. A stone's throw away is an ancient buffalo wallow, still visible in the prairie grass.

Standing in the wallow, hearing in the wind the thunder of millions of hooves, one can see the upper branches of Coon Creek snaking from the west, the innominate and innumerable gullies coalescing to become one body moving inexorably toward the sea. Shaded by gnarled oaks, it seems more ancient than its downstream cousin, Elm Creek. But like all streams, all rivers, each has its own personality and place. One branch of the Oregon Trail crossed the Blue Earth River at the confluence of Elm Creek, and Coon Creek was both icehouse and community swimming pool in the early days of Waterville. Now, both are mostly forgotten.

But not without voice. They possess a song and language older than mankind, and nowhere along their respective courses is that most evident than in the bittersweet adagio performed in their final moment before becoming another entity: confluence.

I longed to hear the parting melody of Coon Creek, so one afternoon, with the sun slanting through the trees and an icy breeze flowing from the north, I parked at a spot west of the juncture with the idea of following the railroad tracks to the trestle bridge and then skirting the creek to its demise. It was a good plan but I didn't know about the gunman.

I felt like I had stepped back in time, walking the steel rails like a hobo. They stretched before me, the crossties hidden beneath a patina of fallen leaves, crowded with encroaching trees and the open fields beyond. Pleasurable walking, with the bridge coming all too soon.

I hesitated there, undecided over which side of the creek to follow. Three deer bounded onto the tracks in front of me, pausing to eye me up, and then they were off, white tails waving goodbye.

I crossed the bridge to follow them, the waters of Coon Creek far below me, vertigo dizzying me as I tiptoed from tie to tie. Once across, I dropped down through the undergrowth and broke into a field. At that moment a rifle boomed. I froze.

The shooter was near. Was it a poacher, blasting at the deer I'd kicked up? What were my odds for being hit, either by ricochet or purposely? Time to leave, I thought.

But I couldn't. I was so near the confluence that I was lured on. Backtracking over the bridge, I slipped into the woods hedging the creek. Down I went, as silently as possible, following the twists and turns. Each step took me nearer to the gunman, so I cut for the river. Before breaking onto the open along the Little Blue, I scanned a wooded ridge where I thought the shot had come from. Another blast hammered the silence, and another.

I could see the confluence. The Little Blue, blocked by the ridge, curved to the north in a broad sweep, and at the base of the hill Coon Creek joined it.

I moved closer, keeping to the trees. More shots rang out. Either someone was target practicing or slaughtering an entire herd of deer. Each shot made me flinch.

Something moved in the trees just below the crest of the ridge. Through the binoculars I glimpsed a man carrying a rifle before the woods swallowed him. Pistol shots rapped out like a string of firecrackers exploding.

*Leave*, I told myself. The confluence was only a hundred yards away, but it might as well have been on the moon.

So close.

I backed through the woods. *BAM*. Crossed the open field and gained the railroad tracks. *BAM*. Each step weighted with defeat. *BAM*. Crows flooded through the treetops like oily black smoke, mocking me. *BAM*.

# SINGING STONES AND CONFLUENCES

*C*onfluence. The word possesses a liquidity as if formed from the very waters it describes. To say it slowly, lingering on each syllable, is to taste the river itself. It is the loveliest member in a long repertoire of synonyms, as graceful and lovely as the braiding of currents.

After having spanned the juncture of tiny Elm Creek and the Blue Earth River, and after being dissuaded by gunfire from doing the same at Coon Creek and the Little Blue, I set out one crisp autumn morning to see the conjoining of rivers. If the merging of the smaller tributaries had been minimalist, I reasoned, surely the meeting of bigger waters would increase in degree, even in a time of drought. No small thing this, but confluence on a grand scale, seven hundred combined miles of riverflow coming together, the hydrological equivalent of community.

From my vantage at Prospect Hill Cemetery, where I parked to begin my trek, the valley opened at my feet. Farm ponds slept beneath their coverlets of ice. Clouds drifted in from the west. The confluence was hidden behind a thicket of woods, but the distant Little Blue glinted in the sun and the Blue Earth River came in on my right, and somewhere past that first long bend they merged.

Descending through dark cedars, I crossed the dirt road, passed through a narrow bird-filled copse, and stepped into a plowed field. The river made a broad sweep before me, deeply eroding the banks. Skirting the edge of the bluff, I worked my way down to the sandbar and strode across the damp sands. The slow drawl of the current soundlessly slipped by. A solitary Harlan's hawk, black as night, perched in a tall cottonwood, as if sentinel to whatever the river might bring down.

Walking the broad sandbar was easy but slow-going, for studded among the tracks of raccoons, deer, and turkey were brightly-colored rocks that seemed to reach out to me. There were flints the color of chestnuts and shards of Sioux quartzite and dark geodes, and after slipping a few in my pocket I recalled that in my former life I used to collect one special stone at the end of each fishing year. It was always a bittersweet moment, reeling in the line and hooking the fly into the keeper, but for a memento I'd find a flat stone on which I would write the name of the stream and the date. A record of my time and place. And here, again, I was collecting bones of the earth.

These stones, too, told a record, one of fathomless time. The gravel and sand I walked on had washed down hundreds of miles and centuries, carving through layers of the earth's crust, the foundations of mountains, the stuff of stardust. Smooth-polished, they remember the sound of rapids, the soft lullaby of a riffle, the gentle lap of current in streamside coves and confluences. They rattled in my pocket, clicking, clacking, as if speaking a forgotten language.

As I moved along the curve of the river the confluence slowly came into view. The Little Blue River, looking broader but shallower, rolled in from the west, and the Blue Earth River bore down from the right, almost hidden behind a wooded bank. Together they formed a wide pool painting a mirror image of the barren cottonwoods lining the banks. Just downstream was a shallow riffle, and the sound of cascading water was the first music the two rivers made together.

I took to the woods when the mud became too deep, crossing through beaver-felled trees with their sharpened trunks glowing ashen in the gray light. Tall desiccated weeds blocked my view of the confluence, but I broke through onto a muddy bank and stood beside the junction. Mussel shells glittered like broken pottery. A scrim of ice crusted the shallows.

All was still and silent. The waters melded with neither sound nor ripple, each river blending seamlessly into the other. Wedded, Kaw-bound.

I closed my eyes and thought of river time. Spring floods, summer surges, autumn slumber, winter ice. Ebb and flow. Constant and timeless change.

The noon siren wafting across the fields shattered my reverie, pulling me back to the present. Clouds had blocked the sun. The temperature began dropping as if anticipating the next storm.

There were more rocks to collect on the way back, and one bronzed, fossilized bone with the heft of iron. Gifts of the river. By the time I reached the truck my pockets were bulging.

When I got home I scattered the rocks in a little garden area in front of our house, adding them to my repository of found things: cow skull, deer skull, rocks taken from the crests of these flint hills. But these stones were different. Marked and shaped by waters, they remembered the sound of the river, the feel of it like a lover's caress. They longed to return to its embrace.

Ingrained in our souls is the yearning for home. Even for stones. At night, lying in bed, I imagine them singing, singing the song of the river, and none but themselves to hear. The bones take on flesh and roam the plains. The river rises. In a confluence of time and longing, these stones will sing.